Authoritarianism Goes Global

Authoritarianism Goes Global

The Challenge to Democracy

Edited by LARRY DIAMOND, MARC F. PLATTNER,
and CHRISTOPHER WALKER

Johns Hopkins University Press

Baltimore

Johns Hopkins University Press
2715 North Charles Street
Baltimore, Maryland 21218-4363
www.press.jhu.edu

Library of Congress Cataloging-in-Publication Data

Names: Diamond, Larry Jay, editor. | Plattner, Marc F., 1945– editor. |
    Walker, Christopher, 1964– editor.
Title: Authoritarianism goes global : the challenge to democracy / edited by
    Larry Diamond, Marc F. Plattner, and Christopher Walker.
Description: Baltimore : Johns Hopkins University Press, [2016] | Series: A
    journal of democracy book | Includes bibliographical references and index.
Identifiers: LCCN 2015038214| ISBN 9781421419978 (pbk. : alk. paper) | ISBN
    9781421419985 (electronic) | ISBN 1421419971 (pbk. : alk. paper) | ISBN
    142141998X (electronic)
Subjects: LCSH: Authoritarianism. | Democracy.
Classification: LCC JC480 .A93 2016 | DDC 320.53—dc23 LC record available at
    http://lccn.loc.gov/2015038214

A catalog record for this book is available from the British Library.

*Special discounts are available for bulk purchases of this book. For more information,
please contact Special Sales at 410-516-6936 or specialsales@press.jhu.edu.*

CONTENTS

ACKNOWLEDGMENTS

This volume emerged from a two-year initiative by the National Endowment for Democracy's International Forum for Democratic Studies examining the phenomenon of resurgent authoritarianism. This project was organized around a series of roundtables addressing various aspects of the broader subject, but also featured a number of larger public presentations. We extend our deepest gratitude to the participants who played a key role in these discussions. In addition to those who contributed to this book, these included Bernard Haykel, Steven Heydemann, Karen Elliott House, Judith Kelley, Thomas O. Melia, Christopher Sabatini, Jean-François Seznec, and Jan Surotchak.

We also wish to express our thanks to the Smith Richardson Foundation (SRF), which provided critical financial support for this project. We are especially grateful to Nadia Schadlow, SRF senior program officer, International Security and Foreign Policy, for her advice and cooperation.

Christopher Walker, executive director of the International Forum, has been the driving force behind this project, championing the idea since he first proposed it in 2014. Given our own long history as coeditors of both the *Journal of Democracy* and numerous *Journal of Democracy* books published by Johns Hopkins University Press, we soon saw the potential that this initiative had for generating articles for the *Journal* and for eventually culminating in an edited volume. In fact, we published all fourteen of the chapters in this book as essays in the *Journal* between January 2015 and January 2016.

Once we made the decision to aim at producing a book on this subject, we immediately thought of asking Chris to join us as a coeditor. Not only had he led the Forum's comprehensive study of resurgent authoritarianism, but he also was instrumental in providing advice as we set about commissioning articles on this subject. We are delighted that he accepted our invitation to serve as a coeditor, playing a central role in drafting the introduction and also contributing an excellent concluding essay.

In addition, we are indebted to our colleagues at Johns Hopkins University Press. Editorial director Greg Britton provided valuable assistance and encouragement in the preparation of this volume, and managing editor Juliana McCarthy, also of the Books Division, helped with the production process. It has also been a pleasure to work once again with Bill Breichner, Carol Hamblen, and Angela Taylor of the Journals Division.

Most of all, however, we thank the members of the *Journal of Democracy* staff for their indispensable contributions to the preparation of this volume. As always, the essays that follow benefited from the remarkable editorial efforts of executive editor Phil Costopoulos and senior editor Tracy Brown. Managing editor Brent Kallmer brilliantly met the myriad layout and production challenges of this volume, and assistant editor Hilary Collins provided substantial assistance in drafting the introduction and managing the editorial correspondence during the volume's planning and production phases. And we cannot conclude without expressing our appreciation to the National Endowment for Democracy's President Carl Gershman and the Board of Directors for the longstanding support that they have provided to the International Forum for Democratic Studies and the *Journal of Democracy.*

—*Marc F. Plattner and Larry Diamond*

Authoritarianism Goes Global

Introduction

THE EDITORS

T HE QUARTER-CENTURY since the collapse of communism has been marked by three trends, the most recent of which has caught many observers by surprise. The first was the "democratic surge" that began with the "third wave" of democracy in the mid-1970s and kept pace into the first half-decade of the new century. Although democracy's momentum slowed in the mid-2000s, the overall pattern from 1990 to 2005 was clear. Continuing a trend that had begun well before the Cold War ended, the list of countries categorized by Freedom House as "electoral democracies" grew from 76 in 1990 to 119 in 2005. During this same period, the countries rated Free by Freedom House grew from 65 to 89, indicating a significant expansion in the number of countries that had established democratically accountable systems.

In the mid-2000s, a second trend came into view. Authoritarian regimes that had regained their footing reacted to democratic forces pushing for governance systems that were more accountable and responsive—and less corrupt. As part of this "backlash" against democracy, repressive regimes began to apply measures meant to limit independent voices and institutions, including civil society groups and the media. While the outlines of systematic resistance to democracy had begun to emerge in the early 2000s, the backlash really took off in reaction to the popular uprisings known as "color revolutions." These mostly peaceful citizen uprisings against rampantly corrupt authoritarian regimes swept out incumbents in Georgia, Ukraine, and Kyrgyzstan in 2003, 2004, and 2005, respectively. Remaining repressive regimes, seeing what might be coming their way, responded by beginning to apply fuller restraints on freedoms of expression and association, with special emphasis on progressively narrowing the space available to nongovernmental organizations.

The signs of this squeeze (in some places it was sharp enough to be called a crackdown) were visible from the outset, yet for a while at least the whole thing seemed relatively circumscribed and episodic. Writing in the *Journal of Democracy* in 2006, Carl Gershman and Michael Allen characterized the backlash as a "problem that involves a relatively limited number of countries—approximately 20 out of the more than 80" where democracy assistance was being provided at the time.[1] Most of what the authoritarians were doing was domestic in focus: They forced local activists and democracy-oriented organizations in countries as diverse as Egypt, Russia, Venezuela, and Zimbabwe to contend with rafts of obstructive new laws and regulations, but authoritarian maneuvers within regional or even global settings had not yet begun.

Writing at about the same time as Gershman and Allen, Thomas Carothers foreshadowed some of the more acute challenges that were gaining steam. He noted that, in addition to the restrictive measures being pursued by undemocratic regimes, the broader international context for promoting democracy was changing.[2] Greater resistance and less receptiveness to external support for democracy were taking root. Since then, the global context has changed even more dramatically, and so too has the environment for supporting democracy.

The third and most recent trend in the post–Cold War context is one that has emerged from the backlash but is distinct from it. We might most aptly call it the "authoritarian surge." Led by the "Big Five" authoritarian states of China, Russia, Iran, Saudi Arabia, and Venezuela, the authoritarian powers have taken more coordinated and decisive action to contain democracy on a *global* level.[3]

Over the course of this period, authoritarian governments have become bolder and more adept at stopping dissent before it starts. Restrictions on democratic voices at home have become increasingly sophisticated. Repressive governments have learned how to use the forms of law to repress independent civil society, while also developing sophisticated techniques to manipulate the media, both traditional and new. Even more striking than the refinement of domestic repression is the extent to which these regimes have learned to project influence beyond their own borders.

Authoritarianism has gone global. The characteristic features of the present authoritarian surge include amply funded media initiatives such as Russia's RT, China's CCTV, and Iran's Press TV. Each enjoys a global reach and projects messages that seek to undermine Western and U.S. prestige while shaping attitudes toward democracy. The new challenge to democracy is also evident in the authoritarians' efforts to alter the democracy and human-rights mechanisms of key rules-based institutions, including the Organization of American States, the Council of Europe, the Organization for Security and Cooperation in Europe, and international bodies concerned with the governance of the Internet. These regimes and their surrogates are increasingly seeking to insinuate themselves into the democratic political space with the goal of influencing—whether openly or furtively—the political dynamics of countries in one world region after another.

The extent of the authoritarian challenge forces us to confront the disconcerting prospect that the most influential antidemocratic regimes are no longer content simply to contain democracy. Instead, they want to roll it back by reversing advances dating from the time of the democratic surge. Just a decade ago, few political observers could even have imagined such a development.

In order to aid the cause of coming to grips with this challenge to democracy, the International Forum for Democratic Studies at the National Endowment for Democracy organized an effort to study the new authoritarian activism and grasp its inner workings. This volume is a product of that intensive project, which was carried out during the years 2014 and 2015.

The present book is meant to stand on its own, though it is also worth mentioning that it builds on earlier essay collections published in the *Journal of Democracy* since the close of the Cold War. Taken together, these volumes illuminate key trends and offer a guide to the shifting landscape that democracy and efforts to promote it have had to cope with over the last several decades. In their editors' introduction to *The Global Resurgence of Democracy* (1996), Larry Diamond and Marc F. Plattner recognized democracy's significant achievements up to that time and concluded on a note of "qualified optimism" about democracy's prospects. Diamond and Plattner observed that "for the near term, and perhaps for some time to come, democracy will benefit from the absence of any alternative regime form that could appeal across regions and cultures."[4] Twenty years later, it remains true that no such alternative has emerged. Some might wish to nominate China's developmental-authoritarian model, with its stress on economic growth without political rights, as a candidate. Yet China's own troubles with political repression, social restiveness, and general uncertainty (economic and otherwise) make its system an unlikely one for direct export.

In 2001, when the world political landscape had begun to shift in unpromising ways, *The Global Divergence of Democracies* examined the challenges that were then taking shape and asked how the behavior of China and Russia might affect democratic prospects.[5] In the years since, each of these leading authoritarian states has not only become more authoritarian, but has taken the lead in countering democratic developments.

The present volume consists of two parts. The first analyzes the growing influence of each of the "Big Five" authoritarian states: China, Russia, Iran, Saudi Arabia, and Venezuela. These countries have mobilized in pursuit of shared goals—to challenge the liberal international political order and to contain the spread of democracy. Iran is the subject of two chapters, one on the Islamic Republic's methods of domestic political control and another on the clerical autocracy's influence beyond Iran's borders.

This volume's second part contains seven chapters that inventory the "soft-power" tools that authoritarians are using to reshape the international system. These tools include challenges to the democratic norms that have taken root since the end of the Cold War; strategies for repressing free media and civil society; and underhanded assaults on the integrity of election monitoring. Additional chapters examine the ways in which authoritarian powers are molding the Internet to their liking while developing international media outlets as vehicles for spreading authoritarian views to a global audience.

Authoritarianism's "Big Five"

Part I opens with a chapter by Andrew Nathan examining the influence of China's international policies on the fortunes of democracy across the globe. Under Xi Jinping, who became head of the party-state in 2012, China has become increasingly assertive in pursuing its economic and strategic interests. While the Chinese Communist Party (CCP) is willing to work abroad with any type of regime, it denounces "universal values" and calls instead for state sovereignty and noninterference. Nathan observes that "for now, at least, China displays no missionary impulse to promote authoritarianism." Yet this does not mean that the world's largest authoritarian state exerts no adverse effect on democracy.

Nathan outlines six ways in which Beijing objectively works against liberal democracy. First, there is the sheer power of its example: China is the model *par excellence* for illiberal regimes that wish to achieve economic growth while preserving authoritarian rule. Second, the Chinese regime can be said to promote this model through the propaganda—meant to burnish China's international image—that it steadily pumps out via foreign media outlets. Third, China is a world leader in developing and teaching the technologies and techniques of censorship and political repression. Fourth, says Nathan, Beijing aims to "roll back existing democratic institutions or to stifle sprouts of democratic change in territories where it enjoys special influence." Fifth, China provides diplomatic support, favorable economic access, and investment opportunities to authoritarian regimes that function as key economic and strategic partners. Sixth, Beijing works with other illiberal powers to change the norms governing international organizations, the goal being to block outside scrutiny of authoritarian practices. But as Nathan concludes, "China's influence on the fate of democracy in the world, and its ability—if it wants to—to promote authoritarian transitions beyond its borders will depend on how the democracies perform."

In the second chapter, Lilia Shevtsova traces the Putin regime's efforts to maintain the system of personalized power that it has created to rule Russia. This system, she argues, is already in decay; the Kremlin's top priority is to shore it up. With this objective in mind, the regime uses the "Putin Doctrine" to legitimize harsh authoritarian measures at home and abroad. Domestically, there are crackdowns on political opponents, civil society activists, and independent media outlets. Foreign policy, too—be it the invasion of Ukraine, the annexation of Crimea, or the recent intervention in Syria—is bent to the task of sustaining personalized power and the *sistema* (as Russians call it). Belligerence and adventures in the countries on Russia's periphery and overseas are intended to distract the Russian public from the country's acute social and economic problems and to allow Putin to pose as a restorer of national greatness.

The specific aims of Russian international policy include containing Western influence both inside and outside Russia, undermining cooperation among Western democracies, and building a pro-Kremlin lobbying network in the West. Moscow also seeks to bolster fellow illiberal states by exerting influence within regional organizations such as the Eurasian Economic Union, the Collective Security Treaty Organization, and the Shanghai Cooperation Organization. Within these bodies, the Kremlin actively shares techniques for information warfare and propaganda with like-minded regimes. While the future remains uncertain, Shevtsova argues that "the Kremlin will not mellow with time"—any signs of backing down from its current strategy could be interpreted as weakness. This situation will push the Russian regime closer to its tipping point and, as it becomes more desperate, will turn it toward even harsher authoritarian measures, including more intensive repression at home and provocation beyond its borders.

Chapters 3 and 4, authored by Abbas Milani and Alex Vatanka, respectively, outline the central elements of Iran's domestic and international policy. Milani sheds light on the inner dynamics of what he calls Iran's "paradoxical regime." Despite it authoritarianism and brutal repression, a young and vibrant movement of democratic advocates has persisted since the 1979 Islamic revolution. Although Iran's authoritarian rulers have been forced to accommodate these liberal voices to a degree, power remains highly concentrated in the hands of a narrow elite. As Milani writes, Supreme Leader Ayatollah Ali Khamenei appoints the head of the judiciary; chooses members of influential political bodies; has representatives in every institution; controls the country's key mass-media outlets; and selects all Friday-prayer leaders and dictates the agenda of their weekly sermons. Despite these efforts to dominate every aspect of life in Iran through propaganda and even raw force, Milani argues that the populace remains restive while "cracks in the regime have become more apparent." Milani concludes that while some observers see the regime's "cracks" as belonging to a shrewd strategy of "repressive tolerance"—one in which the regime lets dissidents waste their energy on relative trivia while saving its own energy for truly crucial fights—others believe that even small acts of resistance can chip away at the edifice of clerical authoritarianism.

The Islamic Republic of Iran's key domestic priority is regime survival, and its international policy aims at forging alliances with partners around the world who share its agenda of containing democracy. In the fourth chapter, Alex Vatanka argues that international recognition and legitimacy have always been the goal of Iran's leaders. "As Iran's international isolation over its nuclear program has tightened," Vatanka writes, "Tehran has upped the ante in the race to influence global public opinion." The landmark July 2015 nuclear deal between Iran, the United States, and five other world powers will significantly affect how Iran engages the rest of the world. Whether the Iranian regime comes to behave—as Western advocates of the deal hope it will—in a more open and liberal manner as a result of this rapprochement remains a large question with serious implications for democracy both within Iran and beyond its borders.

As part of the broader trend of authoritarian cooperation, Iran has sought to build ties with like-minded nondemocratic countries, especially China and Russia. Iran's desire to collaborate with other illiberal powers reflects both its economic and its diplomatic needs, according to Vatanka. As it expands its surveillance techniques and cyberspace-policing strategies, Tehran looks to Beijing for new ideas. Meanwhile, following China and Russia, Iran has built an extensive international media presence, as the clerical regime projects its own form of "soft power" into countries in the Middle East, the Balkans, and elsewhere. Through these actions, Iran and its authoritarian partners have formed a "common bond." The thread that unites them is their shared quest to hang on to power. In forming alternative blocs in the global arena, Vatanka argues, these countries seek to undermine democratic norms, share technology to limit free speech online, and utilize international broadcasting to promote their illiberal values.

In Chapter 5, Javier Corrales dissects Venezuela's slide into authoritarianism under the late President Hugo Chávez and his handpicked successor, Nicolás Maduro. Corrales describes this descent in terms of the spread of "autocratic legalism" at home and the creation of an international strategy meant to armor the *chavista* regime against criticism from abroad. He writes that Chávez, a former army officer who was elected president in 1998 after having led a failed coup attempt in 1992, leveraged Venezuela's vast oil resources to build an "alliance of tolerance." The countries that benefit from Venezuela's largesse—in Latin America and beyond—are generally unwilling to criticize the Venezuelan government for its human-rights violations or undemocratic governance.

Corrales argues that Venezuela's rulers have concentrated their power through the "use, abuse, and non-use of the law." Both Chávez and Maduro have used procedures that are constitutional in form in order to pass laws that are autocratic in nature—a ploy that has served to shield them from criticism even as they have drawn ever more power into the executive branch. This trend of autocratic legalism has exerted especially harmful effects on Venezuela's civil society, independent media, and political opposition. The sharp falloff in world oil prices has put the regime under excruciating economic pressure, but Maduro continues to pursue Chávez-inspired soft-power initiatives. Perhaps most prominent among these is Telesur, a state-funded regional outlet that uses both traditional and new media to spread throughout Latin America messages hostile to the West in general and the United States in particular.

Much like Venezuela, the Kingdom of Saudi Arabia is heavily reliant on oil revenues. It also is currently beset by high unemployment and a good deal of domestic uncertainty. These domestic pressures, coupled with the monarchy's ongoing fear of Arab Spring–style political mobilization, have led to a shift in Saudi Arabia's regional foreign policy. In Chapter 6, Frederic Wehrey assesses the sources of this turn and considers its implications for democracy. The Kingdom's authorities are worried by the threat of "ideological mobilization incited from abroad" and remain anxious that Saudis might imitate the popular-protest tactics that rocked the Arab world in 2010 and 2011, when long-entrenched and seemingly secure autocrats found themselves run out of their own capitals almost overnight.

The Saudi regime's counterdemocratic activities, says Wehrey, are basically defensive in intent. The monarchy is most concerned to guard itself and the smaller countries that line its edges against destabilizing external influences. Thus Riyadh seeks to suppress democratic forces that it fears could open the way to rivals such as the Shia radicals of Iran (about a tenth of all Saudis are Shia, and they reside near the oil fields) or the Sunni radicals of the Muslim Brotherhood. The Saudis' main tool is money: The Kingdom uses its petrodollars to help its regional allies buy arms and stabilize their economies. Riyadh also has in hand a new antiterror code—like all Saudi laws, it is the decree of an absolute monarch who rules a polity with no elections and only an appointed, largely advisory parliament—that can support the task of suppressing dissent at home. Such policies, concludes Wehrey, may not come accompanied by heaping helpings of explicitly antidemocratic rhetoric, but it is clear that their "ultimate effect has been damaging to the spread of democratization and political pluralism." Looking ahead, it remains likely that the Saudi authorities will stick to their status quo policy despite swelling domestic pressures for change and the deep political shifts that are underway in the region.

Arenas of "Soft-Power" Competition

The size, location, and political and economic clout of the "Big Five" countries mean that any attempt to analyze the authoritarian resurgence must reckon with them. But such an analysis must also consider the critical "soft-power" arenas in which authoritarian regimes today are projecting influence regionally and globally. The second part of this volume therefore focuses on the strategies and methods that authoritarian states utilize to advance their agendas at home and abroad. It includes chapters covering the authoritarian influence on international norms, election observation, civil society, international media, and the Internet, respectively.

In Chapter 7, Alexander Cooley leads off this section with an essay shedding light on the authoritarians' efforts to challenge the liberal-democratic order. Long-held assumptions about the historical trajectory of norms, he notes, are being tested. Thanks to their determination and assiduous cooperation with one another, the authoritarians have achieved a dismaying degree of success in reshaping international bodies founded to promote human rights and democracy into forums more favorable to regimes that have scant regard for either.

In pursuing this goal, the authoritarians have challenged the universality of democracy and sought to erode liberal-democratic norms, replacing them with new counternorms that emphasize "state security, civilizational diversity, and traditional values." Sensing an opportunity in the rise of counterterrorist and security concerns since 9/11, authoritarians have grown increasingly assertive. They have expanded their own blacklists of domestic terror suspects and enlisted the help of their fellow authoritarians in repressing any groups or individuals whom they deem a threat. Cooley also highlights "respect for civilizational diversity" as the counternorm pushed by regional groups such as the Shanghai Cooperation Organization (whose members include China, Russia, and four Central Asian states). A third counternorm, pioneered by Russia, is the emphasis on defending "traditional values." Cooley argues that civil society has borne the brunt of these three antidemocratic counternorms.

The color revolutions that shook Georgia, Ukraine, and Kyrgyzstan from 2003 to 2005 made authoritarians elsewhere fear the possible rise of prodemocracy mobilizations in their own countries. Out of this fear came the crafting of a "counterrevolutionary playbook" that targets NGOs and democracy monitors." Authoritarian tactics include new legal restrictions on foreign funding for civil society groups, plus the promotion of "pseudo-NGOs" and "zombie election monitors" that serve to sow confusion and lend illiberal governments a façade of legitimacy. In order to further bolster their influence abroad, authoritarian regimes have created new regional bodies that challenge democratic norms while promoting illiberal counternorms. Hard cash helps too: China and the wealthy Gulf states have not been afraid to reinforce counternorms with flows of aid and investment money.

Such efforts, writes Cooley, "have turned a world that was once relatively favorable to the spread of democratic norms into one where authoritarians can push back—and have learned to do so in innovative ways." The focus of such authoritarian efforts is no longer merely preserving authoritarianism at home, but reshaping the international norms that stigmatize such governance. Cooley concludes by stressing that democratic states must remain committed to liberal values and a rules-based international order. Only then can the West and its allies hope to succeed in stemming the tide of the authoritarian resurgence.

The next chapter, by Patrick Merloe, examines the growing challenge posed by authoritarian states that want to rewrite electoral narratives. Following the onset of the post-1974 third wave of democratic transitions, Merloe writes, nonpartisan citizen election monitoring became key to promoting accountability and citizen participation during elections. More recently, however, with the decline in confidence in democracy, authoritarian regimes have become more assertive in the electoral realm, just as they have in the areas of communications and international organizations. These regimes have learned to employ a variety of tactics—including denial of access to information, cyberattacks, abuse of legal powers, electoral fraud, and manipulation of results—to undermine citizen election-monitoring efforts. In a typical ploy, state-run media can pump out disinformation, dwelling on the findings of authoritarian-friendly monitors while ignoring or marginalizing the reports of independent monitors. Public understanding is distorted while incumbents manufacture positive coverage for themselves and loudly lay claim to electoral legitimacy.

To illuminate the extent of the new challenge in this sphere, Merloe provides case studies of recent elections in three countries—Azerbaijan, Zimbabwe, and Venezuela—to show how authoritarians utilize these tactics to manipulate electoral processes. "Electoral transparency," Merloe concludes, "is absolutely and inescapably fundamental to genuine elections." Without credible elections, both democracy and stability are at risk.

Chapters 9 and 10 consider the impact of growing authoritarianism on civil society. In the first of these two chapters, Anne Applebaum turns to history in order to explain the varying attitudes toward civil society among postcommunist countries. Applebaum opens with classic statements by Edmund Burke and Alexis de Tocqueville praising what would come to be known as "civil society." She then turns to the great opponents of civil society, the Bolsheviks who seized power in Russia during the First World War. They insisted that the public sphere must be "unitary and univocal," then set about taking over or crushing all independent organizations. As Applebaum writes, the Bolsheviks loathed independent organizations "because they gave people the power to control their own lives, because they encouraged independent thought, and because they made people more critical of state power." Driven by this antipathy, Soviet rulers systematically destroyed all independent organizations—even apolitical ones. After 1945, the Soviet Union's communist satellite regimes in Central and Eastern Europe did the same thing in their own countries. Even today, communist powerholders in China and North Korea act out repressive policies first conceived and enforced by Lenin and his Bolsheviks.

Ironically, however, as Applebaum notes, "Lenin did not see that by attempting to control every aspect of society, totalitarian regimes would eventually turn every aspect of society into a potential source of dissent." After communism ended, people regained a degree of control that made possible a return to what Václav Havel called the "independent life of society." Yet the work required was often arduous, and the obstacles daunting: Independent initiatives and the legal infrastructure that enabled them had been wiped out, and many in these societies opposed efforts to rebuild them.

Countries such as Poland managed to break out of this pattern and become places where civil society could flourish again. Others, such as Russia, were weighed down by long histories of stubborn state efforts to suppress freedom of association, and remained places where independent civic organizations aroused much mistrust and suspicion. As Applebaum writes, "the return of the KGB to power has been marked by the slow but systematic elimination of all kinds of independent groups and organizations from Russian society." This includes a series of repressive laws restricting foreign funding and handing the Kremlin authority to shut down any foreign organizations deemed "undesirable." Fear tactics such as these threaten to erode Russia's already fragile civil society. Moreover, as Applebaum warns, they could spread beyond Russia and make other postcommunist societies centers of hostility to a free and robust associational life.

In Chapter 10, Douglas Rutzen examines the growing list of restrictions that authoritarian governments are using to suppress civil society and analyzes the gaps in the international legal framework that governments exploit in order to impose these restrictions. Rutzen argues that the fall of the Berlin Wall ushered in an era of unprecedented civic engagement. Following the 9/11 terrorist attacks, however, the climate for civil society grew increasingly frigid. Concerns grew that civil society organizations might be linked to terror groups. Moreover, as we have seen, the color revolutions fed authoritarian governments' already robust readiness to fear anything that could promote prodemocracy mobilization. Thus came the limits and bans.

Governments invoke national security and state sovereignty while protesting that they desire only to improve the effectiveness of development assistance, promote transparency, and keep civil society reasonably accountable to national laws and standards. Although international law contains a variety of mechanisms designed to protect civil society, these are undermined by "exceptions that permit national governments to enact restrictions under certain circumstances." As Rutzen writes, these circumstances include restrictions that are "prescribed by law," seek to fulfill a "legitimate aim," or are deemed "necessary in a democratic society"—a set of large loopholes indeed. But we should make no mistake: With regime security foremost in mind, authoritarian governments have been imposing restrictions on civil society groups' ability to receive funds from abroad in order to weaken the opposition and suppress independent associations.

In Chapter 11, Peter Pomerantsev draws on Russia's experience to examine how authoritarians have refurbished their techniques of media manipulation. Under Putin, the Kremlin, through control and deft use of television, has expanded its efforts to promote an alternative political reality for Russian—and increasingly international—audiences. As a result, the political process in Russia today has come to resemble a reality television show starring Putin as the "superhero-czar." Russian coverage of the war in Ukraine highlights this system's main aims—to insulate Putin and his allies from negative coverage while making his opponents look bad. This strategy has granted the Kremlin control over all forms of discourse, paving the way for it to blur the lines between fact and fiction in order to suit its needs. Kremlin-controlled channels deliberately spread cynicism among Russians and make them vulnerable to conspiracy theories.

Beyond Russia's borders, the Putin regime advances its interests by making allies of parties across the political spectrum, doling out money-making opportunities, and waging an information war against its critics. Perhaps the regime's most potent weapon in this war is RT, the Kremlin's international television broadcaster, which is a force not only via the airwaves but also on social media. Lavishly funded and active in a number of languages, RT has entered into editorial partnerships with a variety of countries, including Argentina and Syria (where Putin has become the mainstay of the Assad regime). Brimming with anti-Western content, RT "muddle[s] the information space and sow[s] doubt and confusion." Through censorship and the use of modern media, Pomerantsev writes, the Kremlin "has created a cynical citizenry, shaped by propaganda and conspiracy theories, that is bereft of hope." Perhaps most distressing is the example that Russia has set for other authoritarian regimes seeking to maintain control through media manipulation.

Like Russia under Putin, China under Xi Jinping has built up a formidable media apparatus with broad reach and refined its foreign-propaganda strategy. In Chapter 12, Anne-Marie Brady traces China's efforts to improve its international image, shape global norms, and expand its own "soft power." Since Beijing's brutal response to the 1989 Tiananmen Square protests, China's image has suffered. To undo the lingering reputational damage of the Tiananmen crackdown, the Chinese Communist Party works tirelessly—especially among the large diaspora of "Overseas Chinese"—via the Internet and other media to portray itself favorably while isolating critical voices. To sway elite non-Chinese audiences abroad, the Beijing regime has (as of 2015) created more than a thousand Confucius Institutes and classrooms worldwide to teach Chinese language and culture on college campuses in dozens of countries. The goal, writes Brady, is to "raise awareness of China's social, economic, and political stability, and the nation's incredible economic growth."

Although Beijing has already invested billions of dollars in these soft-power initiatives, Xi Jinping has pledged to spend still more on them. Given China's size and growing political ambition, its international mass-media gambits must be taken very seriously. Brady writes that since Xi announced the launch of a new global media strategy in 2014, "China's foreign-propaganda efforts have taken on a new level of assertiveness, confidence, and ambition." The same ambition can be seen in Beijing's efforts to get more of China's almost 1.4 billion people online even as authorities keep censoring the Internet and doing their best to strangle the possibility of any meaningful political speech or organization.

In Chapter 13, Ron Deibert takes a broader, global look at the influence of authoritarian powers on the Internet. Once trumpeted as "tools of liberation," cyberspace technologies are now being harnessed by authoritarian regimes to repress opposition and shrink civic space. Deibert sheds light on the arsenal of cyberspace-control techniques that authoritarians have developed and suggests responses. Deibert lists three "generations" of information controls. The first generation includes "defensive" strategies that seek to restrict access to information; the second consists of legal regulations intended to constrain the private sector; and the third relies on "offensive" techniques, such as surveillance and targeted cyberattacks. Deibert writes that a fourth generation of information controls could be added to this list: the expanding role of authoritarian regimes in Internet-governance forums. Even more worrisome is the growing use of regional groups such as the Shanghai Cooperation Organization and the Gulf Cooperation Council to reshape online norms.

Deibert outlines the driving forces behind the authoritarian cybersurge. One driver is the emphasis on protection against extremism and terrorism—especially in response to new threats from groups such as the Islamic State and Boko Haram. While cybercrime and terrorism are genuine threats, authoritarian regimes often overstate them to justify their use of repressive practices in policing cyberspace. Another driver is the growing spread of digital technology across the global South. The spread itself is not the problem, but it does carry with it the risk that authoritarian regimes will turn the newly accessible technologies into new tools of political repression. By sharing "best practices" and expanding their cooperation with one another, authoritarians have become more assertive in seeking to tighten their grip on cyberspace. To counter this threat, Deibert writes, democratic states must develop export controls, "smart sanctions," and a monitoring system to identify rights violations. Ensuring a "free, open, and secure cyberspace," Deibert concludes, "should loom as an urgent priority."

In the concluding chapter, Christopher Walker examines the challenge posed by the authoritarian resurgence. He analyzes the ways in which today's authoritarian regimes have turned the tables on the democracies by exploiting the opportunities presented by globalization and integration since the end of the Cold War. Walker writes: "Although authoritarian regimes are today integrated in many ways into the global system, they have not become more like the democracies; rather, they have developed policies and practices aimed at blocking democracy's advance." Over time, the authoritarians have "jiu jitsu–like" systematically turned integration against the democracies, seeking to hollow out the democracy and human-rights components of the most important regional and global rules-based institutions.

A critical part of this effort has been the creation of an "authoritarian toolkit" that includes government-organized nongovernmental organizations (GONGOs), "zombie election monitors," and well-funded international media enterprises, such as China's CCTV and Russia's RT. Through dedicated authoritarian learning, as well as the development and application of simulated instruments of democracy, authoritarian regimes have effectively hijacked the concept of "soft power." Walker concludes that "a renewed struggle between democracy and authoritarianism has emerged." So far, however, the democracies have not taken seriously the authoritarian challenge to the democratic order. If, in the end, the democracies continue to rely on a reactive approach that allows the autocrats to maintain the initiative, "we can expect the grim prospect of an even greater erosion of democratic space in the years to come."

Looking Forward

Authoritarian influence has been growing at a time when the United States and the European Union have scaled back their own ambitions with respect to supporting democracy and the values underlying it. Hence, more than a quarter-century after throngs of jubilant Germans tore down the Berlin Wall, the trajectories of influence of the world's leading democratic and antidemocratic powers are moving in opposite directions. The challenge presented by regimes in Moscow, Beijing, Tehran, Caracas, and Riyadh is being taken to an entirely new level by virtue of their projection of illiberal values and standards beyond their own national borders.

Lately, the leading authoritarian regimes have been riding high. Perhaps it is no surprise that the authoritarian surge has taken off at a time when malaise seems to grip the world's leading democracies. Some of their weakness in the face of the growing authoritarian challenge likely stems from the global economic crisis and the lingering loss of confidence that it has bred in the West. More generally, the established democracies have been distracted and at times even consumed by their own internal political debates and challenges. But the democracies underestimate the authoritarian challenge at their peril. Ironically, in the era of globalization—a phenomenon that many had assumed would give democracies an advantage in world affairs—it is the undemocratic states that have been the nimblest at exerting influence, especially in critical "soft-power" arenas. The democracies, quite simply, need to take the authoritarian challenge far more seriously than they have so far, and improve their game.

Over the past half-decade, as the authoritarian surge has taken clearer shape, four of the "Big Five" countries have been supported by high oil revenues. With the price of oil having moved much lower in 2015, it remains to be seen how Venezuela, Russia, Saudi Arabia, and Iran will manage over the longer haul. All suffer too from the scourge of corruption, which for each is a way of life but also a running sore and even an Achilles' heel.

Given low oil prices, Venezuela and Russia already are facing stiff challenges, which are increasingly raising questions about their regimes' legitimacy. China, unlike the others, does not depend on oil exports, yet it has its own serious problems. This was made glaringly clear during the latter half of 2015, when turmoil beset the Chinese economy amid a grave stock-market tumble. Much of the Chinese system's allure and prestige since the late Deng Xiaoping's stint as paramount leader (1978–92) has been based on the country's prodigious export-led economic growth. But should this growth ever slow, as inevitably it must and as it has recently shown signs of doing, many of those who have been drawn to the Chinese model of authoritarian governance will cast a colder eye upon it and its coercive ways. Presiding over growth and prosperity is easy. The test comes when times get tough and a system's capacities for resilience and self-correction are sorely tried. It remains to be seen how China's rulers, and indeed all the Big Five's authoritarian elites, will respond if they have to cope with long periods of poor economic growth. The Chinese Communist Party has relied heavily on a vast and repressive coercive apparatus even during times of prosperity; during times of hardship the system as it is presently configured may be pushed past its breaking point.

The authors of the essays collected in this volume explain the threat posed by these resurgent authoritarians, but also identify their inherent political and economic weaknesses, including rampant corruption. The established democracies have been slow to recognize the determined challenge that today's authoritarians present, perhaps out of hope that these regimes will be undone by their flaws. But given the resilience that the authoritarians have displayed so far, it would be rash for the democracies to underestimate the seriousness of the dangers that they pose.

Notes

1. Carl Gershman and Michael Allen, "The Assault on Democracy Assistance," *Journal of Democracy* 17 (April 2006): 36–51.

2. Thomas Carothers, "The Backlash Against Democracy Promotion," *Foreign Affairs* 85 (March–April 2006): 55–68.

3. Christopher Walker, "The New Containment: Undermining Democracy," *World Affairs* 178 (May–June 2015): 42–51.

4. Larry Diamond and Marc F. Plattner, "Introduction," *The Global Resurgence of Democracy* (Baltimore: Johns Hopkins University Press, 1996).

5. Larry Diamond and Marc F. Plattner, "Introduction," *The Global Divergence of Democracies* (Baltimore: Johns Hopkins University Press, 2001).

PART ONE

The Authoritarian "Big Five"

CHAPTER ONE

China's Challenge

ANDREW J. NATHAN

THE PEOPLE'S REPUBLIC OF CHINA (PRC) under President Xi Jinping has begun to flex its muscles as a major power. Setting aside Deng Xiaoping's mantra of "hide our light and nurture our strength" and Jiang Zemin's policy of "increase trust, reduce trouble, develop cooperation, and do not seek confrontation," Beijing today actively challenges its neighbors. It also confronts U.S. interests in the South and East China Seas, builds up its navy and missile forces to oppose a U.S. intervention should an armed clash erupt over Taiwan, and promotes the creation of alternative global institutions such as the "BRICS bank" and the Asian Infrastructure Investment Bank that are designed to exclude U.S. and European influence. There is growing worry among Western analysts about the extent to which China, as its power grows, will seek to remake the world in its authoritarian image.

China expert Michael Pillsbury, for example, argues that if the country's economy continues to grow at its current pace and hard-liners retain control over Chinese policy, by midcentury China will oppose democratization around the world, control information about China available globally through censorship of the Internet and influence over mass media, and intimidate critics by means of cyberattacks and the withholding of economic favors.[1] Retired U.S. general Wesley Clark points out that China "has rejected both the move toward democracy and the acceptance of human and civil rights that Americans had hoped would emerge from China's astonishing economic rise. . . . China's foreign policy relies on keenly calculated self-interest, at the expense of the international institutions, standards and obligations the United States has sought to champion."[2]

For the time being, however, China's strategic situation does not permit an all-out challenge to democracy beyond its shores, and whether it will ever undertake such a challenge is uncertain. China's foreign policy remains essentially defensive. First, the country's policy makers are concerned about the fragile security situation at home, caused by dissatisfaction among ethnic minorities, displaced peasants and property owners, disgruntled workers, liberal intellectuals, and others—opponents who, Beijing believes, are incited and supported by hostile foreign forces.[3] Second, policy makers have to worry about relations with the two-dozen countries around China's borders, including powerful states with territorial disputes and other tensions with China, like Japan, Vietnam, and India, as well as countries with a dangerous potential for instability such as North Korea, Pakistan, and Tajikistan. Third, China has to worry about regional crises that could break out at any moment in places such as the Korean Peninsula and the Taiwan Strait. And fourth, it has to worry about access to resources and markets around the world.[4]

Facing this array of challenges, the Chinese leadership seeks to maintain good relations with whatever regime is in power in any country where China has diplomatic and security interests or does business, regardless of the character of that regime. To be sure, it is often easier for Beijing to do business with narrow authoritarian elites than to navigate within complex democratic systems. But attempting to undermine a foreign democratic regime would, in business terms, cost more than it would be worth. And even if it wanted to, China does not have the economic, military, or soft-power resources to exert substantial influence over the domestic political systems of faraway countries. It has not been able even to prevent a democratic transition in its close neighbor Burma or to persuade its only formal ally, North Korea, to adopt liberalizing economic reforms.

This "regime-type-neutral" approach has not been a permanent feature of Chinese foreign policy. The situation was different in the later years of Mao Zedong's rule, when China was economically self-sufficient (though poor) and placed priority on undermining Soviet influence wherever it could. Mao declared, "With great turmoil under heaven, the situation is excellent." Beijing gave material, diplomatic, and propaganda support to pro-China, avowedly Maoist movements in Burma, Cambodia, Indonesia, Malaysia, the Philippines, Thailand, Angola, Rhodesia, and South-West Africa, among other places. A famous poster showed Mao surrounded by smiling revolutionaries of every race, from every continent, inscribed "We Have Friends All Over the World!"

Today, however, China accuses the United States and the European Union of contaminating their foreign policies with "ideology." When revolutionaries in Nepal wanted to emulate Mao, they had to do so without any help from Beijing, which continued to deal with the conservative monarchy in Kathmandu until the king was overthrown and the Maoists became part of the governing coalition, at which point Beijing was willing to deal with them.[5] China views democracy promotion, human-rights diplomacy, humanitarian interventions, and the rise of international criminal law through the lens of strategic gain and loss—as efforts by Western powers to weaken rivals and expand their own influence. To blunt these efforts, Beijing advocates the principles of sovereignty, noninterference, cultural pluralism, and mutual respect. China denounces the idea of "universal values" as a form of Western subversion of states that try to protect their autonomy from Western influence. Speaking at UNESCO headquarters in Paris in March 2014, Xi Jinping declared, "All human civilizations are equal in terms of value."[6] In May 2014, China joined Russia in blocking a UN Security Council referral of the Syrian civil war to the International Criminal Court on the grounds that nations' internal conflicts should be settled internally.

Today's policy of neutrality toward other countries' regime types is as much a product of China's strategic interests as was yesterday's policy of promoting Maoist revolution. If China's strategic situation changes, its policy of regime-type neutrality may change as well. For now, at least, China displays no missionary impulse to promote authoritarianism. But this does not mean that its policies are inconsequential for the fate of democracy. Beijing's pragmatic efforts to protect the regime from challenges at home and to pursue its economic and security interests abroad have a negative impact on the fate of democracy in six ways.

1) ENCOURAGING AUTHORITARIAN REGIMES BY THE POWER OF ITS EXAMPLE. The enterprise of democracy promotion has long benefited from the belief that democracy is the only form of regime compatible with modern society. By demonstrating that advanced modernization can be combined with authoritarian rule, the Chinese regime has given new hope to authoritarian rulers elsewhere in the world.

Some lessons of the Chinese model are as old as Machiavelli. The decisive use of force to suppress resistance intimidates most potential opponents. Repression should be paired with a show of pious fealty to traditional values in order to help citizens rationalize their faith in the benevolence of their leaders. But the post-Mao Chinese Communist Party (CCP) has updated the authoritarian model in several ways. Among other accomplishments, Beijing created a large middle class and then succeeded in coopting it politically; established a rule-of-law framework and then used those institutions to outlaw authentic civil society, political dissent, and independent religious activity; developed a diversified professional media and then maintained effective political censorship over it; and accepted aid from international foundations, governments, and civil society organizations while delegitimizing and making illegal international support for domestic civil society actors and organizations that the regime regards as dangerous.

Many countries facing problems of ethnic diversity are closely observing Beijing's handling of its ethnic minorities. China's ethnic-minorities policies include a combination of economic modernization, linguistic assimilation, and demographic mixing. This approach has succeeded among populations like the ethnic Mongols and the Hui (a Muslim minority population that is interspersed with Han populations around the country). Although there is visible resistance in Tibet and Xinjiang, these policies may also be working there, as majorities of the indigenous populations adapt to urban life, learn the Chinese language, and find ways to make a living in the modern sectors of the economy.

For authoritarian regimes seeking to build modern infrastructures, Beijing's success in using technocrats and experts is encouraging. China has sent more than two-million students abroad to study science, engineering, economics, finance, public administration, and the like.[7] It has created employment conditions sufficient to attract many of these students back home to work in universities, institutes, and government bureaus. It has given the experts enough freedom to work productively in their areas of specialization without allowing them to violate the ban on criticizing the regime. And perhaps most remarkably, the people with real power have learned to listen respectfully to the experts and to take their advice on technical subjects. This helps to create a strong incentive for technocrats to continue serving the regime.

Other authoritarian regimes have looked to China's management of the Internet as a model. Beijing so far has reaped the benefits of rapidly employing information technology without suffering the political consequences that many commentators predicted were inevitable. China has created a panoply of measures that work together to achieve Internet control, including the configuration of the Internet pathways (which allows the authorities to surveil traffic in real time and turn off and on access to specific websites), the legal regulations that require both Internet providers and customers to take responsibility for what is posted, and the deployment of vast numbers of Internet police who inspect what is posted and intervene directly to add and delete material. China has used this system to scrub the Chinese Web clean of references to sensitive topics such as June Fourth (the date of the 1989 Tiananmen Square crackdown), Falun Gong, and troubles in Tibet and Xinjiang. The Great Firewall prevents most Chinese citizens from accessing international news media and foreign websites that the government views as unfriendly or critical. The government has also extended this model of control to other social media like cellphone messaging and chat services.

China has pioneered flexible, tailored police practices for controlling political dissidents. While blunt force applied by the paramilitary People's Armed Police, the regular police, and hired thugs remains useful for dealing with civil unrest and the unruliness of ordinary citizens, the Ministry of Public Security has also created a shadowy bureau referred to as the *guobao* (*Guonei anquan baoweiju* or "Bureau to Guard Domestic Security") that specializes in dealing with high-value targets, such as intellectuals or journalists, whom the regime would like to dissuade or deter. The guobao form special work teams to spy on their targets, "invite" them "for tea" in order to interrogate and threaten them, "host" them away from Beijing during sensitive meetings or anniversaries, and sometimes detain them for indefinite periods of time in order to drive home the message that the dissident individual is helpless against the state.[8]

It would not be easy for other countries to emulate all of what China has done. The Chinese model requires large fiscal resources, technological sophistication, a well-trained and loyal security apparatus, and sufficient political discipline within the regime not to take power struggles public. Nonetheless, as the prestige of the Chinese model grows, even without Chinese efforts to propagate it, other authoritarian governments are encouraged by the idea that authoritarianism is compatible with modernization, and they try to adapt, to varying degrees, Chinese methods of control. As Azar Gat put it in 2007, "Authoritarian capitalist states, today exemplified by China and Russia, may represent a viable alternative path to modernity, which in turn suggests that there is nothing inevitable about liberal democracy's ultimate victory—or future dominance."[9]

2) ATTEMPTING TO BURNISH ITS NATIONAL PRESTIGE ABROAD, PARTLY THROUGH INTERNATIONAL PROMOTION OF AUTHORITARIAN VALUES. In recent years China has mounted a large soft-power offensive around the world.[10] This has included the global expansion of the official Xinhua News Agency, increased world broadcasts by China Central Television (CCTV), Xinhua TV, and China Radio International, and the establishment of nearly five-hundred Confucius Institutes in foreign universities and other institutions.[11] In regions such as Africa, where local media are underfinanced, free content supplied by Xinhua has become an important source of material. Much of this material is straight news, but with a good deal of pro-China content; none of it, of course, is anti-China. Where local media are better financed, organs like the *China Daily* are able to purchase multipage sections to tell China's story. Beijing's themes have also achieved dominance in Chinese-language media in diaspora communities around the world.[12]

The primary theme of Chinese international propaganda is not regime type but China's benevolence—as a civilization, as a culture, and as an international partner. An important secondary theme running through such propaganda, however, is the upholding of the Chinese style of rule, via polemics touting the benefits of Chinese-style socialism, identifying CCP rule with traditional Confucian values like social harmony, and explaining the suitability of China's political system to China's "national conditions" (*guoqing*). In addition, Chinese organs respond to Western attacks on Chinese human-rights violations by pointing out flaws in Western human-rights practices. For example, the Chinese government issues a report on human-rights problems in the United States in response to criticisms of China in the U.S. State Department's annual reports on human-rights practices around the world. Xinhua carries reports on events like the protests against police abuse in Ferguson, Missouri, in an attempt to show international audiences that U.S. human-rights diplomacy is hypocritical, and even to persuade U.S. audiences that the West should stop bashing China.

Chinese propaganda does not, however, cross the boundary of suggesting that democratic countries should adopt authoritarian institutions. That argument would contradict the themes of respect for sovereignty and cultural pluralism that dominate Chinese diplomacy. Indeed, Chinese propaganda does not explicitly characterize China's system as undemocratic, instead describing it as "socialist democracy," "Chinese-style democracy," and "people's democratic dictatorship," among other locutions. Nor is the idea of "Asian values," floated by officials in Singapore and Malaysia and endorsed by Chinese officials, meant to imply that there is any single political model suitable for all of Asia, but only that liberal democracy is not suited to all Asians. It is rare to find an argument, even by proregime independent intellectuals, that portrays the Chinese experience as a universal model that should be adopted everywhere. Yet despite these self-imposed limits, Beijing's polemics, transmitted over its growing international media network, contribute to the weakening of democracy's international prestige. And since everyone knows that the Chinese system is authoritarian (even if Chinese propaganda does not label it as such), the polemics enhance the prestige of nondemocratic rule.

China's soft-power efforts bleed over into what is in effect subversion of other countries' democratic institutions when China tries to censor the way that it is presented by journalists and academics abroad.[13] Prominent examples include the denial of visas to journalists for Bloomberg and the *New York Times* who wrote reports that the regime did not like; denial of visas to academics who offended the Chinese government; pressure on the Frankfurt Book Fair, the Melbourne Film Festival, and other venues not to invite cultural figures disapproved of by the regime; and Confucius Institute efforts to veto programs on China held by other units at U.S. universities.[14] Such measures have promoted self-censorship by media and academic figures abroad.[15] Meanwhile, with its growing economic influence, China has been able to encourage the rise of influential lobbies in democratic countries that favor eliminating issues related to human rights and democracy from their countries' diplomacy with China.[16] Except for Google, foreign Internet providers working in China have been forced to varying degrees to cooperate with Chinese censorship practices in ways that are inconsistent with these companies' principles of operation elsewhere.[17] In these diverse ways, Beijing's efforts to promote a favorable image abroad have, as collateral damage, undermined the vitality of free institutions in some democratic countries.

3) PLAYING A KEY ROLE IN A CIRCLE OF AUTHORITARIAN STATES THAT PICK UP TECHNIQUES OF RULE FROM ONE ANOTHER. Public information about these exchanges is thin. We know that China offers training in its schools of law, journalism, public administration, and police work to professionals and officials from other countries, especially from Africa. China also trains foreign students in a variety of academic disciplines. It conducts joint counterterrorism exercises with the militaries of Kazakhstan, Kyrgyzstan, Russia, Tajikistan, and Uzbekistan—its fellow member-states of the Shanghai Cooperation Organization (SCO). Little information is available about these programs and their effects. But it is reasonable to expect that students trained in Chinese professional schools learn techniques that China uses at home to manage its authoritarian system, and those learning science or liberal arts absorb some attitudes favorable to authoritarian institutions.

Other states have emulated the rhetorical strategy developed by China and some other authoritarian states of labeling their own regimes not as authoritarian but as a new type of democracy. For example, in July 2014 Hungarian prime minister Viktor Orbán expressed his support for "illiberal democracy" as a form of rule, explicitly modeled on that of China, as "a way of organizing communities, a state that is most capable of making a nation competitive."[18]

Perhaps the most important technique that authoritarian states have learned from one another is how to use the forms of law to support repression. China's criminal-procedure code allows the police to detain people repeatedly for thirty-day investigation periods; its criminal code allows dissidents to be sentenced for "picking quarrels and provoking troubles"; its law on lawyers requires defense attorneys to demonstrate loyalty to the state rather than to the interests of the defendant; and its trial procedures do not require a presumption of innocence and can be legally conducted in a single day and without hearing from defense witnesses.

China has pioneered the imposition of regulations punishing those who use the Internet to criticize the regime, and these have been copied by authoritarian regimes elsewhere.[19] China and its Eurasian partners in the SCO concluded secret treaties that allow for the *refoulement* (coerced return despite the well-founded fear of political persecution) from one SCO member-state to another of any of its own citizens whom the receiving state designates as a terrorist.[20] Outside the SCO, China has gotten Cambodia, Malaysia, and Nepal, among others, to cooperate with this new norm, allowing Chinese citizens of Uyghur ethnicity to be returned to China on the grounds that China has designated these individuals as terrorists. China and Russia have spearheaded the use of registration laws and banking controls to prevent their civil society organizations from receiving financial support from overseas. These methods have also been emulated by authoritarian rulers elsewhere.

China also exports some of the hard technology of authoritarian rule. Rebecca MacKinnon writes, "Chinese networked authoritarianism serves as a model for other regimes—such as Iran—that seek to maintain power and legitimacy in the Internet age."[21] Although it is not easy to trace the exchanges of hard and soft technology among regimes seeking to control the Internet, China is reported to have supplied Internet-control technology to Iran and other countries. Amnesty International published a report in 2014 on "China's Trade in Tools of Torture and Repression."[22] China is also a source of facial-recognition software. Of course, China is not the only or indeed the main country to export such technologies—that is probably the United States—but it is believed to be a leading low-cost supplier of technologies not produced in the domestic markets of most authoritarian countries, and it has no export controls on such sales.

4) SEEKING TO ROLL BACK EXISTING DEMOCRATIC INSTITUTIONS OR TO STIFLE SPROUTS OF DEMOCRATIC CHANGE IN TERRITORIES WHERE IT ENJOYS SPECIAL INFLUENCE. These are Hong Kong and Macau—two Special Administrative Regions that came under PRC control in 1997 and 1999, respectively, when they were returned to Chinese sovereignty by their former colonial rulers—and Taiwan, a territory over which China claims sovereignty and over which it has growing economic influence. In none of these places has China denounced democracy in principle, but in all three it has undermined it in practice.

Before China regained sovereignty over the British Crown Colony of Hong Kong in 1997, Chris Patten, the last British governor, had introduced new, more democratic procedures for the election of the colony's

Legislative Council (LegCo). Beijing viewed this as a poison pill designed to undermine its future control over the new Special Autonomous Region. It denounced the reforms as illegitimate, and after retrocession of the territory to Chinese rule, it dissolved the sitting LegCo and installed a new LegCo, elected under procedures even less democratic than those that had been in place before Patten's reform.

At the same time, however, in handing back Hong Kong, Britain had acquired Beijing's commitment that it would allow Hong Kong to retain its rule-of-law institutions and civil freedoms for fifty years, and that Hong Kong would be ruled by the people of Hong Kong. Accordingly, the Basic Law that Beijing granted to Hong Kong provided that its "residents shall have freedom of speech, of the press and of publication; freedom of association, of assembly, of procession and of demonstration; and the right and freedom to form and join trade unions, and to strike." Beijing also promised eventually to introduce "universal suffrage" in the elections of both the LegCo and the Special Autonomous Region's chief executive. These commitments became inconvenient as sentiments critical of Beijing emerged in some sections of the Hong Kong electorate. Instead of launching a frontal attack on democracy as a principle, however, Beijing worked to frustrate democratic impulses in more indirect ways. It postponed its commitment to introduce democratic elections and, in 2014, proposed a nomination method for the 2017 chief-executive election that would have guaranteed Beijing's control over the slate of candidates—a decision that led to a weeks-long series of massive demonstrations by citizens who wanted more far-reaching democratic reforms. In addition, observers believe that Beijing has acted through local businessmen, officials, and underworld figures to threaten, dismiss, and sometimes physically attack journalists and academics who are perceived as excessively liberal.

Beijing faces a less challenging situation in the former Portugese colony of Macau. When Macau returned to Chinese sovereignty in 1999, Beijing provided a Basic Law guaranteeing individual rights similar to those in Hong Kong, but the Basic Law's provisions for electing the Macau chief executive and Legislative Council were less democratic than those promised to Hong Kong. Macau elites have worked closely with Beijing, and Macau's prodemocracy forces so far remain weak. In August 2014, Macau authorities arrested five prodemocracy activists who called for more democratic procedures.

In Taiwan, Beijing has expressed its distaste for democracy selectively, depending on the policies that democratic institutions produce. In 2000, when pro–Taiwanese independence politician Chen Shui-bian was running for president, Chinese premier Zhu Rongji went on television to threaten Taiwan voters with dire consequences if they elected Chen. He won the election anyway, and subsequently placed referenda before the voters on strengthening Taiwan's self-defense capabilities and seeking to rejoin the UN. Beijing denounced these votes as illegitimate, claiming that Taiwan had no right to self-determination. The PRC has prevented Taiwan from gaining observer status in the UN and representation in other intergovernmental bodies because such representation would, Beijing believes, be a step toward independent statehood. The PRC has also sought to exert influence over Taiwanese media to get more favorable coverage of Chinese society and Beijing's policies—the most prominent example being the 2008 purchase of the China Times media group by a pro-mainland Taiwanese businessman. By contrast, when Taiwanese voters in 2008 elected current president Ma Ying-jeou, someone whom Beijing viewed as unlikely to pursue independence, Chinese authorities expressed no objection and rewarded Ma with a free-trade agreement and other policy benefits.

Beijing's opposition to democracy in these three territories aims to protect the regime from challenges that might embarrass it, inspire opponents on the mainland, or require suppression by force. Although the damage done to democratic institutions is incidental to Beijing's drive to exercise control over territories where it claims sovereignty, it is damage nonetheless.

5) HELPING TO ENSURE THE SURVIVAL OF AUTHORITARIAN REGIMES THAT ARE KEY ECONOMIC AND STRATEGIC PARTNERS. Beijing's engagements with nearby North Korea, Cambodia, Burma, the SCO states, Pakistan, and Nepal have sought to preserve buffer states; gain favorable economic access; obtain cooperation in extraditing Uyghurs, Tibetans, and democratic activists; and secure cooperation on its diplomatic priorities, such as isolating Taiwan. China has also cooperated with the governments of Russia, Iran, Venezuela, Sudan, and Zimbabwe in order to gain access to economic resources and diplomatic cooperation in checking the spread of Western influence. In cultivating such relationships, China supplies investments, markets, arms, diplomatic backing, and other benefits that help such regimes to survive.

China has not always approved of the authoritarian regimes with which it deals. For example, it has long been dissatisfied with North Korea's regime—not only because it does not defer to China's strategic priority of maintaining stability on the Korean peninsula, but because Chinese leaders believe that the Kim dynasty has missed opportunities to place itself on more stable ground by failing to carry out Chinese-style economic reforms. Similarly, Chinese leaders were disdainful of the crude, superstitious practices of the Burmese junta. For strategic reasons, however, China contributed to the survival of these and other authoritarian and semiauthoritarian regimes.

6) WORKING TO SHAPE INTERNATIONAL INSTITUTIONS TO MAKE THEM "REGIME-TYPE-NEUTRAL" INSTEAD OF WEIGHTED IN FAVOR OF DEMOCRACY. In the UN Human Rights Council (UNHRC), for example, China has cooperated with like-minded states to promote the principle of "universality," which reduces the degree to which individual countries are singled out for attention. The UNHRC's process of Universal Periodic Review, which China helped to promote, subjects every state—the United States as much as China—to review by the Council, and does so in a way that allows the state under review and its sympathizers heavy influence in shaping the agenda of the review. Similarly, China was a supporter of a UNHRC initiative to have each state submit a Human Rights Action Plan, something China has done. Under this initiative, each state can put forward its own view of how international human-rights norms should be interpreted for application in that country. China also has worked to restrict the role of NGOs in the Council and in the human-rights treaty bodies (expert committees that oversee the implementation of the ten main human-rights treaties), and to restrict the length and content of mandates given by the Council to the so-called Special Procedures (independent experts who, according to the Council's website, report and advise on human rights). The net effect of these efforts has been to position China in compliance with self-set priorities and to insulate it from serious censure in the UNHRC, thereby reducing the pressure that China had felt from the Council's predecessor, the Human Rights Commission, in the early 1990s.[23]

China has sought to establish as a norm that government-to-government complaints about human-rights issues should be delivered in private, and that public airing of such interventions is disruptive of diplomatic courtesy. With respect to state-to-state human-rights dialogues, China has promoted the norms that they should be secret, that they should be bilateral rather than multilateral, that foreign dialogue partners should not coordinate with one another, and that invitees to the nongovernmental-specialist components of these dialogues need to be vetted by both sides (that is, China can veto participants proposed by the other side).[24]

China is one of the many states that have gone along only partially with the normative shift in favor of humanitarian intervention while emphasizing the need for continued respect for the previously dominant norm of nonintervention. Beijing participated in the negotiations over the emergent norm of "Responsibility to Protect" (R2P), but it placed emphasis on the first pillar (of three), which describes the international community's responsibility to help sovereign states to develop their own capacity to protect their people, rather than the third pillar, which addresses the responsibility of the international community to intervene when a sovereign government has failed in its duty.[25]

In the UN Security Council, China has sometimes allowed interventionist resolutions to be adopted (either by abstaining or by voting in favor of them), but it has often delayed, modified, or blocked such resolutions on the grounds that states should settle their internal problems by themselves. When China has allowed such resolutions to go forward, it has usually done so in order to maintain solidarity with Russia and with states in the affected region (for example, the African Union on Sudan, and the Arab League on Libya), to protect Chinese economic interests (for example, Sudan and Libya), and with the proviso that the intervention should not be used to overthrow a regime.[26]

On UN peacekeeping, China has moved from opposing such operations to active support and participation. But it emphasizes the principle of host-state consent and the use of development projects as part of the peacekeeping process. These positions are consistent with China's interest in slowing the erosion of state sovereignty and in positioning itself as a peacefully rising developing country rather than as an assertive great power.[27]

The U.S. State Department under Hillary Clinton pursued an initiative to codify a broad concept of information freedom in several international venues. China (and other like-minded states) pushed back. In the SCO, China supported Russian efforts to define a concept called information warfare and to call for a norm of cyberdisarmament. In 2011, China, Russia, and other states submitted to the UN General Assembly a proposal for a "Code of Conduct for Information Security" that called for greater state-based regulation of the Internet.

China has not joined and does not cooperate with the International Criminal Court. (The United States also has not joined, although it has sometimes cooperated with the Court.) Beneficiaries of China's stance have included the rulers of Sudan, Syria, North Korea, and Sri Lanka.

China rejects the principle of conditionality in the granting of foreign aid and foreign investment.[28] This stance allows authoritarian regimes to shirk pressure on them from the World Bank and Western governments to make human-rights improvements in return for aid. The BRICS bank and proposed new Asian Infrastructure Investment Bank are likely to adopt the same policy.

What of the Future?

If and when China's economy grows to two or three times the size of the U.S. economy, its influence in the world will naturally increase. Yet this does not necessarily mean that China will shift to a proactive, Mao-style effort to promote transitions from democracy to authoritarianism. First, it is not easy to undermine consolidated democracies (to be sure, struggling democracies are another matter). Second, although authoritarian regimes may be easier to do business with, there is no theory of the "authoritarian peace" that says that China would be more secure if more of its neighbors were authoritarian states: Indeed, some of the greatest threats to Chinese security have come from fellow authoritarian regimes, like those of the Soviet Union, North Korea, and Vietnam. Third, China's internal divisions and its geopolitical situation in the middle of Asia are, for the foreseeable future, likely to prevent it from establishing hegemony in its own region, which would be a necessary precondition for it to try to impose on the rest of the world an alternative vision of world order.

But a wealthier China will surely have greater motives and greater capacity to exercise international influence in the six ways analyzed here. Beijing will have greater interests to protect overseas—investments, energy and commodity supplies, citizens, and government personnel. It is likely to view authoritarian regimes as more responsive to its interests, and as more supportive than democratic regimes of the kinds of international norms and institutions that it wants to promote. China's example, its international propaganda, and its technical, financial, and diplomatic assistance will do even more to help authoritarian regimes to survive; its influence in international institutions will be more effective in slowing or even reversing the momentum of the last forty years toward more democracy-friendly and rights-friendly international norms.

But China's influence on the fate of democracy in the world, and its ability—if it wants to—to promote authoritarian transitions beyond its borders will depend on how the democracies perform. Because China's own trajectory is not fixed, it is of course important for the democracies to continue to support Chinese civil society, human-rights activists, and liberal intellectuals. Yet the key to the global fate of democracy lies chiefly within the democracies themselves. Except for its indirect influence on freedoms of speech and the press, Beijing has done little to undermine the performance of democratic systems. Their problems are self-generated. Because the appeal of authoritarianism grows when the prestige of democracy declines, the most important answer to China's challenge is for the democracies to do a better job of managing themselves than they are doing today.

Notes

1. Michael Pillsbury, *The Hundred-Year Marathon: China's Secret Strategy to Replace America as the Global Superpower* (New York: Henry Holt, 2015), ch. 9.

2. Wesley K. Clark, "Getting Real About China," *New York Times,* 10 October 2014, *www.nytimes.com/2014/10/11/opinion/sunday/getting-real-about-china.html.*

3. Andrew J. Nathan and Andrew Scobell, "How China Sees America: The Sum of Beijing's Fears," *Foreign Affairs* 91 (September–October 2012): 32–47.

4. Andrew J. Nathan and Andrew Scobell, *China's Search for Security* (New York: Columbia University Press, 2012).

5. Aditya Adhikari, *The Bullet and the Ballot Box: The Story of Nepal's Maoist Revolution* (London: Verso, 2014).

6. "Speech by H.E. Xi Jinping President of the People's Republic of China At UNESCO Headquarters," 28 March 2014, available at *http://se.china-embassy. org/eng/wjdt/t1142560.htm.*

7. According to the Ministry of Education, 2.25 million students; see Wang

Qingfeng, "China Becomes World's Top Source of Overseas Students: Country Passes India as Top Supplier of Foreign Students to the United States," *Caixin,* 25 September 2012, *http://english.caixin.com/2012-09-25/100441943.html.*

8. Xu Youyu and Hua Ze, eds., *In the Shadow of the Rising Dragon: Stories of Repression in the New China* (New York: Palgrave Macmillan, 2013).

9. Azar Gat, "The Return of Authoritarian Great Powers," *Foreign Affairs* 86 (July–August 2007): 59–69.

10. Anne-Marie Brady, *Marketing Dictatorship: Propaganda and Thought Work in Contemporary China* (Lanham, Md.: Rowman and Littlefield, 2008), Ch. 7.

11. There are "over 480" Confucius Institutes worldwide; see "Confucius Institutes Worldwide," UCLA Confucius Institute, *www.confucius.ucla.edu/about-us/confucius-institutes-worldwide.*

12. Thanks to Anne-Marie Brady for pointing this out.

13. Sarah Cook, "The Long Shadow of Chinese Censorship: How the Communist Party's Media Restrictions Affect News Outlets Around the World," Report to the Center for International Media Assistance, 22 October 2013, *www.cima.ned.org/publications/long-shadow-chinese-censorship-how-communist-party%E2%80%99s-media-restrictions-affect-news-out.*

14. Marshall Sahlins, "China U.: Confucius Institutes Censor Political Discussions and Restrain the Free Exchange of Ideas. Why, Then, Do American Universities Sponsor Them?" *Nation,* 29 October 2013, *www.thenation.com/article/176888/china-u#.*

15. Emily Parker, "Censors Without Borders," *New York Times Sunday Book Review,* 14 May 2010, *www.nytimes.com/2010/05/16/books/review/Parker-t.html?pagewanted=all&_r=0;* Perry Link, "The Long Shadow of Chinese Blacklists on American Academe," WorldWise: Globtrotting Thinkers blog, *Chronicle of Higher Education,* 22 November 2013, *http://chronicle.com/blogs/worldwise/the-long-shadow-of-chinese-blacklists-on-american-academe/33359.*

16. James Mann, *The China Fantasy: How Our Leaders Explain Away Chinese Repression* (New York: Viking, 2007).

17. SecDev Group, "Collusion and Collision: Searching for Guidance in Chinese Cyberspace," 20 September 2011. Among other conclusions, the report says, "Most of the major Western internet companies active in China [except for Google] . . . have acceded to China's demands for information control, seeing this as the price of doing business."

18. "Viktor Orbán's Speech at the XXV Bálványos Free Summer University and Youth Camp, July 26, 2014, Băile Tuşnad (Tusnádfürdő)," *http://hungarian-spectrum.wordpress.com/2014/07/31/viktor-orbans-speech-at-the-xxv-balvanyos-free-summer-university-and-youth-camp-july-26-2014-baile-tusnad-tusnadfurdo.*

19. For example, Robert Herman, "Authoritarian Contagion in Africa," 4 February 2014, Freedom at Issue blog, *http://freedomhouse.org/blog/authoritarian-contagion-africa.*

20. Human Rights in China, *Counter-Terrorism and Human Rights: The*

Impact of the Shanghai Cooperation Organization, Human Rights in China Whitepaper, March 2011, *www.hrichina.org/en/publications/hric-report/counter-terrorism-and-human-rights-impact-shanghai-cooperation-organization.*

21. Rebecca MacKinnon, "Networked Authoritarianism in China and Beyond: Implications for Global Internet Freedom," paper presented at the conference on "Liberation Technology in Authoritarian Regimes," Hoover Institution and Center on Democracy, Development and the Rule of Law (CDDRL), Stanford University, 11–12 October 2010, p. 30, available at *http://iis-db.stanford.edu/evnts/6349/MacKinnon_Libtech.pdf.*

22. Amnesty International, *China's Trade in Tools of Torture and Repression* (London: Amnesty International Publications, 2014), *www.amnesty.org/en/library/asset/ASA17/042/2014/en/7dcccd64-15c2-423a-93dd-2841687f6655/asa170422014en.pdf.*

23. Rana Siu Inboden and Titus C. Chen, "China's Response to International Normative Pressure: The Case of Human Rights," *International Spectator: Italian Journal of International Affairs* 47 (June 2012): 45–57.

24. Katrin Kinzelbach, *The EU's Human Rights Dialogue with China: Quiet Diplomacy and Its Limits* (Oxford: Routledge, 2014).

25. Rosemary Foot, "The Responsibility to Protect (R2P) and Its Evolution: Beijing's Influence on Norm Creation in Humanitarian Areas," *St Antony's International Review* 6 (February 2011): 47–66.

26. Joel Wuthnow, "Beyond the Veto: Chinese Diplomacy in the United Nations Security Council" (PhD diss., Columbia University, 2011); Allen Carlson, "More Than Just Saying No: China's Evolving Approach to Sovereignty and Intervention Since Tiananmen," in Alastair Iain Johnston and Robert S. Ross, eds., *New Directions in the Study of China's Foreign Policy* (Stanford: Stanford University Press, 2006), 217–41.

27. Marc Lanteigne and Miwa Hirono, eds., *China's Evolving Approach to Peacekeeping* (London: Routledge, 2012).

28. Deborah Brautigam, *The Dragon's Gift: The Real Story of China in Africa* (New York: Oxford University Press, 2009).

CHAPTER TWO

Forward to the Past in Russia

LILIA SHEVTSOVA

THE RUSSIAN SYSTEM of personalized power, the antithesis of a state based on the rule of law, is demonstrating an amazing capacity for survival even in the midst of advanced stages of decay. The latest survival strategy that the Kremlin, the central headquarters of this system, is now using to prolong its life includes several parts. The first is a "conservative revolution" at home. The second is the conversion of Russia into a revanchist power that will undermine the rules of the international order if that helps to preserve the internal status quo. The third is the containment of the West, combined with the forging of an anti-Western International.

Throughout its long struggle to keep itself going, the Russian system has defied many predictions and ruined many analytical narratives. At the end of the 1980s, it humiliated the entire field of Sovietology, which had persuaded the world that the Soviet Union was as solid as a rock. In the 1990s, "transitologists" said that the system would move one way, only to find it going in another direction entirely. In the early 2000s, the system discarded the assumption that Russia would partner with the United States in its battle against terrorism. And from 2008 to 2012, the system turned both the U.S. "reset" policy and the EU Partnership for Modernization program into the punch line of a joke.

Over the past two decades, the system has limped on, meeting new challenges with imitation solutions that do not change its essence. At the beginning of the 1990s, it reincarnated itself by dumping the Soviet state, faking adherence to liberal standards, and professing a readiness for partnership with the West. Today, its liberal dress-up game is a thing of the past; it has turned toward harsh authoritarianism and aspires to become the West's chief antagonist.

The system's key innovation is its use of liberal civilization to prolong its life, first by setting out to "contain" that civilization and then by imitating it, which proves that the system's own potential for durability is slight. From the time of the Soviet collapse until recently, the teams of presidents Boris Yeltsin and Vladimir Putin viewed the mimicry of Western institutions and norms, the rise of a rent-seeking comprador class integrated into Western society, the limited pluralism of political life, and the relative freedom of private citizens as aids to survival.

The post–Cold War world, with its "end of ideology" and fuzzy normative lines, created the ideal arena for Russia's game of misleading and pretending. The West's eagerness to engage Russia led it to believe the Kremlin when it paid lip service to Western values, which in turn discredited those values. The system proved to be extremely efficient at turning elections, the justice system, the media, liberal slogans, and even membership in Western clubs (the G-8, the Council of Europe) into instruments of personalized power. What began as a Western partnership with Russia has ended not in Russia's liberal transformation but in its return to one-man rule and the emergence of a powerful lobby of "accommodators" within the West who help the Kremlin to pursue its goals. The general impression was that the system could have gone on like this indefinitely, carried along by corruption (which is a way of compensating for the absence of institutions), public indifference, the lack of viable alternatives, and high oil prices.

Things changed, however, when the election-related protests of late 2011 and early 2012 forced the Kremlin to adopt a new survival strategy. The "Putin Doctrine" legitimates a harsher rule at home and a more assertive stance abroad.[1] Putin's background and character hardly militate against this: He prepped in the KGB; he likes hands-on control, shady deals, and mafia-style loyalty; he hates the idea of anything like a "color revolution" in Russia; and he is hostile to the West and the rule of law. For the first time in Russian history, representatives of the security services, professionally trained to employ coercion, are not just working for the Kremlin—they are running the Kremlin. Russia has had a despotic state throughout its history, but until now it has not had a "triad regime," in which one group has taken control of political power, vast stores of wealth, and the repressive mechanisms of the state.

The irony is that the Kremlin, in looking for a way to keep going, returned to a model that by the end of the 1980s had already caused the system's previous incarnation to fall apart. In another ironic twist, liberal civilization once again became the stimulus for the system's consolidation—this time through deterrence of liberal democracy.

The events of 2014 in neighboring Ukraine—the EuroMaidan protests and the fall of President Viktor Yanukovych—gave the Kremlin an opportunity to test its new doctrine. By annexing Crimea and backing pro-Russian separatists in eastern Ukraine, the Kremlin was able to justify its military-patriotic mobilization of society and its transformation of Russia into a "besieged fortress." This was a traditional survival maneuver, but with a new twist for a new century. The Kremlin's style of "hybrid warfare" used military force without admitting it, and "weaponized" other areas of life. Thus we now have customs wars, natural-gas wars, information wars, culture wars, and history wars. Countering this new type of warfare is a task fraught with difficulties.[2]

Public mobilization around the leader and the motherland rose to a new pitch, aided by the lack of traditional cultural or moral regulators (think of the role that Confucianism plays in Sinitic societies) capable of shielding an atomized society of disoriented, demoralized individuals from the schemes of an overweening state. Ever since Stalinism's relentless assault on all "horizontal" ties (even those of family), Russians have been tragically at the mercy of the state and its claims: Individuals are invited to compensate for their helplessness by looking for meaning in collective national "successes" that promise to bring them together and restore their pride. The annexation of Crimea has become such a "success," giving ordinary Russians a chance to forget their woes and feel a surge of vicarious optimism. The Kremlin has seemed to say, "We will remind you what it feels like to be a great power if you forget your problems and our promises." The confusion that befogs Russian society may be glimpsed in an October 2014 public-opinion survey. Sixty percent of its respondents agreed that Russia was moving toward a crisis, while 64 percent said that it was moving in the right direction.[3]

The Kremlin's shift to a war footing will mean more than higher military spending and a resurgent military-industrial complex. Russian militarism is a unique form of the order-based—as opposed to the law-based—state. Although turning Russia into a Stalin-era armed camp is no longer possible, the Kremlin is militarizing certain walks of life and imitating militarization in other areas where it cannot achieve the genuine article.

This is not the first time, of course, that the Kremlin has tried to deflect attention from its problems by resorting to a military-patriotic mobilization.

One thinks of the Second Chechen War in 1999, and of the five-day war with Georgia over Abkhazia and South Ossetia in mid-2008. The Kremlin is aware that military-patriotic mobilizations tend to be short-lived, need fueling via triumphs over real or imagined foes, and will falter if there is too much bloodshed. By these standards, the Ukraine-Crimea gambit may prove a poor choice. It is dragging on, the fighting is murky, the West has reacted by imposing painful sanctions, and the death toll is already reportedly well into the thousands.

The Kremlin's experimentation with the war paradigm has landed the system in a quandary. There is not enough general well-being and stability to underwrite a return to a peacetime footing, but the war strategy and the search for new threats unleash forces that are hard to control. The consequences of the undeclared war with Ukraine may already be too much to handle. Among them are the strengthening of hawkish forces that demand "victory"; a push for more resources by the military-industrial complex; growing frustration among Russian nationalists and imperialists who expect Putin to subjugate other nations; and those economically crippling Western sanctions.

It is no surprise, then, to find Putin restlessly seeking new ideas to justify his claim to unrestrained rule. His self-selected array of legitimating concepts resembles a stew whose ingredients are simply whatever the chef could obtain: Sovietism, nationalism, imperialism, military patriotism, Russian Orthodox fundamentalism, and economic liberalism. He juggles ideas borrowed from Russian conservatives as well as the Western right. He cites the Russian philosopher Ivan Ilyin (1883–1954), who in 1948 could still describe fascism (he appears to have had in mind Franco's Spain and Salazar's Portugal) as "a healthy phenomenon."[4] Ilyin also called for a "Russian national dictatorship" while warning that "Western nations. . . . seek to dismember Russia."[5] Putin has not yet talked of such a "national dictatorship," but he loves to complain about Western efforts to back Russia into a corner. Putin speaks of freedom as well, but by this he means not individual liberty but rather, quoting Ilyin, "freedom for Russia."[6]

For the Kremlin, ideas are instrumental. If an action is deemed necessary, ideas will be found to justify it. An atomized people is there to be confused and given the impression that everything is fluid and relative. Thus the system's propaganda may claim, "Russian values do not differ dramatically from European values. We belong to the same civilization,"[7] only to posit a moment later that the West is Russia's main enemy. Whether conscious or unconscious, this is a textbook case of cognitive dissonance; the Kremlin is endorsing contradictory propositions, disorienting both Russia and the world, and making chaos its playground.

The Regional and International Dimension

Russian foreign policy has become the Swiss Army knife of the personalized-power system's drive to preserve itself. Like that famously versatile tool, foreign policy has many functions. It is used to guarantee an external environment conducive to personalized power; to compensate for the Kremlin's waning internal resources and the growing dissatisfaction of the most dynamic parts of Russian society; to divert attention away from deep social and economic problems; to contain Western influence both inside and outside Russia; to undermine the unity of the Western (mainly European) community; and to strengthen the network of pro-Kremlin lobbyists and apologists in the West.

Two of the Kremlin's foreign-policy projects are especially important. First, it seeks to create in the post-Soviet space something resembling the old "global socialist system," but without its unifying communist idea. Hence the Eurasian Economic Union (EEU), which includes at present Armenia, Belarus, Kazakhstan, and Russia, with Moscow acting as leader. Second, the Kremlin wants a dual approach to the West, containing it as a normative power and a geopolitical actor while cooperating with it (on Moscow's terms, of course) when that seems advantageous.

The EEU aims at close coordination of economic and political strategy. Moscow intends to preside over a bloc that will counterbalance the EU. Originally, Ukraine was supposed to be a member too, but in fact the EEU is a club of authoritarian states whose main goal is to preserve personalized rule in each state. The member states—especially Armenia and also Kyrgyzstan, which is waiting to join—are ready to take part in this Kremlin project in return for subsidies and security guarantees. But their loyalty is tenuous. They will likely have no trouble betraying the Kremlin or extorting concessions from it if a new sponsor with a better offer appears. Already, Belarus has signaled its restiveness by restarting customs inspections on its border with Russia.

The EEU, an imperial idea, is part of another Kremlin juggling act. In 2014, Putin began borrowing from Russian nationalists the idea of the Russkiy Mir (Russian World), which is supposed to consolidate ethnic Russians globally on the basis of loyalty to the Kremlin. The annexation of Crimea was the first step in implementing this initiative. Putin has also expressed his commitment to helping Novorossiya (New Russia)—that is, Russian speakers—in southeastern Ukraine and has provoked an undeclared war in the region. The Russkiy Mir project is an ethnocentric initiative; its logic runs counter to the imperial or quasi-imperial nature not only of the EEU but (far more importantly) the multiethnic Russian Federation itself. Even Moscow's allies, Belarus and Kazakhstan, refused to back the Crimea takeover, and it is not hard to see why: Both countries have sizeable Russian-speaking communities.

The Kremlin has pushed ahead with both these projects simultaneously, using nationalism in order to strengthen imperialism and even rallying many Russian nationalists to its cause. Most nationalists had long opposed Putin, but with the Russia-Ukraine conflict they began supporting him. Sooner or later, however, the Kremlin will have to come down on the side of the imperial idea, since it is the only one that will allow Moscow's continued control over the multiethnic Russian state (the Kremlin, in fact, has already dropped the idea of supporting Novorossiya in Ukraine). When that happens, nationalists are likely to move back into opposition.

Moscow's resort to contradictory ideas—imperial mythology on the one hand, and a nationalism that undermines Russia's integrity on the other—indicates that the system is growing desperate. It also underlines the lack, more than two decades after the Soviet breakup, of a new identity for Russian society, which remains susceptible to mutually exclusive visions.

Returning to a great-power agenda of expansion and spheres of influence is not an end in itself for the Kremlin. Great-power aspirations are just a way of sustaining personalized power at a time when internal displays of might are no longer sufficient. Russia will have to pay for the revival of its quasi-empire, however, and escalating economic troubles will soon render the Kremlin's imperial ambitions too heavy a burden for the country's budget.[8]

The EEU is not the only integration platform that Moscow controls. In 1992, Russia created the Collective Security Treaty Organization (CSTO), which also includes Armenia, Belarus, Kazakhstan, Kyrgyzstan, and Tajikistan.

In 2001, the Shanghai Cooperation Organization (SCO) was formed by China and Russia together with Kazakhstan, Kyrgyzstan, Tajikistan, and Uzbekistan. The SCO reflects a convergence between two major powers—China and Russia—that are vying with each other for influence in Central Asia while also recognizing a shared interest in keeping Western (primarily U.S.) economic, political, and military influence out of the region. Russia is pushing for closer integration under the framework of these two entities while insisting on retaining its leading role and trying to influence the balance of forces in the member states.

So far, neither organization amounts to much more than a discussion club with loose mutual commitments. The CSTO's collective rapid-response force (meant to be able to intervene in local conflicts and support member states' incumbent regimes) currently consists of a mere four-thousand troops. And the SCO has served mainly to highlight the divergent rather than the common interests of China and Russia: The former sees Central Asia as a market for its products, while the latter is trying to achieve broader integration. It is evident, however, that both projects are directed against the West. It is possible, of course, that if any member state's authoritarian regime is threatened, the CSTO or the SCO could try to come to its aid.

The Kremlin sees the participation of the newly independent states in such projects both as a guarantee of their loyalty to Moscow and as something that legitimates Russian support for the antidemocratic regimes that rule these states. Moscow's efforts to include Georgia and Moldova in the CSTO and the EEU while also influencing the political situation in these countries testifies to its agenda. In November 2014, heavy Russian pressure on Armenia, accompanied by Kremlin support for President Serzh Sarkisian's undemocratic regime, forced that country to drop its bid to sign an association agreement with the EU. The urge to avoid being "integrated" or "cooperated" into de facto subjugation by China or Russia is a feeling that we can expect will remain lively in the smaller countries lying near or between them.

Containing and Influencing the West

As for the Western liberal democracies, Putin has been trying to find a new balance between working with them and containing them. He may even believe that, once the Ukrainian conflict is sorted out, he will be able to go back to business as usual in his dealings with the West. Containment, in Kremlin eyes, has three dimensions: 1) Keep the West from expanding its geopolitical footprint in Eurasia; 2) induce it to endorse "spheres of influence" in the region; and 3) block all channels through which the West can exert influence inside Russia. This last dimension of containment explains why Putin has had his pocket parliament adopt laws stripping Russian civil society of financial aid from the West. In addition to funding bans, anti-Western (primarily anti-American) propaganda remains one of the most effective means of counteracting Western influence.[9]

A further containment effort consists of Kremlin moves to "renationalize" the Russian elite. The system has demanded that Russians with assets abroad repatriate them and give up their Western holdings. Representatives of the power structure have even had to surrender their passports, thus preventing them from traveling to "hostile countries." The comprador elite is to be transformed into an elite that is completely loyal to the leader and ready to cut all links to the West.

But the Kremlin is not (yet!) ready to seal the borders completely and return to a Cold War–like standoff. Cooperation with the West remains powerfully impelled by concrete interests. These include Russia's need to sell its hydrocarbons to Europe; Russian dependence on Western investments, loans, and technologies; Moscow's understanding that its military and economic resources would be sorely strained in the event of a confrontation with the West; the threat of new Western sanctions; and the elite's personal interests in the West.

These circumstances could steer the Kremlin to restore dialogue with the West, but they can neither guarantee that this dialogue would last nor prevent new showdowns. It is still unclear what the Kremlin's terms are. It is far easier to understand what the Kremlin rejects than what it proposes. Among the Kremlin's demands to the West: Do not meddle in Russian domestic life; accept the existence of Russian spheres of influence; halt NATO's expansion toward Russia's borders; refrain from deploying NATO forces in Eastern Europe and the Baltic states; stop inviting former Soviet states into the EU; accept Gazprom's monopoly; recognize Russia's claims in the Arctic; accept the Kremlin's understanding of the international rules of the game; and respect Russia's status as an "equal" (there is never any explanation of exactly what this term means).

Many of these terms have been accepted—but this has not turned the

Kremlin away from aggressiveness. In October 2014, Putin pushed things further by declaring that the old world order is unraveling (the result, naturally, of U.S. misbehavior). He called for the construction of a "polycentric" order, which apparently will prevent the United States from trying to act like a hegemon and guarantee a balance between the liberal and illiberal worlds. Escalation of these demands is a way for the Kremlin to create an unending series of grievances, ready to be used as pretexts for further militaristic behavior.

Even as the Kremlin indulges in such strategic grudge-mongering, however, it will also be willing to experiment on its own terms with various forms of engagement and cooperation with liberal democracies. It will of course be pursuing its own interests and goals, which will surely include the promotion of Western disunity and the provision of support to Western apologists for Moscow and its agenda. The Kremlin and its operators have perfected the arts of provoking conflict, playing states against each other, coopting Western elites, penetrating Western organizations, consolidating support within Western societies, creating international deadlocks, and playing the spoiler's role.[10]

Putin's elite has learned not only to contain but to influence the West. It has stopped the movement of Georgia, Moldova, and Ukraine toward Europe; forced European leaders to accommodate the Kremlin's energy policy; and fostered powerful pro-Moscow business lobbies within Western countries. The Russian leadership has been tenacious in taking advantage of the West's dissensus and dysfunctions as well as Western distaste for new "ideological projects" and the normative aspects of foreign policy. Moscow has carefully studied the ways in which it can exploit the weaknesses suggested by Western longing for a quiet "status quo," to say nothing of the West's willingness to retreat from commitments and the sad lack of ambition and moral strength that today's West brings to the historic task of countering hostile civilizations.

The Kremlin will not mellow with time. The Russian elite and a segment of the Russian people see the Kremlin's anti-Western campaign as evidence of Moscow's prowess. The power structures will demand that Russia stick with its mobilization model, fearing anything that smacks of "backing down" as a sign of weakness. Portions of the brainwashed populace will even accept their privations as a fair price to pay for a chance to bask in claims of Russia's greatness, even if those claims are at heart counterfeit.[11]

All these circumstances will sustain Russia's militarist and imperial behavior on the world stage, unless the system is transformed.

The Kremlin's Survival Toolkit

The Kremlin has demonstrated its ability not only to use the traditional means of autocracy, but also to invent new means of prolonging its life. Among the traditional instruments of influencing the public is the elimination of any remaining channels of self-expression. Under Yeltsin and the earlier Putin, the regime tended to tolerate some protests and preferred "managed political pluralism." Today, the pocket parliament has passed a series of laws that liquidate basic constitutional freedoms and point the way to full-scale dictatorship.

There are several dimensions to this subjugation of society. First, the Kremlin has robbed elections of their meaning by barring popular candidates whom the authorities do not control, and by falsifying results. With no access to television or major newspapers, genuine oppositionists can no longer compete.

Second, the authorities have continued an unprecedented campaign of reprisals against civil society. The NGO and "anti-extremist" laws (the latter is officially aimed at fighting terrorism) feature deliberately ambiguous wording that allows authorities to clamp down on any civil activity. Since Putin left his stint as premier and returned to the presidency in 2012, parliament has imposed new restrictions on civil society. These include a law that limits public assemblies and raises relevant financial sanctions to the level of criminal fines; a law that recriminalizes libel; and a law that may expand the notion of "treason" to include involvement in international human-rights issues.

Parliament has also put new limits on Internet content and foreign ownership of media concerns. Total control over social networks, just as in China and Iran, is next on the list.

In 2012, Russia created the "Unified Register of Prohibited Information." Run by the Federal Security Service (the successor to the KGB), this web-monitoring effort can demand the deletion of "harmful" information without a court order. Decisions to delete content or ban websites are made pursuant to the expanded anti-extremist law, which treats any type of dissent (including the "public slandering" of government officials) as extremism. Liberal websites such as *grani.ru, kasparov.ru,* and *ej.ru (Yezhednevny Zhurnal)* have already been shut down as "harmful."

In 2014, the authorities began considering steps to tighten control over Internet Service Providers (ISPs). The idea is to filter content on all levels of network traffic and to prohibit DNS servers for *.ru* and *.rf* domains from being located outside Russia. There is also a proposal to ban regional and local ISPs from connecting directly to foreign networks. Only Russian national service providers would be allowed to handle regional and local Internet traffic. The possibilities for online censorship are endless. As one report explains, there is proposed legislation that would allow

> the [Russian] government to place offending websites on a blacklist, shut down major anti-Kremlin news sites for erroneous violations, require the storage of user data and the monitoring of anonymous online money transfers, place limitations on bloggers and scan the network for sites containing specific keywords, prohibit the dissemination of material deemed "extremist," require all user information be stored on data servers within Russian borders, restrict the use of public Wi-Fi, and explore the possibility of a kill-switch mechanism that would allow the Russian government to temporarily shut off the Internet.[12]

In effect, the proposed law abolishes Article 29 of Russia's 1993 Constitution, which gives citizens the right to access information freely.[13]

As the new regime of online policing indicates, the security services have been empowered to control citizens' private lives. The institution of local self-government is being replaced by the "power vertical." School "reforms" are being introduced in order to ensure that rising generations will absorb one idea only: The leader is always right!

The Kremlin is especially active in the areas of information warfare and propaganda, both of which are tools that allow it to limit its use of raw coercion. In the course of its military-patriotic campaign, the Russian regime has been able to militarize the media (especially television), turning media organs into war-propaganda outlets. Information warfare has been used to paint the United States as Russia's major enemy, to brand the Ukrainian government a "military junta," and to smear Kremlin critics as "traitors." Unlike in Soviet times, there is no ideology on offer. Instead, the Kremlin and its minions are working "to sow confusion via conspiracy theories" and to spread disinformation with a view to eroding journalistic integrity.[14] War media have bolstered popular support for the war president, created patriotic hysteria in Russian society, and warped public consciousness by broadcasting justifications for hatred, violence, and confrontation.[15]

Russia's external propaganda machine is directed not only at creating a Russian "fifth column" in the West, but also at misinforming Western society and undermining its normative principles. The goal is to prove that the West is just as bad as the regimes that the West is trying to criticize. Everybody can be bought, and Western democracy is a sham: This is the mantra of the Kremlin's media abroad, and they seem to be finding a sympathetic audience. In the nine years since its creation, the Kremlin's RT (formerly Russia Today) television channel, with a budget worth US$300 million—and soon to be increased by 40 percent—has established itself as a strong global media presence. On YouTube, only the BBC's clips are watched more than RT's. In Britain, RT has more viewers than the Europe-wide news station Euronews, and in some major U.S. cities it is the most viewed of all foreign broadcasters.[16]

Through its absurd arguments, lies, and half-truths, the Kremlin's propaganda arm makes normal debate impossible.[17] "A policy of expansionism and conquest has no future in the modern world"—this is what Putin likes to say, even after the annexation of Crimea. "We will not promote Russian nationalism, and we do not intend to revive the Russian Empire," says Putin, while doing both those things. "People . . . have certain rights . . . and they must have a chance to exercise those rights," insists the president as he takes rights away from Russians.[18] The Kremlin claims that the Crimean annexation was a reaction to the threat of Ukraine's joining NATO, though neither Kyiv nor NATO had any such plans. The arguments are false, but given the intended audience's naivety, if repeated often enough they have a chance of hitting home.

The Kremlin has shown itself able to build effective lobbying networks outside Russia.[19] Today the Kremlin has an influential support infrastructure in the West. This includes companies interested in doing business inside Russia; political leaders who run certain errands for the Kremlin; media personalities and experts who try to put a positive spin on the Kremlin's actions in exchange for favors and access; and the bankers and lawyers who launder the Russian elite's dirty money.

Both leftist and rightist forces in the West frequently serve as apologists for the Kremlin's policies. The left and its leading intellectuals view Russia as an alternative model to capitalism and a force opposing the United States, the country that they detest more than any other.[20] The increasingly influential European right, meanwhile, views the Kremlin as an ally in its struggle against the idea of European integration. Its ranks include Nigel Farage and his UK Independence Party, Marine Le Pen and her National Front in France, and Geert Wilders and his Freedom Party in the Netherlands.[21]

The Ukrainian events have triggered the emergence of this left-right International of Kremlin sympathizers. In Europe and elsewhere, politicians and intellectuals of both the right and left can be found among those who back the Kremlin's position on Ukraine. This International is injecting confusion into Western civil society and making it harder for the West to take a consistent stand regarding Putin's Russia.

The Russian and international expert community, often without quite realizing what it is doing, also helps the personalized-power system to legitimate itself. When experts argue that "the 'Medvedevian' line in Russian politics remains alive—the soft-liner strategy of gradual ameliorative change," that NATO expansion is the problem, that the West must "accommodate Russia," that "the EU precipitated matters by blundering into the most sensitive part of Russia's backyard," and that the West's goal is "Putin's ouster," they only help the system to justify its actions and disorient the liberal world.[22]

How Grave a Challenge?

The return of an anti-Western and revanchist Russia to the global scene was a shock to the international community—a fact which tells us that the politicians and intellectuals of the day have failed to understand the processes generated by the Soviet collapse.

What made Russia return to the role of the "anti-West"? Was it the disrespect, even humiliation, that Russians allegedly experienced at the hands of the West? Was it Western expansion into Russia's "areas of interest" and "geopolitical space"? Or was it the liberal democracies' decay? I would argue that this shift was preordained by Russia's failure to use its defeat in the Cold War to transform itself into a rule-of-law state. The Russian political elite, especially the part that presented itself as liberal, failed to play a truly reformist role.

The Kremlin's switch to the military-patriotic mode is a sign of the regime's agony. Here we have a new conundrum: Russia cannot build an effective militarist state because it lacks a genuine consolidating idea, because the Kremlin is bereft of reliable repressive instruments, and because sizeable slices of Russia's elite and society have no wish to live in a "besieged fortress." At the same time, Russia cannot demilitarize and create an open society because other segments of its elite and its wider populace are not ready for life in a rule-of-law state.[23] The current agony could end in some form of "regime change"—a prospect that emerged as a topic of discussion and speculation in the world media during Putin's mysterious disappearance from public view for ten days in early March 2015—but that may only allow the underlying system to reproduce itself in one fashion or another and prolong its own decay.

It would be hard to embark on a new Russian transformation now that the concept of liberal reforms has lost so much credibility. Russians might even have to experience a full-scale dictatorship before they will try again to take the liberal-reformist path. One also has to take into account a formidable civilizational problem: There are no historical experiences or analogues to guide the transformation of a hydrocarbon-dependent, nuclear-armed state that is also a vast, territorially integrated land empire.

A few external factors at least partly facilitated Russia's return to its old authoritarian, anti-Western ways. One was the West's sheer naivety (it thought that it was helping democratization by helping Yeltsin). Others included the liberal democracies' acquiescence in Russia's authoritarian turn and Western cooperation with Russia at the expense of the West's own norms. That liberal democracies ceased to provide a role model for Russia is one of the most tragic developments of the past twenty years.

Today the Kremlin is quite successfully filling the international political and ideological vacuum with its foreign-policy "breakthroughs." When the global order grows unstable, principles no longer matter, "red lines" get fuzzy, and world leaders "lead from behind" (or just plain hide in the rear), opportunities open up for a regime that has the will to give the rules the back of its hand and act as a spoiler.

How sustainable is Russia's military-patriotic mobilization? Russians still support it, but that support is starting to run out of steam. True, today only about 21 percent of Russians would choose the European way for Russia. The "European" camp is a minority, but its members cluster in the big cities and thus can play a decisive role during social upheavals. It is still unclear when this minority will be able to consolidate, to overcome its fear of the regime, and to present an alternative to the system. Much will depend on new waves of protests that only a deep crisis will be able to trigger.[24] There are many potential tipping points, but no one can say whether Russia will suddenly plunge into a systemic crisis or continue a gradual slide into rot and paralysis.

Even if a crisis does break out, the most likely result is that the Russian elite will try to save the system by picking a new authoritarian leader. Society is just too demoralized, and the opposition too weak, to challenge the system itself. It looks, then, as if Russians' illusion that the personalized-power regime is capable of ensuring "normalcy" may endure for a while.

We can be certain, however, that the Russian system will further degenerate. The leader's turn toward provocation and war as expedients for survival tells us that the system has exhausted its stability-maintenance mechanisms. It is experiencing both types of political decay cited by Francis Fukuyama: "institutional rigidity" and patrimonialism, as "officials with a large personal stake in the existing system seek to defend it against reform."[25] We can be certain that a top-down democratic transition—the kind that would flow from a pact between reformers within the system and the opposition—is impossible. Russia can escape the civilizational trap into which it has fallen only by means of a revolution that would dismantle the system and create a new chance to build a rule-of-law state.

Notes

1. On the Putin Doctrine, see Lilia Shevtsova, "The Maidan and Beyond: The Russia Factor," *Journal of Democracy* 25 (July 2014): 74–82. See the 2013 essay by Foreign Minister Sergei Lavrov, "Russia's Foreign Policy Philosophy," available at *www.mid.ru/brp_4.nsf/o/8D9F4382C2ACD54744257B40005117DF*; and Vladimir Putin, "Address by President of the Russian Federation," 18 March 2014, at *http://eng.kremlin.ru/transcripts/6889*. See also his September 2013 speech (in Russian) at *www.rg.ru/2013/09/19/stenogramma-site.html*.

2. Peter Pomerantsev and Michael Weiss, "The Menace of Unreality: How the Kremlin Weaponizes Information, Culture and Money," *Interpreter,* Special Report, 22 November 2014, available at *www.interpretermag.com/wp-content/uploads/2014/11/The_Menace_of_Unreality_Final.pdf*.

3. Alexei Levinson, "The Emergency Situation in the Minds," *Vedomosti,* 11 November 2014 (in Russian).

4. An English translation of Ilyin's brief essay "On Fascism" may be found at *http://souloftheeast.org/2013/12/27/ivan-ilyin-on-fascism.*

5. Ilyin's essay on national dictatorship may be read in the original Russian at *www.pravoslavie.ru/jurnal/ideas/dictatura.htm.*

6. Vladimir Putin, "Presidential Address to the Federal Assembly," 4 December 2014, available in English at *http://eng.kremlin.ru/news/23341.*

7. Putin, "Address by President of the Russian Federation," 18 March 2014.

8. Even before the Crimean annexation, Russia was spending about $18 to $20 billion a year to support unrecognized and dependent "states" such as Abkhazia. The annual spending on Crimea alone could add another $10 or $12 billion to the total.

9. Hostility toward the United States is on the rise in Russia. It reached an unprecedented high in May 2014, when 71 percent of respondents said that their feelings toward the United States were "mostly" or "very" bad. About 60 percent of Russians view the EU negatively now. Against this backdrop, the positive perception of China has risen from 62 percent to 77 percent; 40 percent of respondents called it Russia's closest ally (second only to Belarus). More than two-thirds (68 percent) of respondents named the United States as the most hostile country toward Russia. See *www.levada.ru/05-06-2014/otnoshenie-rossiyan-k-drugim-stranam.*

10. James Sherr, *Hard Diplomacy and Soft Coercion: Russia's Influence Abroad* (London: Chatham House, 2013).

11. The number of those Russians who feel unready to pay for Russian "greatness" is growing. In March 2014, 19 percent of Russians were not ready to pay, a figure that had grown to 31 percent by December. See *www.levada.ru/print/30-12-2014/maidan-krym-sanktsii.*

12. Natalie Duffy, "Internet Freedom in Vladimir Putin's Russia: The Noose Tightens," American Enterprise Institute, 12 January 2015, available at *www.aei.org/publication/internet-freedom-vladimir-putins-russia-noose-tightens.*

13. Lyudmila Klimentjeva, "Kremlin Plans to Toughen Control over Internet Providers—'Kommersant,'" 29 April 2014, available in Russian at *www.vedomosti.ru/politics/news/25959451/kreml-nameren-uzhestochit-kontrol-za-internet-provajderami.*

14. Pomerantsev and Weiss, "Menace of Unreality."

15. Putin secretly gave military medals to three-hundred journalists for backing the Crimean annexation and strengthening military patriotism. On how war propaganda works, see Joshua Yaffa, "Dmitry Kiselev Is Redefining the Art of Russian Propaganda," *New Republic,* 1 July 2014.

16. RT's 2,500 employees support broadcasts in Russian, English, Spanish, and Arabic, with German to be added soon. According to *Der Spiegel,* RT brainwashing has had an effect, at least in Germany. See *www.spiegel.de/international/world/russia-uses-state-television-to-sway-opinion-at-home-and-abroad-a-971971.html.* On the work of Russian propagandists in the Baltic states, see Inga Springe et al., "Spreading Democracy in Latvia, Kremlin

Style," *Baltic Times,* 21 March 2012, available at *www.baltictimes.com/news/ articles/30852.*

17. On this topic, see Paul Goble, "Lies, Damned Lies, and Russian Disinformation," *Kyiv Post,* 14 August 2014, *www.kyivpost.com/opinion/op-ed/paul-goble-lies-damned-lies-and-russian-disinformation-360527.html* and Goble, "Hot Issue—Lies, Damned Lies, and Russian Disinformation," Jamestown Foundation, Global Research and Analysis, 13 August 2014, *http://tinyurl.com/nh35kpp.*

18. These statements are from an interview that Putin gave on 3 June 2014 to correspondents from French radio and television. See *http://eng.kremlin.ru/ transcripts/22441.*

19. On the Kremlin's lobbying efforts in Washington, D.C., see Luke O'Brien, "Putin's Washington: Even Money, Lots and Lots of Money, Can't Buy Him Love—A Story of Lobbying and Its Limits," *Politico Magazine,* January–February 2015, *www.politico.com/magazine/story/2015/01/putins-washington-113894.html#.VKzSHnuigyo.*

20. Von Bernd Ulrich, "The Germans and Russia: How Putin Divides," *Zeit Online,* 10 April 2014, *www.zeit.de/politik/ausland/2014-04/ germans-russia-media-putin.*

21. Doug Saunders, "Vladimir Putin's Fifth Column in the West," *Globe and Mail* (Toronto), 7 June 2014, *www.theglobeandmail.com/globe-debate/ vladimir-putins-fifth-column-in-the-west/article19021604.*

22. Richard Sakwa, "Whatever Happened to the Russian Opposition?" 23 May 2014, *www.chathamhouse.org/sites/files/chathamhouse/field/field_document/20140523SakwaFinal.pdf*; Tony Brenton, "The Unfolding Ukraine Crisis Signals a New World Order," *http://www.theguardian.com/commentisfree/2014/ may/16/ukraine-crisis-signals-new-world-order-russia*; John Mearsheimer, "Why the Ukraine Crisis Is the West's Fault: The Liberal Delusions That Provoked Putin," *Foreign Affairs* 93 (September–October 2014): 77–89; and Dmitry Trenin, "The Ukraine Crisis and the Resumption of Great-Power Rivalry," Carnegie Moscow Center, 9 July 2014, available at *http://carnegie.ru/2014/07/09/ ukraine-crisis-and-resumption-of-great-power-rivalry.*

23. Igor Klyamkin, *Istoria i istoricheskoje soznanie* [History and historical consciousness] (Moscow: Liberal Mission Foundation, 2012), 137.

24. Acute economic hardship could prove a tipping point. In December 2014, 62 percent of respondents said that they were not ready to accept declining living standards as the result of sanctions. See *www.levada.ru/ print/30-12-2014/maidan-krym-sanktsii.*

25. Francis Fukuyama, *The Origins of Political Order: From Prehuman Times to the French Revolution* (London: Profile, 2011), 454.

CHAPTER THREE

Iran's Paradoxical Regime

ABBAS MILANI

JUST AS THE 1979 ISLAMIC REVOLUTION that begat the truncated republic of Iran was notable both for its ironies and incongruities and its novelties and cruelties, Iran today is ruled by a regime of glaring paradoxes. After 35 years of Islamic theocracy, Iran has become a land of myriad contradictions: It is a cruel authoritarian state, personified by the dour, aged faces of its autocratic rulers, where there are more public hangings per capita than anywhere else in the world and where misogynist laws deny women equal rights and status. Yet behind the mirthless face of the regime pulsates a young and globally connected citizenry and a women's movement as impressive in its reach as in its prudence and patience. So while the center is defined by authoritarian control, in the body politic, the "center cannot hold."

Only by deconstructing the nature and origin of these paradoxes can we understand the nature of the ruling authoritarian theocracy, as well as the challenges that it faces in maintaining the status quo. To assess why the Iranian regime has endured, to understand the methods that it uses to coerce and coopt its critics, and finally to gauge its long-term prospects of survival, we must place these issues in their dynamic historical context. The regime's authoritarianism is more flexible and durable than some of its quixotic detractors hope, yet more fragile and endangered than its invested defenders suggest.

The 1979 revolution was, according to a near-consensus among scholars, the most "popular" revolution in modern times—almost 11 percent of the population participated in it, compared to the approximately 7 and 9 percent of citizens who took part in the French and Russian revolutions, respectively.[1] As the political philosopher Hannah Arendt argued, the concept of "revolution" is a creation of modernity. Before the rise of modernity and the birth of the concept of natural rights, the word "revolution" had no political connotation; it referred simply to the movement of celestial bodies. When the idea of a citizenry replaced the notion of subjects, however, the word took on its new political meaning—a sudden, often violent structural change in the nature and distribution of power and privilege. "Subjects" form a passive populace bereft of rights and needful of the guardianship of an aristocracy or rulers invariably anointed by the grace of God (or Allah). "Citizens," by contrast, are imbued with natural rights, including the right to decide who rules over them.

In Iran, notions of popular sovereignty and limited government legitimized by the consent of the people had been part of political discourse since the late nineteenth century. Ironically, however, the 1979 revolution, which had the requisite popular support, was led by Ayatollah Ruhollah Khomeini, who had denigrated the notion of popular sovereignty as a colonial construct meant to undermine the Islamic concept of *umma* (or spiritual community). In Khomeini's treatise on Islamic government,[2] the will of the people is subservient to the dictates of the divine, as articulated by a supreme leader.

In this sense, his concept of an Islamic revolution is an oxymoron, and its concomitant idea of Islamic government—*velayat-e faqih,* or rule of the jurist—is irreconcilable with the modern democratic ideal of popular sovereignty. On the contrary, *velayat-e faqih* posits a population in need of a guardian, in the way that minors or madmen need guardians. In other words, the people are subjects rather than citizens. As conservative clerics such as Ayatollah Mesbah Yazdi and Ayatollah Ahmad Jannati never tire of repeating, the very idea of an Islamic republic is a contradiction in terms. Iran, they say, is the government of God on earth, and certainly no mere republic. In an "Islamic state" (a term they used long before it was appropriated by terrorist groups), the people have no role or capacity to invest legitimacy in a ruler, or to divest it from him. All legitimacy is in the hands of Allah, and the supreme leader is His viceroy on earth. Defying the dictates of the leader, in this narrative, is nothing short of heresy—punishable both in this world and the next.

Yet in 1979, Ayatollah Khomeini called a populace that was expected to be servile and passive to stage a revolution—historically, the defiant act of a citizenry cognizant of its ability and right to demand a new social contract. And in the months before the revolution, Khomeini told the people that it was their right to demand a new social contract. Every generation, he said more than once, has the right to determine its own mode of governance.

As a token of this right, the first government after the fall of Mohammad Reza Shah Pahlavi was led by Mehdi Bazargan, who served as prime minister from February to November 1979. Bazargan was a man of moderate leanings, with a clear proclivity for democratic rights. At the same time, every government office, and soon every institution in the country, also had "special representatives" of Khomeini who increasingly asserted their authority to the detriment of government officials. A dual power structure began to emerge—one representing the will and desire of the people, and the other appointed by the supreme leader. It was not long before Khomeini, along with a coterie of clerics and activists, began talking of *velayat-e faqih* and the divine mandate of the clergy to rule. Thus the most popular of all "modern" revolutions led to the creation of a state whose constitution places absolute power in the hands of an unelected, unimpeachable man (and he shall always be a *man*) and whose basic political philosophy posits people as subjects and pliable tools of a supreme Islamic jurist, the *faqih*.

The democratic forces that had come together to make the revolution and overthrow the shah, however, did not dissipate or disappear, despite the biggest exodus from Iran in its three-thousand-year recorded history—of the country's approximately 35 million inhabitants at the time of the revolution, between six and seven million have gone into exile. Advocates of democracy, women's rights, freedom of expression, the rights of religious minorities (including Bahais) and ethnic minorities (such as Iranian Kurds and Azeri speakers) have, in spite of repeated waves of suppression, persisted. The uneasy reality of an authoritarian regime ruling a still vibrant and defiant society constitutes the most remarkable paradox of the Islamic revolution. Yet the country's many historic anomalies and social disharmonies threaten the status quo.

The 1979 revolution was in a sense a replay of Iran's first assay at democratic constitutional government, which resulted from the 1905–1907 constitutional revolution. At that time, a coalition of secular intellectuals, enlightened Shia clergy, bazaar merchants, the rudiments of a working class, and even some members of the landed gentry came together to topple the oriental despotism of the Qajar kings and replace it with a monarchy whose power was limited by a constitution (*mashruteh*). Indeed, the system established by the new 1906 Constitution emulated a European model of a liberal-democratic polity—one that allowed for elections and separation of powers, yet had a monarch as the head of state.

In those years, the most ideologically cohesive and powerful opposition to this new democratic paradigm was spearheaded by Sheikh Fazlollah Nouri—a Shia zealot who dismissed modern democratic constitutions as the faulty and feeble concoctions of fallible men. He believed instead that the divine and infinite wisdom of God, manifest in *shari'a,* should guide the country. The advocates of constitutional democracy were so powerful, however, that Nouri became the only ayatollah in Iran's modern history to be executed on the order (*fatwa*) of his fellow clerics. For decades, Nouri's name was synonymous with the reactionary political creed of authoritarian rulers who sought their legitimacy in *shari'a.*

The Rise of Authoritarianism

Almost seventy years later, the same coalition of forces that had created the constitutional movement coalesced once again, this time to topple the shah's authoritarian rule. By the 1970s, each of the social classes that had formed that earlier movement had become stronger and more politically experienced. Nevertheless, they chose as their leader Ayatollah Khomeini, a man who espoused an even more radical version of *shari'a*-based politics than what Nouri had proposed. While Nouri had urged that government should be based on *shari'a,* Khomeini advocated the absolute rule of the *faqih,* a man whose essential claim to power was his anointment by the Shia imams based on his mastery of *shari'a.* Moreover, even *shari'a* would become a pliant tool in the hands of the *faqih,* as the new concept of absolute rule of the *faqih* (*velayat-e motlagheh faqih*) meant that even principles of the faith, as well as the rules of *shari'a,* could be suspended by the supreme leader if he should deem it "expedient." So at a time when authoritarianism was gradually receding all over the world—starting in Portugal and Spain in the 1970s and peaking in the late 1980s as Soviet totalitarianism began to crumble—Ayatollah Khomeini was fighting against the tide of history, erecting an authoritarian state founded on the divine edicts of God and the absolute wisdom of the *faqih.*

Just as Nouri's ideas had split the Shia clergy after the constitutional revolution, Ayatollah Khomeini's ideas (as well as those of his successor, Ayatollah Ali Hosseini Khamenei) not only split the clergy, but also were incongruent with the wishes of the people. Today, this split has corroded the core of clerical ruling power itself. It has been reliably reported that Ayatollah Khomeini once said that, after his death (he died in 1989), the survival of the Islamic regime would depend on the continued cooperation of Khamenei and Ali Akbar Hashemi Rafsanjani, who was the second most powerful man in Iran for more than three decades. But in the last few years, the two men—friends and allies for almost sixty years—have been increasingly at odds.

A great deal of unchecked power is concentrated in Khamenei's hands. According to the constitution, the Assembly of Experts (a popularly elected body of theologians) is supposed to supervise the work of the supreme leader and elect a new one when he dies or is deemed to be derelict in his duties. Khamenei's supporters now openly dismiss the supervisory role of the Assembly and unabashedly claim that the body's "elected" members are as duty-bound to follow the wishes of the supreme leader as everyone else. Moreover, by law Khamenei is Iran's commander-in-chief; he controls around US$90 billion in revenue from foundations, endowments, and special accounts; and he can issue at will a *hokme-hokumati*—an order that everyone is expected to follow, and that trumps the letter and spirit of the constitution and all laws.

In addition, the supreme leader appoints not only the head of the judiciary but the head of the country's monopoly radio and television organization. Ever since Hassan Rouhani's election to the presidency in 2013, Khamenei and his conservative allies have taken a page out of the same playbook they used against the reformist president Mohammad Khatami (1997–2005), using the judiciary to intimidate critics, to shut down magazines, and even to forbid all media outlets from publishing the words or images of the still-popular Khatami. Yet in a perfect illustration of the paradox of Iran's clerical despotism, no sooner had the judiciary announced the draconian ban on Khatami than Rouhani and Rafsanjani both defied the blackout by publishing Khatami's photo on their respective websites.

Lately, the 80-year-old Rafsanjani (who served as president in 1989–97), along with many of the top Shia clerics and a surprising number of Khamenei's erstwhile supporters, has begun openly to challenge the supreme leader, the embodiment and symbol of clerical authoritarianism. Rafsanjani has even suggested that, after Khamenei, a committee of clerics should assume the responsibilities now held by the supreme leader. Many scholars and activists think that such a development would be a critical step in curtailing the authoritarian powers of the leader.

Yet the 75-year-old Khamenei has at his disposal a vast and varied set of tools for ideological molding and outright political oppression. He appoints all Friday Prayer leaders, and his office sets the agenda for their weekly sermons. The country's media generally give wide coverage to what is said in these sermons. His decisive role in appointing the head of the radio and television organization ensures his ability to control who has access to the airwaves. He appoints his own special envoy to *Keyhan,* which used to be the country's most popular daily paper but is now seen essentially as a Khamenei mouthpiece. Finally he appoints virtually all members of what is called the Supreme Council of the Cultural Revolution, a body of usually conservative figures keen on ensuring that higher education in Iran maintains an "Islamic" texture.

Khamenei has representatives in every institution, including all branches of the armed forces. The Islamic Revolution Guards Corps (IRGC) is the chief tool of suppression and control at home. It is now also an economic juggernaut. The Basij—a paramilitary group of gangs-cum-militia—are literally and metaphorically the foot soldiers of the IRGC; they are used to control the streets, accost intransigent critics, and disrupt concerts or conferences considered "undesirable." Yet another paradox of Iran's authoritarianism is that the regime's conservative ideologues, despite claiming that legitimacy comes only from God, nevertheless constantly use the power of mass rallies (invariably organized and funded by the Basij) in order both to underscore the regime's popularity and to intimidate its opposition.

Khamenei also appoints at least six members of the twelve-man Guardian Council, which now vets every candidate for every elective office in the country. In a gesture toward the democratic aspirations of 1979, this clerical dictatorship holds regular presidential and parliamentary elections, whose course clearly traces the ebb and flow of Iran's paradoxical despotism over the last twenty years. On the one hand, Khamenei and his cohort have regularly used their judicial fiat to exclude serious challengers or reformists from seeking elective office; on the other, democracy advocates and the people themselves have tried at every turn to use even controlled elections to inform the regime of their discontent and their desire for democratic reform.

The history of recent Iranian elections is filled with manifestations of the shifting dynamics of authoritarian control and the intermittently assertive democratic demands of the people: the surprising landslide victories of the reformist Khatami in the 1997 and 2001 presidential elections; the surge in popularity of former prime minister Mir-Hossein Mousavi and Rafsanjani in the 2009 presidential election; the unexpected swell of support for Rouhani after he aligned himself with reformists in 2013, enabling him to win that election; and the lack of popular support in 2013 for Saeed Jalili (the intransigent head of Iran's nuclear negotiating team), who, despite having the backing of the regime, won no more than five-million votes.

The Paradox of Control and Weakness

The great paradox of Iran's clerical authoritarianism is that its weaknesses are evident. Even in the regime's ideological and oppressive apparatuses—from the intelligence organizations and government bureaucracy to the clerics who were once regime stalwarts—cracks are visible in the form of leaks, particularly about corruption during the presidency of Mahmoud Ahmadinejad (2005–13), and in comments published in the media and online social networks. For example, at conferences and in interviews, some public intellectuals have recently criticized the regime's nuclear policies and suggested that leaders who can muster only a small percentage of the vote (like Jalili in 2013) are trying to use coercion to maintain power and continue past policies. Meanwhile, as the cracks in the regime have become more apparent, the populace has become more vocal. For instance, when Hossein Shariatmadari, the controversial editor-in-chief of the newspaper *Keyhan,* who is a Khamenei appointee and regime mouthpiece, attempted to give a talk at Tehran University, he was met with angry slogans and spent his entire time jostling with surprisingly assertive students. Every moment of this episode was captured and widely discussed on Iranian social media.

The paradoxes of the Islamic regime's authoritarianism are especially striking in the realm of information technology and social media. Iran has one of the most heavily censored Internet services in the world: The regime boasts of hiring thousands of cyber-jihadists, whose sole job it is to monitor, control, and even influence social media. Facebook and Instagram are officially banned in the country, and many in the regime wish to see a complete shutdown of online social networks—one cleric recently compared them to the biblical golden calf, chastising them as tools of the devil. Some officials advocate the establishment of a "national Internet" that would make it difficult for Iranians to access sites that the regime deems dangerous.

At the same time, close to forty-million Iranians have Internet access, five-million Iranians have Facebook accounts, and about a million use Instagram. Even more remarkably, Ayatollah Khamenei and President Rouhani each have active Facebook and Instagram accounts. There are now open disagreements between different elements of the regime—members of the Rouhani government on the one hand and conservative clerics on the other—about whether and how much control there must be over these kinds of tools and sites. While forces close to Rouhani, including members of his cabinet, insist that censoring or shutting down the sites is no way to fight their potential ill effects, the conservatives consistently advocate imposing more limits on usage. They also occasionally use the judiciary or the IRGC and its intelligence units to arrest social-network users and accuse them of either "collusion" with the enemy or spreading corruption.

A cultural trench war—a subtle battle for hegemony—is being waged in virtually every domain of life in Iran. Draconian laws and harsh sentences meant to intimidate critics are increasingly defied by a surprisingly large number of people. Jafar Panahi, the award-winning filmmaker who has been banned from making films for twenty years as punishment for his support of the democratic movement, has just sent his most recent movie to European film festivals. Every proposed movie must be approved by the government before cameras can roll, but Panahi clearly defied the rule and made his film without a permit. Nasrin Sotoudeh, a human-rights lawyer who has spent much time in prison and been banned from the Iranian bar, has not only continued to protest her banishment by standing vigil in front of the offices of the bar association, but also defied authorities by agreeing to play herself in the Panahi film. Everyday life in Iran now includes a number of permanently underground activities: theater groups, musical bands, film clubs, art exhibits, and an active and thriving publishing network that makes banned books available online and sometimes in print. There is even an underground university; because the regime bans Bahais from enrolling in colleges, members of that faith have created a remarkable alternative university, whose graduates have been accepted to many prominent Western schools.

While the regime maintains a policy of gender apartheid—one objection to Facebook and Twitter is that they allow "illicit" direct contact between members of the opposite sex—women are increasingly visible in every sphere of public life. There are now more women poets, writers, directors, singers, and entrepreneurs than ever before. The country is experiencing a sexual revolution that is unlike anything it has known before and is altogether incongruent with the professed pieties of the regime. There is, sadly, a tsunami of divorce—rooted partly in the many social malaises facing the country but also in the reality of newly assertive women who would rather get divorced (possibly becoming single parents) than suffer the "slings and arrows" of a misogynist relationship.

At the same time, in an apparent effort to intimidate women to dress "modestly" and in line with regime guidelines, there has been a spate of acid attacks on women—the most infamous case happening in the city of Isfahan. Women's groups and other democratic forces in Tehran and Isfahan have demonstrated against what they consider to be the regime's lackadaisical approach to apprehending the culprits. It is striking that a regime which prided itself on arresting almost instantly those who had allegedly committed a small act of armed robbery—four young men, using machetes taking a small sum of cash from someone who had used a cash machine— has been somehow unable to arrest the culprits in the acid attacks.

The regime has tried to stem the tide of this cultural revolution by force and through propaganda. It occasionally arrests leaders of the Bahai underground university and raids some of the other cells of cultural resistance. But so far it has utterly failed to dissuade the population from participating in them. Thus, while the specter of Procrustean cultural control is never far from the horizon in Iran, defiant resistance through the sophisticated use of metaphors in every discursive form manages to persevere. When a regime tries to engineer and control every facet of life—from sartorial style to quotidian minutiae—then all facets of that life become potential loci of resistance. A scarf worn an inch higher on a woman's head, revealing just a few more strands of hair, or a name for a newborn baby chosen from the lexicon of pre-Islamic Persian mythology rather than the roster of Islamic saints, becomes a tool of resistance and an indicator of defiance.

Students of Iranian politics have interpreted in varying ways the paradox of having so many loci of "underground" resistance in a severely repressive authoritarian regime. Some observers argue that the regime, in an attempt to forestall the necessity of structural change, has opted for what social theorists have called "repressive tolerance." According to this narrative, the regime has consciously decided to allow these private, underground, and ultimately apolitical forms of resistance not as a gesture of toleration, but rather as a way of placating and pacifying the dissatisfied masses in order maintain the status quo.

Others, however, argue that after the traumas of the last twenty years—the failed promises of the eight-year Khatami presidency, the suppressed Green Movement of 2009, and the ongoing and near-apocalyptic destruction in Syria and Iraq—the Iranian people, recognizing the regime's willingness to brutally suppress any direct threat to its power, have chosen a new way to engage in politics. Instead of directly challenging the power of the state, they use elections to send messages of discontent and to help elect less undesirable leaders (such as Rouhani). More crucially, they have begun to chip away at the regime's capacity to control and shape daily life. Politics is, after all, as much about the quality of life in the private sphere as it is about control of the centers of power.

According to this narrative, the gradual, corrosive, and inexorable power and persistence of such micropolitical defiance—these myriad sites of life lived in a manner incongruent with the regime's "social-engineering" designs—will inevitably break the clerics' authoritarian grip. Also helping to loosen their hold is the serious economic crisis that the regime currently faces, a result of longtime corruption, incompetence, the siphoning off of government rents and sky-high black-market profits by the elite, all augmented by international sanctions and the falling price of oil. The only way for Iran to resolve this crisis is by instituting the rule of law and putting an end to corruption, crony capitalism, and the rentier state that subsidizes authoritarian rule.

Notes

1. See Charles Kurzman, *The Unthinkable Revolution in Iran* (Cambridge: Harvard University Press, 2004).
2. Ruhollah Khomeini, *Islamic Government,* trans. Joint Publications Research Service (New York: Manor Books, 1979).

CHAPTER FOUR

Iran Abroad

ALEX VATANKA

SINCE ITS FOUNDING IN 1979, the Islamic Republic of Iran has dedicated considerable resources to constructing new international norms that reflect the practices, worldview, and aspirations of the ruling authorities in Tehran—all with the goal of enhancing its legitimacy and devaluing its domestic critics. From recasting the conventional principles of human rights and political participation to launching alternative international media and working to reshape and restrict access to the Internet, the Islamic Republic's quest to forge counternorms is moving ahead unabated. In the course of these efforts, it seeks out global partners that share its agenda. Tehran has found Russia and China, in particular, to be useful role models, facilitators, and collaborators.

Ayatollah Ruhollah Khomeini, the founder of the Islamic Republic, considered the very notion of "democracy" to be an undesirable Western concept. He insisted that "Islam itself is democratic" and set out to define Islam's provisions for political life. In the infant days of the 1979 revolution, few dared to defy the icon of the anti-shah movement over a single word, allowing Khomeini to prevail in this matter. Iran thus became an "Islamic republic," leading to an ongoing struggle to define the system's republican character. Khomeini and his inner circle in the Islamic Republican Party quickly formulated the new polity's characteristics, which over the years became the regime's counter to democracy. Those who opposed the new constitutional arrangement, starting with Prime Minister Mehdi Bazargan in November 1979, were sidelined or imprisoned. Some, including the Islamic Republic's first elected president, Abolhassan Bani Sadr, even fled.

Although the popular uprising against the monarchical dictatorship of Mohammad Reza Shah Pahlavi (1941–79) had been a rainbow movement with strong prodemocracy leanings, less than two years later Khomeini had installed himself as Iran's supreme leader and "God's representative on earth." The democratic struggle had ironically produced an unabashedly illiberal theocracy that soon proved resourceful in its quest to survive, predatory in its political behavior, and unprincipled in its disposition. Before Ayatollah Khomeini died in June 1989, he cemented this Machiavellian approach by decreeing that the interests of the "Islamic Republic" superseded even the tenets of Islam. Thus the very few who can define the interests of the system, principally the supreme leader himself, were made invincible.

Two constant features have been part and parcel of the political process in Iran ever since: First, there has been a continuing struggle among key regime personalities, factions, and institutions to define, own, and defend the revolution of 1979 and "Iranian national interests." Second, thanks to intense intraregime competition for influence—most visible in the violent schism that followed the disputed 2009 presidential election—the Islamic Republic has faced a hemorrhaging of support from within its ranks. Accordingly, although the regime has managed to consolidate its institutional grip, the system's basic legitimacy is no more secure today than it was in 1979.

The regime's many critics see Iran's "Islamic democracy" as a façade that allows the current supreme leader, Ayatollah Ali Khamenei, to maximize control while making minimal concessions to a society hungry for genuine political rights. When President Mahmoud Ahmadinejad opportunistically began to challenge Khamenei during Ahmadinejad's second term in office (2009–13), Khamenei publicly warned that the presidency could be eliminated altogether. The notion of "Islamic democracy" is perhaps the most blatant counternorm conceived by the Islamic Republic, but Ayatollah Khamenei is not stopping there.

Global Soulmates

Although the regime's formulation of "Islamic democracy" remains unconvincing inside the country, this has never prevented Tehran from seeking to assert its values on the international stage. It does so on the pretext of defending local non-Western cultural norms. In the course of promoting its substitutes for democratic norms, the regime frequently attacks the accepted standards of human rights—a particular weak spot of the Islamic Republic.

Mohammad Javad Larijani, the head of the Iranian judiciary's Human Rights Council, has been spearheading the defense of the country's record. In late 2014, for example, Larijani responded to a UN report condemning the lack of civil liberties in Iran by alleging that the Islamic Republic was a target of Western "media and political terrorism."[1] Larijani's rebuttal as well as his proclamation that Iran should be the "flag bearer of human rights in the world"[2] has baffled observers. While many ordinary Iranians considered these comments laughable, Tehran's desire to challenge global human-rights standards is anything but flippant. After all, if what constitutes democratic practice can be reinterpreted by the Islamic Republic, as it has done since 1979, then so too can the concept of human rights.

In Larijani's words, "Iran will defend its values" in the realm of human rights. "Today, [the issue of] human rights has become a pressure tool against the Islamic Republic," he bemoaned, insisting on the need for a strategy to deal with this perceived Western subversion. Yet neither Larijani nor his predecessors have ever really sought to withdraw from the international human-rights bodies that they accuse of partisanship. Instead, they want to use Iran's membership in such bodies to form alliances with like-minded nations in order to shape the global agenda "at every opportunity," as Larijani put it.[3]

While Iran's Human Rights Council endlessly weighs its "strategic options"[4] as part of its campaign to influence the global human-rights agenda, its lobbying efforts are at the very least partially shielding Tehran from international scrutiny. For example, during the October 2014 UN Universal Periodic Review[5] of Tehran's compliance with basic human-rights standards, Iran's record—including violations of the rights of religious and sexual minorities—was broadly censured. Yet delegations from states such as Russia, China, Syria, and Cuba opted to refrain from any serious probe into the human-rights situation in Iran.[6] By now, it has become routine for Tehran to rely on sympathetic states in such forums.

While Khamenei considers the issue of human rights to be a tool that mighty states use to pressure weaker ones, he nonetheless seems to recognize that the issue does carry weight. But he has yet to devise a convincing alternative to the accepted conventions. Back in 1987, before becoming supreme leader, he explained: "We do not believe that Roosevelt, Churchill and Stalin and their like had the smallest consideration for human rights in the true sense of the word," adding that the Allied leaders were insincere "in forming the United Nations and drafting the Universal Declaration of Human Rights."[7] But "what is the remedy?" he asked. The solution that he proposed was "return to Islam, and recourse to Divine revelation."[8] Due in part to the Islamic Republic's limited appeal even among Muslim states, however, its attempts to promote "Islamic human rights" have made little headway. Its unsuccessful approach rests on what human-rights scholar Reza Afshari has called the "mirage of cultural authenticity."[9]

Despite its failure to sell its version of human rights, the Islamic Republic still covets support in international forums when its record is under scrutiny. In this context, its efforts have not been entirely in vain. For example, when the UN Human Rights Council voted in March 2014 to renew the special rapporteur's mandate to investigate Iran's record, 21 states supported the motion, but nine opposed it. Among the nine that came to Iran's aid were Russia, China, Cuba, and Venezuela.[10] Despite the vote, Iranian authorities continued to ban UN Special Rapporteur Ahmed Shaheed from visiting the country. Larijani called Shaheed's appointment "illegal" and asked him to resign. Meanwhile, states such as Belarus and Russia continue to give Iran cover by echoing Tehran's claim that the UN's human-rights charges are politically motivated.

International recognition and legitimacy, if not respectability, have always been a goal of Iran's leaders, regardless of whether they are hard-liners or moderates. In other words, even as the pendulum has swung from Ahmadinejad's reckless international populism to current president Hassan Rouhani's pursuit of global integration and acceptance, certain drivers of Iran's policy approach have remained constant. Tehran has always sought out similar and sympathetic states to collaborate with—be they China, Syria, and Libya in the 1980s, Cuba and North Korea in the 1990s, or Venezuela, Bolivia, and Nicaragua in the 2000s.

In most cases, Iran's relations with other nondemocratic regimes first developed as a means to fulfill material needs and gain geopolitical support aimed at countering the country's international isolation. Although these remain key priorities, Iran is now also seeking to form alternative blocs within international forums, and it views like-minded nondemocratic countries as collaborators in this quest.

Tehran's courting of other illiberal powers such as China and Russia therefore rests on two pillars—economic and diplomatic. First, this approach seeks to meet Iran's basic economic and trade needs given that its behavior at home and abroad has made democracies wary of dealing with it. One example of such a policy is Iran's trade relationship with China. Trade between Iran and China increased from US$4 billion in 2003 to $36 billion in 2013, making China Tehran's biggest trading partner by far. More recently, in the aftermath of Russia's falling out with the West over the crisis in Ukraine in early 2014, Tehran and Moscow penned an oil-for-goods barter agreement reportedly worth $1.5 billion per month. It was said to be a win-win deal that enabled both countries to circumvent troublesome Western states.

Second, forging ties with other illiberal powers provides Tehran with a diplomatic comfort zone and a claim to international inclusion, even if it fails to convince the West. Tehran has earnestly sought to join the Shanghai Cooperation Organization (SCO), a six-member bloc led by Russia and China that touts itself as a counter to the West. Iran currently has observer status in the organization. At the SCO's September 2014 summit, President Rouhani urged the organization to establish a mechanism to negate Western-led sanctions.

In addition to its diplomatic efforts in international organizations, Iran carries out an active policy in its drive to become a regional power. This includes backing certain forces, especially among Shia populations that either are receptive to or in need of Iranian patronage. As of 2015, thousands of Iranian military advisors, under the leadership of General Qassem Suleimani, who heads Iran's extraterritorial Qods Force and is answerable only to Ayatollah Khamenei, were propping up Tehran's allies in Syria, Iraq, and Lebanon. In each of these countries, the armed component of Iran's intervention has been complemented by a methodical messaging campaign aimed at the local populations. Traditional and social media are fully utilized as part of Tehran's campaign to legitimize its agenda.

Policing Cyberspace

The SCO also looks for ways in which its members can cooperate in cyberspace to confront "the use of information technology aimed at undermining [the] political and economic security" of SCO member states.[11] In late 2010, Iran's largest telecommunications firm purchased a "powerful surveillance system capable of monitoring landline, mobile and internet communications" as part of a $130 million contract with a Chinese company.[12] The deal was signed only a few weeks after the EU decided to impose restrictions on the sale of communications equipment to Iran. Supplying technology is not the only way in which China collaborates in Iran's quest to control the Internet. Iranian authorities also look to China as a model for shaping the discourse in cyberspace.

In April 2003, Iran became the first country to prosecute a blogger. Given that the media environment in Iran is one of the most restricted in the world, it is not surprising that the advent of the Internet age in the mid-1990s resulted in a mushrooming of blogs. Although there is no exact count, there are now tens of thousands of Persian-language blogs—and this number was even higher in the years before the rise of social media.

The staggering popularity of blogs has undoubtedly been the direct product of censorship and the lack of outlets for civil society activists. The administration of reformist president Mohammad Khatami (1997–2005) had loosened some restrictions on civil society. According to official statistics, when he left office there were 6,914 registered nongovernmental organizations (NGOs) operating in Iran. His successor Mahmoud Ahmadinejad (with the blessing of Khamenei) put NGOs under increasing pressure and many were closed.[13] Civil society activists of all stripes therefore turned to cyberspace as an alternative venue for conducting their work.

This did not go unnoticed by the regime, particularly after the popular uprisings that followed the disputed June 2009 presidential election. According to Freedom House, "since June 2009, the authorities have cracked down on online activism through various forms of judicial and extra-legal intimidation," and "an increasing number of bloggers have been threatened, arrested, tortured" while "others have been formally tried and convicted."[14]

The months of unrest in 2009 were broadcast to the world in a way that both surprised and embarrassed the Iranian authorities. The regime intended to prevent any such "Twitter revolutions" from happening again. Thus the state took extraordinary measures to impose its control over all Internet activities. In one famous incident in September 2011, authorities banned a water-gun fight in a public park in Tehran simply because text messaging and social media had been used to organize the event. They objected not to the water-gun fight itself, but to the use of social media as a tool that could enable people to organize without the regime being aware it.

In the post-2009 environment, with the proliferation of opposition activism across a host of social-media platforms such as Facebook, Twitter, and YouTube, identifying and harassing dissidents has become more challenging for Iranian state agencies. The regime has been particularly concerned about the increasing availability of online instructional videos and other materials teaching civil-disobedience tactics, prompting it to intensify efforts to discourage dissent, including meting out harsher punishments. Iranian authorities have also extended their pursuit of dissidents beyond the country's borders. The regime often digitally tracks activists based abroad. If they return to Iran, they will be punished even for such minor acts as posting comments critical of the regime on social media. In addition, the regime has reportedly put pressure on local relatives of foreign-based activists.

As Tehran blatantly engages in political repression, Ayatollah Khamenei consistently defends the actions of his regime by invoking the defense of "Islamic democracy." In November 2009, at the peak of the postelection unrest, he justified the Internet crackdown as a way of repelling a "Western cultural invasion" and a "soft war" against the Islamic Republic. Seemingly under Khamenei's close direction, the Islamic Republic launched a two-pronged campaign to further restrict Internet access and to fund and promote proregime sites to counter online voices critical of the regime. Following the example of Beijing, which has had considerable success in steering bloggers and online debate toward nationalist themes that complement the stance of the central government, the Iranian regime tasked the Islamic Revolution Guards Corps (the armed steward of the regime) and the progovernment Basij paramilitary force with producing a legion of proregime cyber-warriors under such names as the Iranian Cyber Army.

If Iran's 2009 protests served as a wake-up call for the regime, alerting it to the potential dangers of technology, the avalanche of unrest in the Arab world that began in 2011 drove home the point. By March 2012, Khamenei had issued a directive creating the Supreme Council of Cyberspace (SCC), which would serve as the hub for managing Iran's Internet policies. Like the Guardian Council, which filters out undesirable political candidates and legislation, the SCC is supposed to black out online materials that the regime finds unpalatable. Given the vastness of cyberspace, the SCC has called upon the general public for help in identifying and filtering out objectionable websites. Thousands of sites have since been blacklisted.

Despite having developed sophisticated censoring processes, Iranian authorities are still grappling with the increasing availability of antifilter technologies. Thus Tehran has looked abroad—especially to China—for ideas, and it has now set out to create a closed national Internet that is separate from the World Wide Web.[15] (Other nondemocracies such as Burma, Cuba, and North Korea have already established parallel Internet systems.) To justify this move to the public, Khamenei in a March 2014 speech again made reference to the uniqueness of the Islamic Republic and warned against open communications with the world: "Today's youth are exposed to all these harmful propaganda tools. They are exposed to the Internet, through which the enemies are trying hard to make our youth deviate from the right path."[16]

Within the ranks of the regime, there are voices that question the feasibility of such a hidebound approach. In September 2014, President Rouhani said in a speech that "some people think by building walls problems will be solved." He added: "When you make [Internet] filters, they will make filter-breakers."[17] Still, in the Islamic Republic it is the unelected supreme leader who has the final word on all matters of state.

International Broadcasting

If Iran shares with China and other illiberal regimes a common interest in regulating cyberspace as a purportedly defensive strategy, it also shares with them an equally strong desire to go on the offensive in the realm of international broadcasting. Tehran has long considered this arena worthy of investment in order to counter the influence of Western broadcasters such as the BBC and Voice of America.

The state-run Islamic Republic of Iran Broadcasting (IRIB) has been airing in a number of foreign languages since 1979. Then, in early 2003, Tehran launched the Al Alam Arabic-language television network to rival Qatar's Al Jazeera Arabic, which had been on the air since 1996, and Saudi Arabia's Al Arabiya (which also made its debut in 2003). But it was with the launch of the 24-hour English-language Press TV in 2007 that Tehran really sought to become a significant player in international broadcasting. Both China and Russia had already set up English-language news services: China's CCTV News in 2000, and Russia's RT (formerly Russia Today) in 2005. Qatar launched Al Jazeera English in November 2006. The timing of Press TV's launch was not coincidental; it sent a clear message that Tehran was expanding its ambitions from the regional level to the global one.

Al Alam and Press TV target regional and international audiences in Arabic and English, respectively, with overtly politicized content. Their *modus operandi* is simple: They defend Iran's policies and those of its allies, while criticizing Western policies. The programming on both stations includes a pervasive questioning of the basic international norms of political and human rights.

As Iran's international isolation over its nuclear program has tightened, Tehran has upped the ante in the race to influence global public opinion. In 2012, it launched Hispan TV with the aim of reaching the Spanish-speaking world at a time when Ahmadinejad and Venezuelan president Hugo Chávez were jointly endorsing a rejection of the established global order. In 2005, Chávez had launched Telesur, a station broadcasting messages similar to those that would later be adopted by Press TV. Although the launch of Hispan TV may appear to have been tied to Ahmadinejad's rejectionist worldview, in reality the Islamic Republic's efforts to challenge conventional standards through international broadcasting pre-dated Ahmadinejad and have continued without interruption since he left office in August 2013. Regardless of the likely return on its investments, Tehran is committed to stay in this race.

Beside the financial burden, Tehran's involvement in foreign-language broadcasting has also had diplomatic costs, from Press TV being fined by the British in 2012 for breaching broadcasting codes, to Al Alam's offices in Egypt coming under physical attack, to authorities in Bahrain accusing Iranian media of inciting sectarianism. Yet the regime has clearly concluded that Iran has no choice but to stay in this game, broadcasting its alternative values and defending itself against the "soft war" that it claims its adversaries are waging on the airways.

Expediency versus Democracy

The Islamic Republic was born of a popular movement that was in many ways democratic in its aspirations. But the faction that prevailed in the 1979 revolution—the Islamists who are today led by Ayatollah Khamenei—has spent the last 36 years violating democratic practices at every possible turn. Whether in the manipulation of electoral processes, the defining of free speech in ways that serve the regime, or the stifling of debate both in print and online, the Islamic Republic has not refrained from acting in predatory and unprincipled ways. Ultimately, the regime's sole concern is hanging on to power, and all its policies are designed to serve this simple objective.

It is this unprincipled approach that has led the Islamic Republic to collaborate with other illiberal states such as China, Russia, and faraway Venezuela. It is why the Iranian regime—an Islamist regime that claims to be carrying out Allah's wishes on earth and preparing the ground for the coming of the Mahdi—counts among its most treasured foreign partners an atheist China and a Russia led by a self-declared champion of Christianity. It is not a common set of values that brings them together, but rather the desire to preserve their own power and to limit their sense of isolation in the international arena. If there is a succinct way in which to describe the goal of such alliances, it is what has been aptly called the doctrine of "democracy containment."[18] This approach has already brought Russia and China to Iran's aid in UN human-rights forums, and Tehran is eagerly pursuing membership in the SCO, an organization whose outlook on political and human rights mirrors that of the Islamic Republic.

Joining forces with the SCO and with states such as Russia and China at least offers Ayatollah Khamenei's system (*nezam*) a means of avoiding global ostracism. Given the dissimilarities that exist among Iran and its international partners, few in Tehran presumably expect a real partnership to emerge from their country's cooperation with its illiberal allies. Yet a common bond has arguably been in the making, as these countries jointly question standard international norms, exchange technologies and techniques for repressing free speech online, and employ global broadcasting to promote and defend their illiberal worldviews. The Islamic Republic and its authoritarian allies will likely double down on this approach in the years to come.

Notes

1. "Iran's Larjani Slams West's 'Bias' on Human Rights," *Euro News*, 7 November 2014.

2. Javad Larijani, "Iran Has to Be the Flag Bearer of Human Rights in the World," *Islamic Republic News Agency*, 12 August 2014.

3. Larijani, "Iran Has to be the Flag Bearer of Human Rights in the World."

4. High Council for Human Rights, "An Opportunity for the Development of

International Human Rights and the Promotion of the Islamic Republic," available in Persian at *www.humanrights-iran.ir/news-42945.aspx*.

5. According to the website of the UN Office of the High Commissioner for Human Rights, the Universal Periodic Review "is a unique process which involves a review of the human rights records of all UN Member States. . . . It is a cooperative process which, by October 2011, has reviewed the human rights records of all 193 UN Member States."

6. "A Look at the Second Review of Iran's Human Rights Record," BBC Persian, 13 November 2014, *www.bbc.co.uk/persian/blogs/2014/11/141107_l44_nazeran_upr_iran*.

7. Ayatollah Khamenei, "Human Rights in Islam," delivered at the 5th Islamic Thought Conference, 29–31 January 1987, 4, available at *www.iranchamber.com/history/akhamenei/works/human_right_islam.pdf*.

8. Khamenei, "Human Rights in Islam," 6.

9. Reza Afshari, *Human Rights in Iran: The Abuse of Cultural Relativism* (Philadelphia: University of Pennsylvania Press, 2001), 3–8.

10. International Campaign for Human Rights in Iran, "Iran's Human Rights Showing Little Progress, UN Votes to Renew Special Mandate," 28 March 2014, *www.iranhumanrights.org/2014/03/unhrc-2014*.

11. "Sanctions Against Iran 'Unacceptable'—Russia, China, Other SCO Nations," *RT*, 13 September 2013, *http://rt.com/news/nuclear-iran-sco-summit-833*.

12. Steve Stecklow, "Special Report: Chinese Firm Help Iran Spy on Citizens," Reuters, 22 March 2012, *www.reuters.com/article/2012/03/22/us-iran-telecoms-idUSBRE82L0B820120322*.

13. See Iran Human Rights Documentation Center, "Attack on Civil Society in Iran," Arseh Sevom Report 2005–2010, *www.iranhrdc.org/english/human-rights-documents/ngo-reports/arseh-sevom/3214-attacks-on-civil-society-arseh-sevom.html*.

14. Laurent Giacobino et al., "Whither Blogestan: Evaluating Shifts in Persian Cyberspace," Iran Media Program, Annenberg School for Communications, University of Pennsylvania, March 2014.

15. Christopher Rhoads and Farnaz Fassihi, "Iran Vows to Unplug Internet," *Wall Street Journal*, 28 May 2011.

16. "Supreme Leader's Speech in Meeting with Members of Assembly of Experts," 6 March 2014, Center for Preserving and Publishing the Works of Grand Ayatollah Sayyid Ali Khamenei, *http://english.khamenei.ir//index.php?option=com_content&task=view&id=1881&Itemid=4*.

17. "Rouhani's Strong Criticism of Internet Supervision and Gender Segregation," 8 September 2014, available in Persian at *www.farhang.gov.ir/fa/article/3516*.

18. Christopher Walker, "Authoritarian Regimes Are Changing How the World Defines Democracy," *Washington Post*, 13 June 2014.

CHAPTER FIVE

Autocratic Legalism in Venezuela

JAVIER CORRALES

T HE CONCEPT OF HYBRID REGIMES—those that exhibit both demo-cratic and authoritarian features simultaneously—is by now well established in the field of comparative politics. Hybrid regimes are sometimes called "competitive authoritarian" because, while the ruling party competes in elections (usually winning), the president is granted an array of autocratic powers that erode checks and balances. Such re-gimes are now common across the developing world. If we use Freedom House's classification of Partly Free as a proxy for hybrid regimes, then in 2014 they were slightly more common than classic authoritarian regimes.

The dynamics of hybrid regimes—why some remain stable over time while others become either more democratic or more autocratic—are less well understood. Venezuela under Hugo Chávez (1999–2013) is a case of a hybrid regime that rapidly moved toward increasing authoritarianism. In the *Freedom in the World* report for 1999–2000, Freedom House lowered Venezuela's rating from Free to Partly Free. Venezuela's turn toward greater autocracy accelerated over the years, reaching new levels under Chávez's successor Nicolás Maduro (2013–present). Today, Venezuela ranks as the least free of all Partly Free regimes in Latin America.

This raises two questions. First, what are the *mechanisms* by which a competitive authoritarian regime turns more autocratic? By definition, a hybrid regime is one in which the executive branch concentrates powers to the detriment of nonstate and opposition actors. But what else needs to happen for us to say that it has turned more autocratic? This essay examines Venezuela since 1999 to show how such a transformation can take place. My argument focuses on the use, abuse, and non-use of the rule of law.

Second, what were the *causes* of Venezuela's rapid move toward greater authoritarianism, especially in the last five years of *chavismo*? Drawing from my previous work (often in collaboration with other authors), I offer two basic arguments. One focuses on domestic factors: The ruling party's declining electoral competitiveness since the late 2000s, together with path dependence, helps to explain Venezuela's turn toward greater authoritarianism. The other focuses on foreign policy: By 2010, Venezuela had succeeded in creating a foreign policy that shielded it from international pressures. Although other factors were no doubt at play, these two served as the most essential drivers.

During Chávez's presidency, Venezuela became the paradigmatic Latin American case of competitive authoritarianism. The ruling party, known since 2007 as the United Socialist Party of Venezuela (PSUV), competes in elections against a legal multiparty opposition, as one would expect in a democracy. At the same time, the PSUV helps the executive branch to weaken checks and balances, treat the opposition unfavorably, and reduce the autonomy of civil society. Over the years, the regime's autocratic practices have become more pronounced.

Three Key Elements

The primary mechanism facilitating Venezuela's increasing authoritarianism could be termed "autocratic legalism." Autocratic legalism has three key elements: the *use, abuse,* and *non-use* (in Spanish, *desuso*) of the law in service of the executive branch.

Let us begin with the *use* of autocratic laws. Since it first came to power, the ruling party has taken advantage of its dominance in the country's legislative bodies (the 1999 Constituent Assembly, the 1999–2000 "small congress" or *congresillo,* and the 2000–present national legislature), in conjunction with its total control of the Supreme Court since 2005, to enact laws that empower the executive branch at the expense of other branches of government. By the time of Hugo Chávez's death in March 2013, there were many such autocratic laws on the books:

1) The *1999 Constitution*, despite many democratic innovations, increased the power of the president: It eliminated the Senate (an important veto player); banned public funding for political organizations (which is interpreted to mean political parties); and empowered the president to call for referendums to recall legislators, dissolve the legislature under certain conditions, and propose constitutional amendments and rewrites.

2) *Enabling laws* grant the president the right to rule by decree. The *chavista*-dominated legislature passed enabling laws four times under Chávez—in 1999, 2000, 2007, and 2010—and one time (so far) under Maduro—in 2013.

3) The *Organic Law of Telecommunications* (2000) allows the government to suspend or revoke broadcasting concessions to private outlets if it is "convenient for the interests of the nation, or if public order and security demand it." This law was modified in 2011 to include all audiovisual production (including cable TV) and to reduce concessions to radio networks from 25 to 15 years.

4) The *Law for Social Responsibility* (2004) bans the broadcasting of material that could incite or promote hatred and violence. It was extended in 2010 to apply to the Internet. Accordingly, electronic media may not transmit messages that "foment anxiety in the public or disturb public order," "incite or promote disobedience to the current legal order," "refuse to recognize legitimately constituted authority," or "incite or promote hatred or intolerance."

5) The *2005 penal-code reform* expanded the *desacato* (insult) law, which makes it illegal to be "disrespectful of government officials," to cover an even greater number of officials to whom this law applies. It also seriously restricted the use of public spaces for protesting.

6) *Laws governing "communal councils"* (the Organic Law of Popular Power [2010], the Organic Law of Public Planning [2010], the Organic Law of Social Auditing [2010], and the Organic Law of Communes [2010]) provide public funding and legal prerogatives to

these ill-defined bodies, which are required to work with the state to offer services, carry out public works, and participate in community development. In doing so, they often supersede the roles of elected mayors and municipal councils. None of these laws requires the councils to hold competitive elections for their representatives.

7) The *Law for the Defense of Political Sovereignty and National Self-Determination* (2010) blocks Venezuelan human-rights defenders from receiving international assistance. Nongovernmental organizations (NGOs) that "defend political rights" or "monitor the performance of public bodies" are barred from receiving any foreign funding. Foreigners invited to Venezuela by such groups can be summarily expelled from the country if they express opinions that "offend the institutions of state, top officials or attack the exercise of sovereignty." The NGOs could face stiff fines, and their directors could lose their right to run for public office for up to eight years.

8) The *Law Against Illicit Exchange Transactions* (2010) grants the government a monopoly over all currency trades, including government bonds. Foreign currency from exports must be sold to the Central Bank of Venezuela (BCV) at the official exchange rate. The law also bans "offers" in foreign currency made between Venezuelan entities or individuals for the sale of goods and services.

9) The *Law of Partial Reform of the Law of Political Parties, Meetings and Protests* (2011) bans deputies from any conduct that departs from the "political orientation and positions" adopted by their party during election times. This law is intended to deter legislators from voting in opposition to the party line.

10) The *Organic Law of Fair Prices* (2014) is an update to the 2011 Law of Fair Costs and Prices, which legalized the regime's broad system of price controls and essentially did away with the price system. The 2014 version stiffened the earlier law, expanding the number of infractions to include the reselling of "essential" merchandise and the commission of acts causing "economic destabilization." It also bans profits over 30 percent. Sanctions include

fees, imprisonment, confiscation of assets, and the like. Further-more, with the addition of "economic destabilization"—which can be interpreted to mean even the spreading of a rumor—the law expands the subjective justifications that the state can invoke in order to sanction private agents. Since 2011, this law has also been one of the main causes of shortages and informal markets, and an often used justification for cracking down on the private sector.

Venezuela's arsenal of autocratic laws exhibits two features. First, the autocratic aspect of these laws is not always overt. It is often buried among an array of clauses or articles that empower citizens or other political groups, and these surrounding clauses encourage empowered groups to support these laws, at least initially. But there is always one clause that ends up empowering the executive branch far more than other actors, which is what makes these laws so autocratic. Second, these laws have been enacted in a constitutional manner, at least insofar as they have been duly approved by constitutionally sanctioned processes. This paradox poses a twofold problem for the opposition: 1) Such laws bolster the state's capacity to control nonstate actors, and 2) they cannot be easily challenged because they have emerged through constitutional channels.

Abusing the Law: "Communicational Hegemony"

The second element of autocratic legalism is the *abuse* of the law, meaning the inconsistent and biased implementation of laws and regulations. In Venezuela, this has occurred in many domains, but is especially salient in the media world, and it helps to explain how, under Chávez, the balance between private independent media and government-controlled media shifted in favor of the latter. Today, an ordinary Venezuelan with little access to the Internet is more likely to be exposed to public or pro-PSUV media, which is usually more easily available and economically accessible than private independent media. The consequence has been a significant decline in press pluralism. This shift in the media, known locally as "communicational hegemony," has been a deliberate strategy of *chavismo*.[1]

By 2014, through the use and abuse of the law, communicational hegemony was extensive in both print media and television. For instance, in

TABLE I   Independent print and television media (percentage)

	1998	2014
Print		
All newspapers nationwide	100%	56%
Of which, local and regional newspapers	100%	49%
Television		
All television channels nationwide	88%	46%
Of which, local and regional channels	50%	39%

NOTE: Independent means 1) privately owned; 2) covering politics; 3) not communitarian; and 4) not systematically censoring information that is favorable to the opposition.
SOURCE: See endnote 2.

1998, there were 89 newspapers in Venezuela.[2] All were private and independent. By 2014, Venezuela had 102 newspapers, of which 56 percent were privately owned; 8 percent were state-owned; 15 percent were "not independent," meaning that they systematically leaned pro-PSUV; and 22 percent were "undetermined," meaning that they were either too small or unavailable online to determine their orientation.[3] State-owned newspapers are atypical in democracies. In Venezuela, they are also overtly biased. While the private press is often criticized for being too prone to *denuncias* (accusations)—seen as both a sign of its non-neutrality and proof of the presence of democracy in Venezuela—a state-owned press that systematically censors positive information about actors other than the state is no indication of democratic vitality. The Maduro administration is committed to continuing the policy of expanding the public press. It has already established public newspapers in the cities of Valencia, Maracay, Cojedes, Guárico, and Petare, and in 2014 the president stated that he wanted to have one in every town.

The shrinking of independent media is even starker in the realm of television. In 1998, there were 24 television channels nationwide, of which only 3 were public (and they were nonbiased). In 2014, there were 105 TV channels, but only 46 percent were private. (If one looks at local channels alone, the decline in the share of independent media is less steep, from 50 percent in 1998 to 39 percent in 2014.) State-owned channels now account for 17 percent of all television channels (14 percent if one looks only at local and regional television channels). In addition, under *chavismo* a new category emerged—"communitarian channels," located mostly in smaller cities, accounting for 37 percent of television stations in 2014. Communitarian channels technically are supposed to be independent, and many of them struggle to assert some autonomy vis-`a-vis the state.[4] But only progovernment channels receive state funding and support. Given that there are few other funding sources, communitarian channels inevitably end up complying with state directives.

Venezuela's rising communicational hegemony has come about as a result of both the *use* and *abuse* of the law.[5] The government has used existing regulations to set up public newspapers. Several of these circulate free of charge, easily displacing private competition—a practice that is within the law, but is meant to crowd out the independent media. The state also abuses the law by harassing many independent newspapers, imposing legal fines based on allegations of corruption or violation of the media law, or arbitrarily denying access to foreign exchange, which is necessary to buy paper. According to Reporters Without Borders, at least 37 newspapers have had to reduce circulation due to lack of paper.[6] Other tactics have included preventing state agencies from buying ads in targeted private newspapers; informally pressuring editors to publish the "right" stories; and banning reporters from covering government events. The regime's goal is to abuse the law to force private independent newspapers into financial distress, thereby encouraging cutbacks (as in the case of the daily *Tal Cual,* which had to scale back to weekly publication in early 2015) or even the sale of a paper to new owners (as with *El Universal*). If a newspaper's editorial line changes, the government will forgive the fines and grant it foreign exchange.

The same use and abuse of the law has been applied to television. The big decline in pluralism started in 2003, when Diosdado Cabello, the second most powerful *chavista* politician today and president of the National Assembly, took charge of the National Telecommunications Commission (Conatel), the agency that regulates broadcast television and radio, and restructured media regulations. Conatel is now in charge of determining whether a station qualifies as a communitarian channel (and thus also whether it is eligible for state funding). Conatel has also targeted private television channels by arbitrarily refusing to renew their licenses (as with RCTV in 2007) or by levying excessive fees for supposed violations of the media law (as with Globovisión until 2013). In Venezuela, the only way that a television station can guarantee its financial survival is by staying out of politics—that is, by self-censoring (as Globovisión has done since it was sold to new owners in 2013) and refraining from coverage of political events (as Venevisión and Televén normally do).

This rise of state-owned and nonindependent media has had a clear effect on information availability. In January 2015, for example, the opposition held a major march in downtown Caracas. No television channel broadcast the march or speeches, continuing instead with regular programming. Later that day, Globovisión reported on the opposition leaders' statements, but for no more than five minutes. In contrast, most public television stations broadcast the one-hour-plus speech that Maduro delivered the same day. Globovisión showed Maduro's speech live for fifteen minutes. Venevisión and Televén did not televise Maduro's speech, due to their tacit agreement with the state not to cover politics.

The Non-Use of the Law: Electoral Irregularities

The third element of autocratic legalism is, paradoxically, reliance on illegality. This has been especially significant in electoral politics. One of Chávez's most important authoritarian legacies is an electoral environment plagued by irregularities and governed by a biased regulatory agency, the National Electoral Council (CNE). Indeed, in the sixteen elections held during the *chavista* era, by my count there have been more than 45 types of electoral irregularities, usually involving biased enforcement of electoral laws and often outright violations—for example, the government allows the PSUV to exceed spending or airtime limits; allows polling centers to stay open past their scheduled hours; arbitrarily bans candidates or observers; manipulates voting rules to the ruling party's advantage; cajoles state employees or welfare recipients to vote a certain way; harasses voters at the polls; threatens to deny funds to districts that elect opposition candidates; and conducts cursory audits of results.[7] Over time, some irregularities get corrected for good—often due to pressure from the opposition—but other types persist, and new irregularities tend to emerge with each new election.[8]

This irregularity-prone electoral environment has only deteriorated since Chávez's death in March 2013, beginning with the election for his successor the following month. In that contest, Maduro, who was then acting president, prevailed over his opponent, Henrique Capriles Radonski, by a mere 235,000 votes (a 1.5 percent margin). The opposition claimed that, in the run-up to the election and on election day itself, there were repeated and new irregularities (for example, PSUV sympathizers were seen escorting voters to polls under the pretense of assisting them; harassing electoral observers and voters; paying citizens to bring people to the polls; and maybe even engaging in fraud at a few polling centers), which gave Maduro his narrow victory. After the results were announced, protests broke out in Caracas and several other cities. The government put down the demonstrations; in the end, seven people were killed and dozens were injured. The opposition called for a full audit, which was refused (although the CNE did conduct an audit of the electronic tallies versus the paper ballots), and then—for the first time since 2005—the opposition challenged the election, formally calling for the election either to be annulled or done over in roughly 5,700 voting tables (in Venezuela, each voting table or *mesa electoral* is associated with a particular touchscreen voting machine).

That request was also denied, so the opposition made a futile attempt to take its fraud complaint to the Supreme Court. Venezuela's courts are a key element in the regime's *non-use* of the rule of law. High-level judges have been overtly partisan since the government packed the courts in 2004, and many lower-level judges are untenured and are often penalized for ruling the wrong way. Furthermore, according to a recent study, not one of the 45,474 rulings issued by the Supreme Court since 2005 has gone against the government.[9] So it was no surprise that the Court dismissed the opposition's fraud suit.

While municipal elections the following December saw fewer cases of irregularities at the ballot box, they did see the full force of state power being leveraged in favor of PSUV candidates during the campaign period, including overspending and the illegal use of public funds and state media. Moreover, at the time of the election, the terms of three of the five members of the CNE—a body with only one nongovernment representative—had expired. With the 2013 elections, the Maduro administration showed that it had not only inherited Chávez's semi-authoritarian legacy, but was building on it.

The heightening of autocratic legalism under Maduro has proved destabilizing.[10] To begin with, in early 2014 the opposition split over how to respond to the faulty electoral process and the government's refusal to address irregularities, with one faction calling for and carrying out street protests. The outbreak of popular demonstrations led to the worst repression ever under *chavismo*, and perhaps under any elected government in the country's history.

Between February and April 2014, Venezuela was engulfed in demonstrations, first launched by university students in the small western cities of San Cristóbal and Mérida. The government harshly repressed the initial round of protests, which only triggered more—this time coordinated via social media, using the hashtag "#lasalida" ("the way out"). Opposition hard-liners, including Leopoldo López (a former mayor of the Chacao municipality of Caracas), María Corina Machado (an MP at the time), and Antonio Ledezma (the mayor of metropolitan Caracas), soon joined the fray, and the protest issues broadened to include the economic slowdown, food shortages, and unreliable public services, as well as rampant crime.

All told, roughly 800,000 people in at least sixteen states and 38 cities participated in protests for at least three months. Protesters set up street barricades in mostly middle-class neighborhoods; some demonstrators threw bottles, stones, and petrol bombs. The government sent in the National Guard and the national police to put down the demonstrations, and may have encouraged armed progovernment civilians (known as *colectivos*) to intimidate protesters.[11] According to a report by leading human-rights organizations, the government forcibly broke up 34 percent of these protests, far more than the most intense repression under Chávez (7 percent in 2009), and detained more than 3,100 people.[12]

More surprisingly, the government went after opposition leaders, not just ordinary protesters. López was arrested for "inciting violence," despite a lack of any evidence other than his writings in support of a change in government, which allegedly had "subliminally" incited the protesters. Machado was accused of treason for speaking at the OAS about human-rights abuses in Venezuela and was subsequently expelled from the National Assembly. She and other opposition leaders have even been accused of plotting to kill the president, and in December 2014 Machado was officially indicted for conspiracy and treason. Ledezma was arrested in late February 2015 on charges of plotting to overthrow the government.

Domestic and International Factors

If the use, abuse, and non-use of the law account for the mechanics of Venezuela's shift toward greater authoritarianism, what are the causes behind it? The main domestic driver is a combination of path dependence and declining electoral competitiveness, as Michael Penfold and I argue in our forthcoming second edition of *Dragon in the Tropics*. By path dependence, we mean that once sufficient domestic institutions are established to permit the state to govern in authoritarian ways, these institutions become the preferred instruments for making policy choices. Given that Chávez had already erected the framework and acquired the tools to facilitate government repression, the Maduro administration—because it had the necessary institutions, legal instruments, and a political ideology—naturally used them to crack down harder on the opposition.

But a second important reason for the heightening of authoritarianism is more systemic—namely, the decline in the ruling party's electoral competitiveness. In the 2006 presidential election, Chávez defeated the opposition overwhelmingly with 63 percent of the vote. Since then, however, the opposition has been steadily gaining ground on the PSUV at the polls. The PSUV's electoral decline slowed in the 2012 presidential election, the last one in which Chávez competed (he won 55 percent of the vote), but intensified immediately after Chávez's death. In the April 2013 presidential election, Maduro won just 51 percent of the vote. Even though the PSUV performed much better in the December 2013 municipal elections, its gains were not substantial: If the votes for all the opposition parties are tallied together, the PSUV's margin of victory was a mere 2.7 percentage points, a far cry from the double-digit margins that it enjoyed in the mid-2000s.

As the ruling party in a competitive authoritarian regime loses its ability to compete electorally, it has greater incentives to stress its authoritarian side as a means of survival. It should come as no surprise that a hybrid regime would opt to become more authoritarian when the traditional voter enticements that it needs to compete for the vote (ideological appeal, economic resources, policy innovation, and competent governance) are unavailable or are becoming exhausted. Together with the availability of the tools of autocratic legalism, the PSUV's electoral decline is the most important cause for the intensification of repression under Maduro.

The second reason that Venezuela has managed to turn more authoritarian is the creation of an international shield.[13] During Chávez's presidency, Venezuela began using its foreign policy to build an "alliance of tolerance"—that is, an alliance of countries unwilling to criticize Venezuela, let alone join any international effort to sanction it for domestic wrongdoings. In essence, Venezuela used its oil resources to expand this alliance across Latin America and beyond. Between 2003 and 2012, the country's oil revenues vastly exceeded those of any other country in the region—accounting for more than 30 percent of Venezuela's GDP during that time.[14] But Venezuela has also experienced a steep decline in oil production since 2000.[15] Consequently, since then Venezuela has been one of the two OPEC members that have most strongly advocated maximizing oil prices, much to the frustration of oil-importing countries. In order to improve its reputation among oil importers and build Venezuela's "soft power," Chávez expanded foreign aid, which he touted as promoting a more pro-poor form of development than Western aid.[16]

Building an "Alliance of Tolerance"

Chávez's best-known foreign-aid program is Petrocaribe. Formed in 2005, this trade deal allows seventeen small Caribbean and Central American countries to purchase subsidized oil from Venezuela under favorable financial terms. Compared to similar earlier agreements, Petrocaribe increased the number of country beneficiaries as well as the volume of oil that they receive, raised the price subsidy, and made repayment terms even more favorable for recipient countries. By 2013, Petrocaribe was supplying 59 percent of Cuba's total oil consumption, 93 percent of Haiti's, 70 percent of Nicaragua's, and 13 percent of El Salvador's.[17] Venezuela has similar oil-subsidy and soft-finance agreements with Argentina.[18]

Chávez's expansive economic aid extended beyond Petrocaribe in at least four additional domains: 1) allowing debt retirement, forgiveness, or tolerance for countries that have trouble paying their debts; 2) making Venezuela a major importer of goods and services (to the great benefit of Brazil and Colombia); 3) opening the oil and energy sectors to allied countries such as China, Brazil, Russia, and Iran; and 4) expanding international information services (namely, Telesur).

The flow of petroproducts, petrosubsidies, petrodollars, and petrocontracts from Venezuela to foreign countries won Chávez remarkable diplomatic support. Even though many countries disliked Chávez's policy of keeping oil prices high and frowned on the restriction of civil liberties inside Venezuela, his generous foreign economic aid was welcomed by recipients as well as ideologues who saw the aid policy as another example of the regime's commitment to anticapitalism.

Venezuela has also been known to threaten cutting economic ties with developed nations as a way to secure support. For example, in 2014 Venezuela was rumored to have pressured the Netherlands into blocking the extradition of Hugo Carvajal, the former head of Venezuelan military intelligence, from Aruba (a Caribbean-island country that is part of the Kingdom of the Netherlands) to the United States by threatening to ban Royal Dutch Shell and Unilever from operating in Venezuela. In February 2015, a Spanish daily reported that the Venezuelan government officially threatened several large Spanish multinationals with expropriation if they did not pressure the Spanish government to adopt a more pro-Venezuela policy.[19]

The establishment of Venezuela's alliance of tolerance was facilitated by the reluctance of Latin American governments, despite their commitment to human rights, to censure sitting presidents for their failings. Due in part to this regional reticence, the United States decided to take a stronger stand, declaring Venezuela a "national security threat" in March 2015, thereby paving the way to put sanctions on seven key Venezuelan officials. But Maduro will probably use this so-called U.S. aggression to his advantage in order to justify further state encroachments.

Not all of Venezuela's foreign-policy aims have been achieved. With Venezuela's foreign largesse, Chávez set out to do more than just establish an alliance of tolerance. He wanted not only to preempt foreign critics, but also to expand the number of like-minded regimes in the region. Venezuelan foreign aid has contributed directly to the electoral campaigns of *chavista*-like movements across Latin America (Argentina, Bolivia, Colombia, Ecuador, Paraguay, and El Salvador) and even outside the region (Spain), often with success. A recent study of Venezuela's influence in El Salvador shows how this petrodiplomacy works. Venezuelan aid helped El Salvador to establish Alba Petróleos, a state-owned company that distributes oil within the country. Alba Petróleos, which is run almost entirely by El Salvador's ruling party and therefore rarely audited, provides funding mostly to municipalities governed by ruling-party mayors and also spends heavily on social projects during electoral campaigns. The company does not always pay back its debts to Venezuela, which Venezuela condones (the alliance of tolerance works both ways).[20]

Despite some early successes (notably in Bolivia, Ecuador, and Nicaragua),

TABLE 2   Telesur and competitors on Twitter

Account	Joined Twitter	Avg. No. of Tweets/Month	Avg. Increase in Followers/Month
CNN en Español	April 2009	794	165,038
BBC Mundo	November 2007	698	15,316
Telesur	June 2009	8,570	16,236
NTN24 (Colombia)	April 2010	2,602	47,254

SOURCE: Tabulated by author based on *www.twitter.com.*

the strategy of using foreign aid to create clone regimes has backfired. In recent years, Venezuelan efforts to support particular political factions abroad have generated virulent counterreactions in countries such as Colombia, Peru, Mexico, Honduras, and Paraguay. Anti-*chavista* leaders became all the more popular, and leftist candidates began to disavow ties to *chavismo*. Furthermore, a number of Latin American notables, including five former Latin American presidents, have criticized Maduro's 2014–15 crackdown. In sum, Venezuela's effort to mold clone regimes has had mixed results at best, but its attempt to create an alliance of tolerance has been a major success, enabling Chávez to rule more autocratically without having to face much international criticism.

Beyond the Neighborhood

One of Chávez's most important foreign-policy initiatives was the creation of the television news channel Telesur. Founded in 2005, Telesur is based in Caracas but broadcasts internationally. Its mission is to compete with "imperialist" news sources such as CNN and provide a "Latin American" and "south-oriented" perspective. Telesur offers a free-to-air signal, which means that it can be picked up by anyone with the appropriate equipment. According to the Venezuelan government, the channel is interested in acquiring a mass audience, not profits. Telesur, whose annual operating budget is estimated to be in the range of US$10 to 15 million, claimed to have 7.7 million "subscribers" worldwide in 2014.

Like Chávez's other foreign-policy initiatives, Telesur has a mixed record. On the one hand, Telesur has secured international partners who have helped to fund the enterprise, including Argentina, Bolivia, Cuba, Ecuador, Nicaragua, and Uruguay. In addition, Telesur has information-sharing agreements with numerous organizations including Al Jazeera, the BBC, Russia's RT, Iran's IRIB, and China's CCTV, among others. Initially launched solely as a Spanish-language channel, it began broadcasting in Portuguese in 2008 and in English in 2014.

On the other hand, Telesur's actual viewership is probably low. Venezuela's information minister recently admitted that he does not know how many people are actually watching the channel, claiming that Telesur lacks the resources to collect data on viewership.[21] The private firm AGB Nielsen, which does collect viewership data in Venezuela, reports that between 2008 and 2012 Telesur had an average share of 0.48 percent, making it one of the least-viewed channels in the country (by comparison, Venevisión's share ranged from 23 to 36 percent).[22] Although there are no data on Telesur's international viewership, we can use Twitter to get an idea of the channel's popularity. Compared to its competition, Telesur is enormously aggressive on Twitter, at least in terms of tweets posted per month (see Table 2). At the same time, however, Telesur is significantly underperforming in terms of Twitter followers: Its average increase in number of followers per month pales in comparison to that of CNN en Español.

Telesur is emblematic of the Venezuelan regime's efforts to disseminate its worldview as widely as possible: The government pushes hard for modest returns, but seems not to be too worried about this poor investment-to-return ratio. In the battle against "imperialism," Venezuela is committed for the long haul.

Venezuela's active foreign policy extends well beyond its neighborhood. The regime has established fairly close ties with nondemocracies across the globe, including China and Russia, as well as such pariah states as Iran, Syria, and Libya under Qadhafi. These extrahemispheric partnerships have been motivated by general goals as well as specific bilateral ones.[23] In terms of the former, the regime has sought to forge opaque (and therefore insulated from public scrutiny) economic and business relationships, something that is easier done with nondemocracies, and to create more diplomatic complications for the United States by teaming with its adversaries. It is widely known that Venezuela's regime under both Chávez and Maduro has partnered with countries such as China, Russia, Iran, and Syria on lucrative deals and economic investments.

The specifically bilateral goals are numerous. Venezuela hopes to find a reliable alternative market for its oil in China, and to further increase the more than $50 billion that China has already invested in the Venezuelan economy. Meanwhile, the regime is a huge buyer of Russian weaponry; Venezuela is estimated to have purchased about three-quarters of the $14.5 billion that Russia earned from arms sales in Latin America between 2001 and 2013.[24] Finally, Venezuela had hoped that Iran would join it in a subgroup within OPEC to counterbalance Saudi Arabia's efforts to keep oil prices down. The United States feared for some time that the Venezuelan-Iranian partnership would lead to nuclear projects in Venezuela as well as Iran-sponsored terrorism across Latin America, though Western concern over Iranian influence in the region appears to have subsided somewhat since 2012.

Today, with Venezuela facing a severe economic crisis that makes it a less lucrative business partner and a less attractive role model, the regime's ability to project power globally is dwindling. So Maduro has had to change tactics. Rather than trying to reshape the outside world, his main goal now is to convince Venezuela's global partners that, in terms of their economic interests in Venezuela, a change in the status quo is likely to be harmful to them. This is just another way of using economic ties abroad to promote regime survival at home.

During sixteen years of *chavismo,* and especially since 2006, Venezuela's regime has steadily moved toward harsher authoritarian practices. This trajectory was not preordained. Not all hybrid regimes move in this direction. Many factors contributed to Venezuela's rising authoritarianism: high oil prices in 2003–2008 and 2010–2012, which gave the state vast resources with which to coopt and repress opposition; the decline in Western democracy-promotion initiatives; the growing influence of new nondemocratic powers such as China and Russia; the intensification of U.S. unilateralism between 2001 and 2008, which provoked Venezuela's nationalist impulses; the global shift toward greater tolerance for statism after two decades of neoliberalism; and even the errors and weaknesses of the Venezuelan opposition.

All these factors no doubt played a role. But in hybrid regimes, state officials also have at their disposal the necessary instruments to steer their countries toward deeper forms of authoritarianism. In the case of Venezuela, such instruments have included the clever use of electoral majorities at home and petrodollars abroad. Now that both of these are scarcer, the regime is under unprecedented strain. It is facing newer pressures from international critics (though still too few from Latin America) and from a reenergized domestic opposition determined to reverse the regime's course. Economics and elections have left Maduro cornered to a far greater degree than Chávez ever was. Will Maduro yield to these pressures or will he counterattack? Based on his presidency so far, Maduro appears to be confident that he has enough institutional control at home and support abroad to stay the course. So it is entirely possible that one of Latin America's most politically restrictive regimes could turn even more restrictive in the years to come.

Notes

1. See "Grandes Objetivos Históricos y Objetivos Nacionales," Programa de la Patria 2013–2019, *http://blog.chavez.org.ve/programa-patria-venezuela-2013-2019/idependencia-nacional/#.VPmcVuGLiJ8*.

2. This figure for Venezuelan newspapers is based on Juvenal Mavares's annual media directory, *Directorio de relaciones públicas y medios de comunicación social* (Caracas: J&M Asociados, 1998); see also Prensa Escrita's list of Venezuelan newspapers at *www.prensaescrita.com/america/venezuela.php*.

3. I am grateful to Franz von Bergen and Juan Gabriel Delgado for their research assistance. In order to determine if a private newspaper was independent, we checked whether former staff reporters or other news media reported cases of censored information in the coverage of news that was favorable to the opposition. No doubt, some qualitative judgments were employed. But leaving aside my count of nonindependent print media, the evidence is still clear: The size of private independent print media has declined considerably under *chavismo*.

4. See Sujatha Fernandes, *Who Can Stop The Drums? Urban Social Movements in Chávez's Venezuela* (Durham: Duke University Press, 2010).

5. Philip Bennett and Moisés Naím. "21st-Century Censorship," *Columbia Journalism Review*, 5 January 2015, *http://moisesnaim.com/columns/21st-century-censorship*.

6. "Unos cuarenta periódicos, afectados por la escasez de papel en Venezuela," Reporteros Sin Fronteras, 12 September 2014, *http://es.rsf.org/venezuela-unos-cuarenta-periodicos-afectados-12-09-2014,46951.html*.

7. Javier Corrales, "Electoral Irregularities Under Chavismo: A Tally," *Americas Quarterly*, 11 April 2013, *www.americasquarterly.org/electoral-irregularities-under-chavismo-tally*.

8. Miriam Kornblith, "Latin America's Authoritarian Drift: Chavismo After Chávez?" *Journal of Democracy* 24 (July 2013): 47–61.

9. Edgar López, "En nueve años el TSJ no ha dictado ni una sentencia con-

tra el gobierno," *El Nacional*, 1 December 2014, *www.el-nacional.com/politica/anos-TSJ-dictado-sentencia-gobierno_0_529147208.html*.

10. This section draws from Javier Corrales and Michael Penfold, *Dragon in the Tropics: The Legacy of Hugo Chávez*, 2nd ed. (Brookings Institution Press, forthcoming).

11. International Crisis Group, "Venezuela: Dangerous Inertia," *Latin America Briefing*, No. 31, 23 September 2014.

12. Programa Venezolano de Educación-Acción en Derechos Humanos (PROVEA), "Venezuela 2014: Protestas y derechos humanos," *Informe*, February–May 2014, *www.derechos.org.ve/pw/wp-content/uploads/Informe-final-protestas2.pdf*; "Maduro supera a Chávez en represión," *Hoy* (Quito), 8 July 2014, *www.hoy.com.ec/noticias-ecuador/maduro-supera-a-chavez-en-represion-609719.html*.

13. Javier Corrales and Carlos A. Romero, *U.S.-Venezuela Relations Since the 1990s: Coping with Midlevel Security Threats* (New York: Routledge, 2013).

14. Francisco J. Monaldi, "Oil and Politics: Venezuela Today," paper presented at the Latin American Studies Association Congress, Washington, D.C., 2013.

15. U.S. Energy Information Administration, "Venezuela: Country Analysis Brief Overview," available at *www.eia.gov/countries*.

16. Javier Corrales, "Using Social Power to Balance Soft Power: Venezuela's Foreign Policy," *Washington Quarterly* 32 (October 2009): 97–114.

17. Andres Schipani and John Paul Rathbone, "Oil Price Rout Forces Venezuela to Rethink Petro-Diplomacy," *Financial Times*, 14 January 2015.

18. For a more precise look at Venezuela's petro-aid in its neighborhood, see the table "Venezuela's Petro-Aid: Subsidized Oil Shipments Within Latin America" at *www.journalofdemocracy.org/articles/supplemental-material*.

19. See "Amenazan con expropiar a empresas españolas," *El Nacional* (Caracas), 16 February 2015, *www.el-nacional.com/economia/Amenazan-expropiar-empresas-espanolas_0_575342576.html*.

20. Agustín E. Ferraro and Juan José Rastrollo, "¿Clientelismo político en El Salvador? Estudio de caso de Alba Petróleos y sus empresas relacionadas," Salamanca University, *www.slideshare.net/FUSADESORG/clientelismo-poltico-en-el-salvador-estudio-de-caso-de-alba-petrleos-y-sus-empresas-relacionadas*.

21. See "Telesur celebra cinco años de vida 'haciendo mejor periodismo que CNN,'" *Correo del Orinoco* (Caracas), 1 August 2010, *www.correodelorinoco.gob.ve/comunicacion-cultural/telesur-celebra-cinco-anos-vida-haciendo-mejor-periodismo-que-cnn*.

22. See AGB Nielsen Media Research, "Share por canal inter anual 2008 al 2012: Total individuos," *www.agbnielsen.com.ve/libro2012/SHARE/TOTAL_INDIVIDUOS.html*.

23. Corrales and Romero, *U.S.-Venezuela Relations*, 162.

24. Ilan Berman, "Russia Pivots Toward Cuba, Venezuela, Nicaragua," *Washington Times*, 26 March 2014.

CHAPTER SIX

Saudi Arabia's Anxious Autocrats

FREDERIC WEHREY

ONE OF THE WORLD's last remaining bastions of absolute monarchy, the oil-rich Kingdom of Saudi Arabia pursues throughout the broader Middle East and beyond an activist foreign policy that is largely nonideological, realist, and defensive in intent, but negative in its implications for democracy. In the aftermath of the 2011 Arab uprisings, Saudi Arabia has intervened in a number of transitioning states with the aim of countering the challenges posed by the Islamic Republic of Iran, the rise of the Muslim Brotherhood, and Salafi jihadism as embodied by al-Qaeda and the Islamic State. While the intent of such interference may not be explicitly antidemocratic, many of the recipients of Saudi support have been authoritarian and antiliberal.[1] The ultimate effect has been damaging to the spread of democratization and political pluralism.

When 90-year-old King Abdullah died in January 2015, the royal regime's Allegiance Council, an appointed panel of 28 princes tasked with ensuring a smooth succession, swiftly named 79-year-old Crown Prince Salman as the new king. The Council then designated his 69-year-old half-brother Muqrin as his successor, with 55-year-old Muhammad bin Nayef as the next in line after Muqrin. However, in an unprecedented move, King Salman divested Crown Price Muqrin by royal edict and replaced him with Muhammad bin Nayef. Then Salman selected his own son, 30-year-old Mohammed bin Salman, to be deputy crown prince. These speedy changes to the royal succession took place in a volatile regional environment where rebels with loose ties to Iran had just overrun the capital of neighboring Yemen, forced out its president, and pushed that already turbulent country closer to full-blown state collapse.

Increasingly, Saudi Arabia's reach is global, with robust trade links to the powerhouse economies of Northeast Asia; burgeoning security and defense ties to South Asia; and longstanding bonds with Muslim communities across Asia, Africa, and Latin America. Although Saudi Arabia is not a revolutionary power bent on exporting its brand of authoritarian governance, its foreign policy is counterdemocratic in effect. Within the region, Saudi money and influence have been used to block the ascendance of groups that the royal family deems a threat to its security at home. The Saudi regional strategy is rooted in the monarchy's view of the 2011 uprisings not as the Arab Spring but as the Arab Troubles—upheavals that brought sectarian strife, Iranian expansionism, newfound prominence for the Muslim Brothers, and fresh strains of jihadism such as the one that drives the Islamic State.

Under King Abdullah, key targets of Saudi interference included the Islamists of the Muslim Brotherhood. Although the Brothers once found shelter in Saudi Arabia after Egypt cracked down on them during Gamal Abdel Nasser's presidency (1956–70), the relationship soon soured as the Brotherhood's ideology mixed with the Kingdom's quietist form of Salafism, imbuing it with a political activism that was threatening to the ruling family. This commingling spawned the rise of the so-called Sahwa (Awakened) clerics, many of whom came to dominate the theological faculties of Saudi universities. During the 1990s, these popular figures mounted an unprecedented political critique of the royal family, and more hard-line clerics inspired the growth of al-Qaeda. A desire to prevent a repeat of this scenario factored heavily into King Abdullah's post-2011 policies toward the Brotherhood.

The authoritarian partners whom Saudi Arabia supports against the Brotherhood, Iran, and jihadism range from fellow Gulf monarchs to neo-Nasserist military rulers in Egypt to Salafi religious figures who stress political quietism. The array of official and semi-official tools used in these efforts includes the sponsorship of transnational Arab media outlets and quietist Salafi charities; personal diplomatic forays by Saudi princes; and even overt military interventions. Looming largest, however, is the massive financial aid that oil-rich Saudi Arabia is able to spread around. Between early 2011 and April 2014, Saudi Arabia pledged roughly US$22.7 billion in regional aid; it ended up distributing $10.9 billion, much of which went to Egypt.[2]

Outside the Middle East—in Bangladesh, Indonesia, and parts of the former Yugoslavia, for instance—Saudi Arabia has been willing to tacitly support elections when they favor diplomatic allies.[3] But closer to home, the *cordon sanitaire* against participatory politics is kept as impermeable as possible.

Saudi authorities may sometimes back democratic institutions in the region or even at home, but only within clear limits and as a pressure-release tactic to coopt elites or counter rivals such as Iran or the Muslim Brothers.[4] Hence Riyadh favored the spread of consultative councils in the Gulf in the 1990s; instituted domestic municipal-council elections in the 2000s; and aided certain candidates in the Yemeni, Bahraini, and Iraqi parliamentary elections. But any serious steps toward democratization nearby, in the states of the Gulf Cooperation Council (GCC), will show where the Saudis draw their red line. As recent history shows, the Saudis fear that longstanding kinship, sectarian, and cultural ties among these states make them highly susceptible to political contagion. The risk that an outbreak of constitutionalism or civil society mobilization in one Gulf country could spread to the others is too much for Riyadh to tolerate.

Saudi Arabia's increasingly assertive foreign policy belies a deep domestic insecurity regarding the future of an oil-based dynastic state (with all the succession worries that this implies) that rules a "youth-bulge" society (most Saudis are under thirty) situated within one of the world's most restive regions. A future convergence of these challenges could make segments of the Saudi populace open to mobilization—particularly ideological mobilization incited from abroad. The House of Saud has long worried that the sharpest threats to its rule come not from "hard-power" foes, but instead take the form of "soft-power" ideological challenges, whether secular (Arab-nationalist Nasserism and Ba'athism) or religious (Shia revolutionary agitation after the Iranian Revolution, Muslim Brotherhood activism, and the Sunni jihadism embodied by al-Qaeda and the Islamic State).[5]

The tumult that has been roiling the Arab world since 2011 represents only the latest dangerous ideological "wave." It has unleashed new forms of democratic agitation, handed new opportunities to the Brotherhood, and fueled new and highly violent strains of jihadism such as the Islamic State. The recent burst of Saudi activism in the region is meant to insulate the Kingdom from these threats—but the net effect has been profoundly harmful for democratization and is ultimately not sustainable.

Domestic Suppression

For decades, Saudi Arabia has been one of the world's most politically closed states. Democracy remains anathema to the country's Salafi Islamic establishment, and the monarchy itself has only recently loosened restrictions. Responding to a wave of petitions from clerics and liberals alike, King Fahd in 1992 promulgated the "Basic Law of Governance." This quasi-constitutional document (which says early on that Saudi Arabia accepts only "Almighty God's Book, The Holy Qur'an, and the Sunna [Traditions] of the Prophet" as its constitution) sets up a 60-person Consultative Council or Majlis al-Shura. In practice, this royally appointed body includes mostly technocrats, albeit drawn from across the different regions and provinces of the country. The Majlis has a statutory right to question cabinet members and to review social and economic policies before the government promulgates them.

The rest of the 1990s and the decade after saw the creation of a number of incipiently democratic institutions, including civil society groups such as engineers' unions. After 9/11 and a spate of high-profile terrorist attacks within the Kingdom in 2003, the monarchy not only took vigorous police measures but also founded the King Abdulaziz Center for National Dialogue in order to (as the Dialogue's website says) "combat extremism." In 2005 came the first municipal-council elections. Adopted at the urging of the United States, this cautious and limited experiment with participatory governance led activists to hail this period as a "golden era" when Saudi citizens, for the first time ever, could begin openly hashing out "issues."

By 2006, as U.S. priorities shifted, tensions with Iran rose, and the fighting in Iraq took on an especially ugly sectarian cast, optimism was fading. The participatory structures proved to be largely cosmetic and lacking in any real authority. Organizations that claimed to be dedicated to civil society and human rights turned out to be closely tied to the royal family. Activists across the sectarian spectrum decried the National Dialogue as a mere "debating society." The elected municipal councils had no capacity to oversee budgets; real power rested with royally appointed governors. And the regime put a cap on the amount and type of dissent that it would tolerate, particularly on the question of a constitution.

As the Arab Spring protests roiled the region in early 2011, the Saudi regime responded with arrests, clerical exhortations against challenging the ruler, and massive subsidies meant to defuse unrest. There were demonstrations within Saudi borders, but most took place in the heavily Shia locale of Eastern Province. This gave the regime an opening—which it ably used—to frame matters in sectarian terms, thereby dampening prospects for cooperation across regional lines within the country and buttressing the case for monarchical rule. Introducing democracy, the regime and its supporters argued, would open a Pandora's box of sectarian, tribal, and regionalist furies. The internecine conflicts in Iraq, Syria, and Yemen have reinforced this narrative.[6]

Recent years have seen intense debates within Saudi Arabia about how to move the country forward economically without overstepping political and religious boundaries. The educational and judicial systems have been crucial battlegrounds. Reformist members of the royal family have been campaigning to purge Saudi universities of Brotherhood-affiliated clerics and officials, and to diminish the influence of hard-line judges.

In tandem, there have been increased efforts to rein in clerics—both those who were critical of King Abdullah's reforms as too permissive, and others who felt that the reforms needed to go further. As a result, Saudi prisons have become filled with a broad spectrum of political prisoners. They include conservative Salafis from the region of Qasim and its capital, Buraydah; Shia from the east; and liberals from Hijaz in the west along the Red Sea. In 2013, there were protests almost every day outside prisons in the conservative heartland province of Qasim—an unprecedented development in an area long known as a bulwark of support for the monarchy.

The proliferation of social media poses new challenges to state control of political discourse. Twitter is hard to police. In many cases, the authorities prefer to forgo efforts at restriction and respond by marshaling "Twitter armies" of their own to push the regime's message. "Many cases" are not all cases, however: Social-media statements seen as "insulting Islam" have been punished by law.

The most notorious case has been that of 31-year-old blogger Raif Badawi and his Free Saudi Liberals website. Convicted of "insulting Islam," Badawi was sentenced to a fine, a ten-year jail term, and a thousand lashes, the first fifty of which were administered in Jeddah on 9 January 2015, with fifty ordered to follow at weekly intervals for nineteen more weeks. Amid a worldwide outcry against this brutal punishment, Saudi authorities ceased the lashes, citing a doctor's opinion that Badawi had not healed sufficiently from the first whipping. Both Badawi and his lawyer, Waleed Abu al-Khair, remain imprisoned. As of August 2015, the Saudi Supreme Court is reviewing his case.[7] In late October 2015, the European Parliament awarded Badawi its Sakharov Prize for Freedom of Thought.

On top of its longstanding laws against apostasy and blasphemy, Saudi Arabia has put into force a draconian antiterror code. These new regulations, shelved back in 2011 after human-rights activists leaked details about them, became law by royal decree in late December 2013. The new laws, along with a related Interior Ministry statement, define terrorism loosely enough to encompass any form of critical speech deviating from Saudi political and cultural norms. Another Interior Ministry document adds that "terrorism" includes "calling [others] to atheist thought . . . or doubting the unvarying principles of the Islamic religion."[8]

The domestic political motives behind the antiterror code are far-reaching. Making no reference to violence beyond "harm to facilities," the code— which is aimed at unruly Salafis and Muslim Brotherhood types as well as "atheists"—focuses almost solely on matters of expression and "public order." Under the antiterror code, authorities have already charged young men for nothing more than "seditious tweets" that put Saudi living standards or the royal family in a negative light.[9] In a country whose rulers brook no political opposition, even apolitical social activism can easily meet the law's criteria for "threatening the national unity" of the country or "insulting the state's reputation or stature."[10] In many respects, the antiterror code was the domestic expression of a broader post-2011 countermovement by the Saudi regime that had its strongest impact in Egypt.

If Syria is the main front in Saudi Arabia's geopolitical struggle against Iran, then Egypt is the main front in the political and ideological struggle against the Muslim Brotherhood. Thanks to its great weight in Arab affairs, Egypt has always been of central importance to Saudi decision makers. Hosni Mubarak's fall in early 2011 hit the Saudi royals like an earthquake—in one stroke, they lost an authoritarian bulwark against both Iran and the Brotherhood. Even more ominously, as King Abdullah noted at the time, they watched the United States discard a longtime ally.

In order to stem the rise of the Brotherhood in Egypt, the Saudis have given financial aid to the government of General Abdel Fattah al-Sisi, to sympathetic media, and to those Egyptian Salafis who have become the military's tacit allies against the Brotherhood. As early as 2011, when

Egypt was under the rule of the Supreme Council of the Armed Forces (SCAF), Saudi Arabia pledged $4 billion in badly needed economic support (Egypt, with a population of 84 million, has difficulty feeding itself). The initial goal was to block any drift toward Iran. The Saudis purportedly channeled money to the Salafist al-Nour party during Egypt's 2011–12 parliamentary elections.

When Brotherhood member Mohamed Morsi won a runoff to become president of Egypt in June 2012, Riyadh shut off its aid. Rumors flew that Prince Bandar bin Sultan (who would soon become Saudi Arabia's intelligence chief) and the Gulf states were working quietly to embolden military opposition to the Muslim Brothers, even as Washington was urging General Sisi to reach a peaceful compromise with Morsi. Saudi support resumed once the military ousted Morsi in July 2013. Together with the other GCC governments, the Saudis have given Egypt $23 billion in aid (in the form of petroleum products and central-bank deposits) since Morsi was ousted—a sum that dwarfs the combined $2.8 billion pledged by Washington and the EU.[11] In interviews, U.S. Defense Department officials have told me that this influx of Saudi aid—together with a shift toward arms purchases from Russia—has significantly eroded U.S. ability to push the military regime in Cairo toward political reforms. Saudi commentators, meanwhile, have defended the move as helping to stabilize Egypt and to restore its capacity to oppose Iranian influence in Syria and Iraq.[12]

It is important to note, however, that Saudi Arabia's policies in Egypt did cause blowback at home. Clerics from the Sahwa branch of Saudi Salafism—the variant that draws inspiration from Muslim Brotherhood ideology—were not shy about taking to the lively Saudi social-media scene in order to criticize Morsi's ouster. A few clerics even called for external aid to Morsi's supporters. Other prominent Salafists, including Mohsen al-Awaji, Saad al-Buraik, and Naseer al-Omar, used Morsi's ouster to point out the Saudi government's failings, though some tempered their comments by implying that Morsi's mismanagement and tilt toward Iran were to blame for his downfall. Thirty-four prominent Sahwa clerics wrote Egypt's al-Nour party to charge it with backing secular forces and "obstructing *shari'a*" during the constitution-writing process.[13]

By August 2013, Saudi authorities had jailed two Sahwa clerics, placed another under house arrest, and banned a Riyadh preacher from public speaking—all because they expressed support for the deposed president or voiced opposition to General Sisi. Ironically, this crackdown prompted the very politicization of Saudi clerical discourse that the monarchy had been so eager to avoid when the Brotherhood held power in Cairo.

To the west of Egypt, across North Africa, the Saudis have offered a similar mix of financial aid to authoritarian, anti-Brotherhood actors—often neo-Nasserist officers—and Salafi quietists. Much of this pre-dates the Arab uprisings. For example, senior Saudi clerics visited Libya in the twilight years of Muammar al-Qadhafi's regime at his invitation in order to support his efforts at deradicalizing former members of the Libyan Islamic Fighting Group.[14] Like the Saudi original that was its model, Qadhafi's program taught nonparticipation in politics and obedience to the ruler. Although Salafists are hardly the whole story in today's post-Qadhafi Libya, this politically quietist current of Salafism (known as Madkhaliyya after its Saudi clerical progenitor, Rabi' bin Hadi al-Madkhali) remains influential.

After Qadhafi's downfall, Saudi Arabia worked quietly through the Emirates and Sisi's government to support anti-Islamist factional forces under retired Libyan general Khalifa Haftar. Since May 2014, the septuagenarian Haftar has become a major player in Libya's multisided civil war. He has been running an armed campaign—dubbed Operation Dignity—that teams eastern tribes, federalists, military officers, and some liberals in a push to drive Islamist militias out of Benghazi. Warplanes and special forces from the UAE, using bases in Egypt, have carried out strikes inside Libya to support Haftar. A broader, unstated goal is to shut political Islamists and especially the Muslim Brothers out of Libyan politics.

As regards Tunisia, Saudi Arabia has given asylum to deposed dictator Zine al-Abidine Ben Ali, while banning from its soil Rachid Ghannouchi, whose Brotherhood-affiliated Ennahda party is the target of Saudi opposition. In recent years, the UAE has stepped to the forefront with its efforts to counter Ennahda's rise by backing its secular rival, the Nidaa Tounes party, which contains many remnants of Ben Ali's old ruling group.

Quarantine in the Gulf and Iraq

Closer to home, in the Gulf region, Saudi policy has been working hard to limit democratic participation, which Riyadh fears as a path to Shia mobilization and Muslim Brotherhood empowerment. Massive cash payouts to local Sunnis and Salafis and even military intervention have been applied. Looking to the longer term, Riyadh has been spearheading GCC integration initiatives that focus on the internal security of member states. The intent is to make each state's domestic stability the concern of all, as well as to ease the task of policing dissent.

Saudi Arabia's strategy has been on clearest display in the neighboring island kingdom of Bahrain. Linked to the Saudi coast by the 25-kilometer King Fahd Causeway, Bahrain has been tightly involved with the mainland at least since Sunni tribes from the Arabian Peninsula helped the Khalifa family (a Sunni clan) to conquer the island back in the 1780s. Sitting atop declining oil reserves, Bahrain depends on Saudi subsidies. The Saudi royals watch events on the island warily, believing that if Bahrain's majority Shia ever mobilize politically, their coreligionists in Saudi Arabia's oil-rich Eastern Province will swiftly follow suit. And this is to say nothing about the energizing impact that an outburst of Bahraini constitutionalism and democratization could have on Saudi Sunni reformists.

Although Saudi media and officials often worry aloud that opening Bahrain to wider political participation could make the island "fall" to Iran, this fear may not be the main driver of Saudi policy. In an admission that surprised me with its frankness, a senior Saudi diplomat told me in 2006 that Saudi Arabia could live with Bahrain having a Shia premier. He went on to say that continued dependence on Saudi subsidies plus differences between Bahraini Shia and Iran's ruling clerics would keep the island out of Tehran's orbit. Hyperbole about the Iranian threat is useful, however, both as a distraction from the Khalifa family's governance failings and corruption, and as a way of maintaining the support of the United States, which bases its Fifth Fleet on the island. (Bahraini Shia leaders back the U.S. naval base too, seeing it as an aid in keeping both the Iranians and the Saudis at a distance.)

Riyadh has counseled the Khalifa monarchy to adopt limited reforms as a pressure-release tactic. Thus Bahrain has held elections (most recently in November 2014) for a parliament that has virtually no legislative or oversight capacity; has hosted talks modeled on the Saudi National Dialogue; and has eased sectarian discrimination in areas such as housing and public-sector hiring. In encouraging participation but seeing that it stays limited, the Saudis have played a double game. To counter the Shia, Riyadh has given money to deeply sectarian (and mostly pro-Khalifa) Sunni elements such as the al-Asala Islamic Society, the National Unity Gathering, and the Sahwat al-Fatih movement.

Saudi leaders have found events in Bahrain disturbing enough to merit the use not merely of "soft" but of "hard" power. In March 2011, as Arab Spring unrest on the island was cresting, Saudi troops in armored vehicles rolled across the causeway under the banner of the GCC Peninsula Shield Force. Backed by Emirati forces and token contingents from Kuwait and Qatar, the Saudi soldiers took over guarding key points while Bahraini security forces violently suppressed protesters. As of this writing in late 2015, an estimated five-thousand Saudi and Emirati troops remain on the island. They are not in direct contact with the public, but fill support roles (such as guarding strategic sites) in order to free their Bahraini counterparts to bring force to bear more quickly should another crisis arise.

Although met with skepticism by most GCC governments and protests by the Bahraini Shia community, the idea of a closer juncture (to be called the Gulf Union) between Saudi Arabia and Bahrain has roused an eager response from conservatives within the Khalifa family. On the sidelines of a May 2013 GCC meeting in Riyadh, the merger idea received a surprisingly formal endorsement from Saudi and Bahraini officials. The need for mutual defense was cited, but political motives were more likely at work— the ruling family of Saudi Arabia wanted to shore up the ruling family of Bahrain, the place in the Gulf region that seems most vulnerable to political ferment. Bahraini Sunni groups that had formed to back the Khalifa monarchy in 2011 marched in favor of the union with Riyadh, as Shia activists noted with irony how often *they* had been charged with wanting to give up Bahrain's sovereignty to a foreign power (in their case, Iran).

Riyadh's efforts to knit the GCC regimes more tightly together have also included a fund set up in March 2011, at the height of the Arab Spring protests, which promised Oman and Bahrain $10 billion apiece over a decade. More recently, Riyadh has been using the regional route to pressure Qatar, which Saudi authorities say has links to terrorism and sponsors the Muslim Brotherhood.[15]

Saudi Arabia long ago concluded that Iraq, its largest neighbor to the north, has fallen firmly into Iran's orbit, with U.S. naivety hastening the process. Saudis speak of Iraq's 2004 parliamentary elections as having unleashed centrifugal forces that sent sectarian shock waves across the region and gave Tehran its decisive opening. The power of this narrative in driving Saudi Arabia's policies at home should not be underestimated: Stray down the path to the ballot box as Iraq did, the Saudis insist, and you will fling open the gates of *fitna* (strife).

Seeking to do what it could to protect its interests in Iraq, Saudi Arabia cultivated ties to powerful tribes such as the Shammar, as well as to Salafist groups, Islamists from the Iraqi Islamic Party, and former Ba'athist officers. In the 2010 elections, Riyadh backed the Iraqiyya list led by Ayad Allawi, a Shia from the Shammar. But then Tehran stepped in and maneuvered its favorite, Nuri al-Maliki, into the premiership even though Iraqiyya had won more votes. After that, Saudi Arabia virtually quarantined Iraq, building along the long border a multilayered fence that was only opened (albeit cautiously) after the rise of the Islamic State and Maliki's September 2014 replacement by Haider al-Abadi, another Shia politician but one who enjoys Saudi as well as Iranian backing.

On its southern border, in Yemen, Saudi Arabia has long worked to sow weakness and division, using billions in cash to build patronage networks among the powerful Ahmar tribal confederation, the Islah party, and southern secessionists.[16] The recent takeover of Sana'a by the Huthis, the Zaydi Shia movement with links to Iran that effectively ousted President Abdu Rabu Mansour Hadi, spurred Riyadh to suspend all economic aid.[17] In another regional irony, Riyadh had been backing Yemen's Salafists, but it was their rise that had mobilized the Huthis as a Zaydi-revivalist countermovement.[18] The Saudis had tried to put down the Huthi rebellion with limited cross-border troop incursions, artillery barrages, and airstrikes, but to no avail. Today, Saudi policy is focused on recovering whatever influence is to be had—perhaps via secessionists in the south—as Yemen disintegrates. Riyadh has rebuffed overtures by the Huthis to form a new national-unity government that includes officials from the former regime, denouncing the Huthi seizure of power as a "coup."[19]

It was against this backdrop that Saudi military forces, along with those of the United Arab Emirates, Bahrain, Qatar, Kuwait, and Jordan launched an air campaign dubbed Operation Decisive Storm on 25 March 2015. At the diplomatic level, Operation Decisive Storm has been a notable success for the monarch. It is the first deployment of the joint GCC military command that was set up in November 2014, and it is a product of the careful royal rapprochement with Turkey and Qatar. The U.S. backing that the operation has drawn is also significant and serves as further confirmation that the mutual estrangement which marked King Abdullah's last years is fading away.

The operation was also a boost domestically for Salman's line, particularly his son Mohammed bin Salman, whose appointment as defense minister was at first met with skepticism due to his youth and lack of experience. Saudi media are now portraying Mohammed as personally spearheading the anti-Huthi operation, with one article explaining that "the sons of King Salman are at the forefront of Decisive Storm both on land and in the air." (Mohammed's brother Khaled bin Salman is an air force pilot.)[20]

On April 21, the Saudi government announced that Decisive Storm was being replaced by Operation Restore Hope, which included a significant ground component, spearheaded by the United Arab Emirates. Thus far, the campaign has failed to dislodge the Huthis from their power base. And the humanitarian effects of the operation have been catastrophic—civilian deaths, massive numbers of people internally displaced, shortages of medical supplies and food.

The Saudis' portrayal of what is happening in Yemen as an Iranian takeover is meant to rally U.S. and Gulf (plus wider Arab) support for the Saudi position in what is essentially a localized power struggle between the center and the periphery in Yemen in which the Saudi bet was on the center. Within the Gulf region itself, a worrisome byproduct of the campaign has been a wave of sectarianism in social and traditional media, stoked by Sunni clerics. Gulf regimes have also arrested critics of the operation.

Countering Iran in the Levant

In Lebanon, Saudi policy is deeply confessional and supportive of patronage politics, but not explicitly counterdemocratic. The goal is to check Iranian and Syrian influence. For many Saudis, the protection of Lebanon's Sunnis is a matter of profound symbolic resonance, tied to the House of Saud's legitimacy.[21] Lebanese premier Rafiq Hariri's 2005 assassination, almost certainly at the hands of Syria, marked a turning point. When its ally was murdered, Riyadh went into high gear with cash payouts for the Lebanese army and sympathetic Sunni religious actors. Saad Hariri, Rafiq Hariri's son, has been the crucial intermediary, providing $52 million (much of it from the Saudis) to the Sunnis of northern Lebanon in a bid to curb the influence of Hezbollah and its sponsor, Iran.

After the 2006 Lebanon War, Saudi Arabia thought that it had worked out a stable power-sharing arrangement with Iran, but the brief interlude of intersectarian calm ended when Hezbollah forces rolled into West Beirut in May 2008. This humiliating blow, followed by the May 2011 naming of a pro-Syrian politician as prime minister, signaled Hezbollah's grip on the Lebanese government. The Saudis are not done trying, however: Recent reports suggest that Saad Hariri is distributing even more Saudi funding—a staggering $3 billion—to Lebanon's military and security agencies in an effort to pry them out of Tehran's orbit.[22]

Jordan is increasingly appearing in Saudi eyes as a frontline state in the struggle to preserve monarchy, contain the Syrian strife, check Iran's influence, rein in the Muslim Brotherhood, and fight the Islamic State. Riyadh led the GCC's stepped-up aid to Amman, pledging $1.37 billion of a total $5 billion in assistance. This money has indirectly had a counterdemocratic effect. The funds from abroad have reduced the pressure on Jordan's King Abdullah II to achieve promised political reforms and have allowed him to opt instead for merely cosmetic reforms, especially as regards improving the electoral law and converting the premiership from a royally appointed post into an elected office.

If Gulf money has played a role in keeping economic concerns from turning into demands for political change, how long can the tactic work? With oil prices falling, some curtailment of Saudi aid to Jordan is likely. In the meantime, however, Jordan has moved Riyadh's way. Abdullah's regime has enacted restrictive censorship and antiterror measures that resemble their Saudi and UAE counterparts in using an elastic definition of "terrorism." The Muslim Brotherhood has not yet been criminalized, but in late 2014 Jordanian authorities arrested a number of Brotherhood figures, including one who had been speaking critically of the UAE.

At the heart of Saudi Arabia's push to reorder regional geopolitics and manage the aftershocks of the Arab Spring stands Syria. Here, the Saudi-versus-Iranian strategic rivalry is especially apparent. Riyadh remains wary of great-power diplomatic initiatives regarding Syria, seeing them as at best dangerously naïve, and at worst as tokens of a deliberate conspiracy (led by Washington) to sacrifice the anti-Assad opposition on the altar of a nuclear deal with Tehran. Believing that local (and especially Arab) states must take the lead, the Saudis have worked through a variety of regional intermediaries to reduce infighting among allies, influence the leadership balance in the Syrian opposition, marginalize factions linked to al-Qaeda, and improve the quality of the opposition's battlefield performance through training and the shipment of advanced weaponry. Riyadh has set up a joint-operations room in Istanbul with Qatar and Turkey, channeled funds through intermediaries in Lebanon's Future Movement, coordinated military training with Jordan, brokered arms shipments from Croatia, and reportedly solicited Pakistan's assistance with training.[23]

The GCC's involvement in Syria bears well-known hallmarks of Gulf diplomacy: A few princes and their trusted advisors personally manage key matters while quasi-official actors such as clerics, charities, and tribal leaders may act on behalf of their respective governments, exert pressure on those governments, or pursue their own initiatives outside government control.[24] As one might expect, policies made under such conditions can be unpredictable and mutually contradictory. The jostling of princes eager to one-up each other can contribute to such erratic moves as Riyadh's impetuous October 2013 decision to become the first country ever to reject one of the ten two-year seats on the fifteen-seat UN Security Council. The troubling role that clerical freelancers can play has been sharply underlined by the funding that Kuwaiti Salafists have given to Jabhat al-Nusra, as al-Qaeda's branch in Syria and Lebanon is known.[25]

The House of Saud has become worried enough by this kind of thing to begin clamping down on Saudi clerics who agitate with reference to Syria. The idea is to ensure that any Saudi aid sent to Syria goes through official channels, thus heading off the clerics behind the freelance aid (who also tend to be critics of the monarchy's cautious reforms at home) before they can undermine the ruling family's legitimacy and Saudi Arabia's security. On 29 May 2013, King Abdullah reportedly summoned to Riyadh a number of prominent Salafi clerics who had formed the Ulema Committee to Support Syria, banning them on the spot from seeking donations for that country. A few days later, this committee's leaders announced on

Facebook that the authorities had canceled its fundraising drive.[26] Several individual clerics who had been raising money for "the brothers in Syria" issued similar notices.[27]

An Unsustainable Strategy

Underpinning all the activism by Saudi authorities is a profound sense of foreboding and malaise at home. To be sure, the House of Saud has often weathered turbulence, repeatedly confounding a cottage industry devoted to predicting the monarchy's doom. But over the next five to ten years, the Kingdom is likely to face a confluence of challenges that will be unprecedented in scope—and will very likely result in a recalibration of its role on the regional stage.

The most pressing issue is on the economic front. In the face of declining oil prices, it is unclear how long Saudi Arabia's massive regional spending can be maintained. Dependent on oil for about 90 percent of its revenue, the Saudi government is expected soon to face a budget deficit equal to 1 percent of GNP—the largest in Saudi history. In the near and middle terms, the ruling family is likely to leave housing and other subsidies untouched, but regional assistance is fair game for cuts. The question is how long the Saudis will rely on reserves in an effort to price shale-oil producers such as the United States out of the market. In the longer term, should the drop in oil prices continue, there will be profound implications for the Kingdom's many young people. In a society accustomed to paying for welfare spending with oil revenue, they will face the prospect of receiving fewer benefits than did their parents.

Official statistics put the first-half 2015 unemployment rate at 11.6 percent—5.7 percent for men and 32.8 percent for women (out of those looking for work)—and most of the jobless are in their twenties and thirties.[28] The government has tried to tackle unemployment by encouraging the "Saudization" of workplaces—that is, increasing the proportion of Saudis in private-sector jobs, many of which are with foreign companies. The Nitaqat (Zones) program has placed sanctions on those companies whose ratio of Saudi-to-foreign workers does not meet a certain threshold. Government sources show a slight improvement, with Saudi employment rising by 13 percent over a 16-month period. But the Saudization program has been criticized for loopholes that allow companies to circumvent the restrictions by creating fake positions for Saudi nationals and firing foreign workers without actually increasing the hiring of Saudis.[29]

Meanwhile, the smooth transfer of the crown that took place in early 2015 has stirred up worries about the royal succession. The removal of Muqrin as Crown Prince and his replacement with Muhammed bin Nayef ushers in a new generation of rulers. The transfer of power from King Abdullah to King Salman has also marked the transfer of power from the sons of King Abdulaziz Ibn Saud (1876–1953), Saudi Arabia's founder, to Ibn Saud's grandsons (Muqrin, moved out of the succession by his decade-older half-brother Salman, is Ibn Saud's youngest living son).

A new generation of princes, headed by Deputy Crown Prince Mohammed bin Salman, will now vie among themselves to take up the mantle of the Kingdom's leadership. Already, Mohammed bin Salman has amassed extraordinary domestic power, using the Defense Ministry portfolio and his oversight of Saudi military operations in Yemen to cultivate something near a cult of personality, as well as a wave of Sunni-based Saudi nationalism. Furthermore, a key unknown is what effects Muhammad bin Nayef's parallel rise will have. As head of the Interior Ministry, Nayef is known to be a stalwart opponent of Islamism and a seasoned counterterror veteran. Although he is well respected in Washington, his tenure at the Interior Ministry has seen the "securitization" of political dissent at home and vigorous interventions abroad to combat jihadism.[30]

Already, it is clear that King Salman sees the Brotherhood secondary status as a threat, behind Iran. With Morsi gone from the Egyptian presidency, the Saudi king has reportedly calculated that the Brotherhood's regional challenge has diminished. The Saudis have reportedly been pushing the UAE—an even stronger Brotherhood foe—to adopt less hard-line views. Much of this stems from a burgeoning Saudi rapprochement with Qatar and Turkey, as well as a Saudi effort to contain the Huthi threat in neighboring Yemen by renewing engagement with the Brotherhood-affiliated Islah party in that country.

These foreign-policy shifts and the lessening of animosity toward the Brotherhood are important, but should not be overstated. At its core, the Kingdom of Saudi Arabia remains an authoritarian state with a ruling family wedded to monarchical privilege and backed by a deeply antiliberal and sectarian religious establishment. If anything, it appears to be becoming more so under King Salman. In contrast to King Abdullah, Salman has been wooing the Kingdom's religiously conservative base of power to shore up public support for his domestic policies and to demonize Iran in the region. The result has been a rollback of Abdullah's limited reforms and a new, more virulent Sunni-based nationalism. In tandem, the reign of Salman has witnessed a new Saudi military assertiveness and a highly securitized foreign policy—spearheaded, in part, with remarkable autonomy by the king's young son Mohammed. Taken in sum, none of this bodes well for the spread of pluralistic politics in the region.

Notes

The author is grateful for the research assistance provided by Ala' Alrababa'h and Varsha Koduvayur, junior fellows in the Middle East Program at the Carnegie Endowment for International Peace.

1. For a discussion of a functional rather than ideological approach to analyzing counterdemocratic powers, see Thomas Carothers and Oren Samet-Marram, "The New Global Marketplace of Political Change," Carnegie Endowment paper (April 2015), *http://carnegieendowment.org/files/global_marketplace. pdf*. They write: "Autocracies do not necessarily promote autocracy when they try to influence political outcomes in other countries. A more accurate analytic umbrella concept for understanding their efforts is a more functional and less ideological one . . . A purely ideological interest in spreading autocracy per se is generally not on display."

2. Martin Dokoupil, "Saudi Could See Budget Deficit Next Year, Risks Draining Reserves—IMF," *Reuters.com,* 24 September 2014.

3. See Laurence Whitehead, "Antidemocracy Promotion: Four Strategies in Search of a Framework," *Taiwan Journal of Democracy* 10 (December 2014): 1–24.

4. Gerd Nonneman, "Security and Inclusion: Regime Responses to Domestic Challenges in the Gulf," *Whitehall Papers* 51 (2000): 107–15.

5. Stephen M. Walt, *The Origins of Alliances* (New York: Cornell University Press, 1987), 216; F. Gregory Gause III, "Balancing What? Threat Perception and Alliance Choice in the Gulf," *Security Studies* 13 (Winter 2003): 303.

6. See Frederic M. Wehrey, *Sectarian Politics in the Gulf: From the Iraq War to the Arab Uprisings* (New York: Columbia University Press, 2013).

7. Chris Green, "Raif Badawi: Saudi Arabia's Supreme Court Reviewing Case of Jailed Blogger," *The Independent,* 12 August 2015.

8. Saudi Arabia, Ministry of Interior Website, *www.moi.gov.sa.*

9. "Saudis Charge Three over Allegedly Seditious Tweets—Paper," *Reuters. com,* 1 April 2014.

10. Saudi Arabia, Bureau of Experts at the Council of Ministers, *www.boe. gov.sa.*

11. Fiona MacDonald and Dana El Baltaji, "Kuwait Egypt Aid Pushes Gulf Pledges to $12 Billion in 24 Hours," *Bloomberg.com,* 10 July 2013.

12. Khalid al-Dakhil, "What Is Riyadh Waiting for from Cairo?" *Al-Hayat* (Cairo), 20 July 2013.

13. "Saudi Religious Scholars Accuse Egyptian Salafist Al-Nour Party of Obstructing Sharia," Middle East Monitor *www.middleeastmonitor.com/news/ africa/9200-saudi-religious-scholars-accuse-egyptian-salafist-al-nour-party-of-obstructing-sharia.*

14. Author's interviews in Tripoli, Libya, 5 July 2012.

15. Bruce Riedel, "Saudi Arabia Moving Ahead With Gulf Union," *Al-Monitor,* 22 December 2013.

16. Stig Stenslie, *Not Too Strong, Not Too Weak: Saudi Arabia's Policy Towards Yemen*, Norwegian Peacebuilding Resource Center Policy Brief, March 2013.

17. Yara Bayoumy and Mohammed Ghobari, "Exclusive: Saudi Suspends Aid to Yemen After Houthi Takeover—Sources," *Reuters.com,* 4 December 2014.

18. Laurent Bonnefoy, "Salafism in Yemen: A 'Saudisation'?" in Madawi al-Rasheed, ed., *Kingdom Without Borders: Saudi Arabia's Political, Religious and Media Frontiers* (London: Hurst, 2008).

19. Rod Nordland and Shuaib Almosawa, "Saudis Unswayed by Houthi Rebels' Overture in Yemen," *New York Times,* 7 February 2015.

20. Translated from the Arabic by the author. The original article is from *alyoum.com* and may be found at *http://tinyurl.com/podveo6.*

21. As'ad AbuKhalil, "Determinants and Characteristics of the Saudi Role in Lebanon: The Post-Civil War Years," in al-Rasheed, *Kingdom Without Borders,* 79–97.

22. Hugh Naylor, "Rivals Tehran, Riyadh Pledge Billions to Lebanon's Army," *Washington Post,* 4 November 2014.

23. Frederic Wehrey, "Gulf Calculations in the Syria Conflict," 9 June 2014, *http://carnegieendowment.org/2014/06/09/gulf-calculations-in-syrian-conflict.*

24. Hassan Hassan, "Tribal Bonds Strengthen the Gulf's Hand in a New Syria," *The National,* 16 February 2012, *www.thenational.ae/thenationalconversation/comment/ tribal-bonds-strengthen-the-gulfs-hand-in-a-new-syria.*

25. Ben Hubbard, "Private Donors' Funds Add Wild Card to War in Syria," *New York Times,* 12 November 2013.

26. For a report in Arabic, see "The Scholars Committee to Support Syria

Declares the Stoppage of Fundraiser," 28 May 2012, *www.almoslim.net/node/165719*.

27. Frederic Wehrey, "Saudi Arabia Reins in Its Clerics on Syria," 14 June 2012, *http://carnegieendowment.org/2012/06/14/saudi-arabia-reins-in-its-clerics-on-syria*.

28. See the website of Saudi Arabia's Central Department of Statistics and Information at *www.cdsi.gov.sa/english*.

29. Jennifer R. Peck, "Can Hiring Quotas Work? The Effect of the Nitaqat Program on the Saudi Private Sector," MIT, April 2014, at *http://economics.mit.edu/files/9417*. See also Steffen Hertog, "The Private Sector and Reform in the Gulf Cooperation Council," London School of Economics, *www.lse.ac.uk/middleEastCentre/kuwait/documents/the-private-sector-and-reform-in-the-gcc.pdf*.

30. This point was made by F. Gregory Gause III, "Saudi Arabia's Game of Thrones: King Salman Amasses Power," *Foreign Affairs* (online), 2 February 2015, *www.foreignaffairs.com/articles/142842/f-gregory-gause-iii/saudi-arabias-game-of-thrones*.

PART TWO

Arenas of "Soft-Power" Competition

CHAPTER 7

Countering Democratic Norms

ALEXANDER COOLEY

SINCE THE GREAT FINANCIAL MELTDOWN of 2008, it has become commonplace to think of the West as being in normative retreat. The meltdown has undercut the perception that Western economic systems are superior, touched off an ongoing crisis in the Eurozone, and seen the sitting prime minister of an EU country (Hungary's Viktor Orbán) openly doubt whether liberal democracies can remain globally competitive. In parallel, revelations about NSA surveillance and the release of the U.S. Senate report on CIA torture have reinforced perceptions that the United States acts hypocritically and applies double standards when it comes to so-called values issues.

Beyond vocal criticism of the West as a problematic champion of democratic norms, a larger international backlash against liberal democracy has grown and gathered momentum. Over the past decade, authoritarians have experimented with and refined a number of new tools, practices, and institutions that are meant to shield their regimes from external criticism and to erode the norms that inform and underlie the liberal international political order. The important debate about whether there has been a democratic recession over the last decade—about how to understand these trends and how to classify stagnating polities and decaying institutions—also requires us to examine the broader global political changes and systemic shifts that have produced new counternorms and counterpractices.[1]

Policy makers and academics have been hesitant to acknowledge some of these recent cross-regional trends. Many deeply held and still highly influential assumptions about the nature of the liberal political order, the normative fabric of global governance, and the diffusion of democratic norms are products of the years just after the Cold War. Back then, in the 1990s, when the Soviet Union had just collapsed and former communist countries had begun economic and political transitions, liberal-democratic values appeared triumphant and free of significant ideological competition. At the same time, U.S. power was unrivaled, U.S. control of global institutions was strong, and there was a broad perception that a U.S.-led liberal world order would continue to set the rules, standards, and norms for international interactions. In light of the "pushback" that authoritarian regimes are now carrying out, upbeat assumptions about liberal democracy's effortless dominance require careful scrutiny.

The truth is that norms privileging state security, civilizational diversity, and traditional values over liberal democracy now enjoy significant backing, and they are reshaping the international environment. The effects are most visible in the narrower political space that nongovernmental organizations (NGOs) are facing, the shifting purposes that regional organizations are embracing, and the rising influence of non-Western powers as international patrons. Together, these effects reveal an international political climate that has made the work of spreading democratic norms far more difficult than it was two decades ago.

Perhaps most disturbingly, authoritarians have pursued these tactics and counterpractices because they are proving effective: The activities of NGOs can be successfully restricted; regional organizations can be repurposed to support the political agendas of authoritarian member states; and international investment and assistance can be procured from new donors without accompanying political conditions. Success breeds imitation, and more authoritarian regimes (plus some backsliding democracies) across Eurasia, Latin America, the Middle East, and Africa are beginning to emulate these practices.

Counternorms versus Liberal Democracy

Just as the backlash against liberal democracy spans different regions and countries, it also contains various alternative narratives and norms. The most commonly voiced critiques stress the primacy of state sovereignty and security, while charging that liberal-democratic governments and international organizations are too prone to meddle in the domestic affairs of other countries. Liberal democracy's universalism—its claim to be the sole legitimate form of human governance—comes under challenge, with liberal-democratic discourse said to be serving as cover for U.S. and Western geopolitical interests. Counternorms are thus grounded in changing power balances, as the post–Cold War era of U.S. hegemony gives way to a more multipolar world—a shift often summed up (not without irony) as the "democratization of international relations."

The single most powerful source of counternorms has been the post-9/11 turn toward counterterrorism and security. Since the 2001 terror attacks, there has been a collective acceptance, stretching well beyond the confines of the United States, that the tradeoff between security and individual liberty should be rebalanced in favor of the former. As Kim Lane Scheppele has observed, this "international state of emergency" has empowered governments to expand executive authority, increase areas of secrecy and state privilege, set up exceptional legal procedures, expand domestic surveillance, bypass national asylum procedures, and establish forms of cooperation between security services that escape transnational oversight.[2] While the 1990s saw the steady expansion of global civil society and transnational networks, the 2000s witnessed the globalization of anticonstitutionalist measures for purposes of fighting terrorism and strengthening state security.

Among the most powerful counterterrorist norms to arise thus far has been the widespread acceptance of organized blacklisting of suspected terrorists and their supporters. The legal basis for this practice dates from almost two years before 9/11, when UN Security Council Resolution 1267 of October 1999 created a committee that became charged with compiling a sanctions list aimed at all al-Qaeda affiliates. Resolution 1373, adopted on 28 September 2001, required states to criminalize terrorist financing and authorized governments to establish their own domestic blacklists. According to scholars and legal advocates, international blacklisting has had ill effects on political rights worldwide.[3] With no clear criteria for listing and no procedure for delisting, the "terrorist" designation has become a weapon that authoritarians can wield against political foes. It has also spawned the rise of "parallel" systems of administrative interventions that supplant the criminal-justice system and weaken the rule of law. Moreover, blacklisting appears to have generated a type of intergovernmental "logrolling" in which states do each other favors by readily accepting each other's decisions to list this group or that as "terrorist."[4]

A related concern, heightened by blacklisting, has been the growing abuse of the red-notice system that the International Criminal Police Organization (Interpol) uses to ask states to find, apprehend, and extradite individuals wanted for prosecution or the serving of a criminal sentence elsewhere. According to the legal watchdog Fair Trials, the governments of Belarus, Indonesia, Iran, Russia, Sri Lanka, Turkey, and Venezuela have played a large role in driving up the number of red notices issued from 1,277 in 2002 to 8,132 a decade later.[5]

Appeals to "civilizational diversity" and the principle of noninterference in the domestic affairs of sovereign states form another class of emerging counternorms. The People's Republic of China is the leading supporter of this manner of critiquing liberal democracy's universalism as well the political conditionality that international institutions adopt to further universal democratic norms.

The "respect for civilizational diversity" counternorm is the operating principle of the Shanghai Cooperation Organization (SCO), a regional group founded in 2001 by China, Russia, and four Central Asian states (Kazakhstan, Kyrgyzstan, Tajikistan, and Uzbekistan). Chinese official statements and commentary repeatedly refer to the group's embodiment of the foundational "Shanghai Spirit," a norm that enshrines respect for state sovereignty and noninterference, promotes the "democratization of international relations," and rejects the imposition of political and economic conditionalities by global-governance institutions.[6] As David Lewis has observed, in Central Asia the SCO's norms have displaced the liberal-democratic principles that the Organization for Security and Co-operation in Europe (OSCE) has traditionally promoted across the former Soviet space, and have even prompted the OSCE to water down its regional projects that deal with "democratic values."[7]

A third distinct group of counternorms concerns the defense of "traditional values." Here, Russia is the main backer. Proponents of the "values" school of thought, which is rooted in strands of neo-Eurasianist thinking and fueled by Russia's stand against what the Kremlin sees as Western encroachment, maintain that Western individualism has gone over the edge into a state of crisis and moral decay. This accounts for the challenge now being posed to Western decadence worldwide by a turn toward sources of national culture, heritage, and religion.

The Kremlin is pushing the traditional-values agenda as normative cement for the new economic and security architecture that it is seeking to build across Eurasia.[8] As part of these efforts, LGBT communities and civil society representatives have found themselves targeted by stigmatization campaigns and legislative restrictions. Eurasian countries are introducing bans on "homosexual propaganda" similar to the one that Russia passed in 2011. Kyrgyzstan's unicameral parliament, widely thought to be one of the region's more pluralistic, in October 2014 overwhelmingly approved a bill criminalizing "propaganda for nontraditional sexual relations" and banned information alleged to promote "homosexual lifestyles." The Senate of neighboring Kazakhstan passed a similar draft bill in February 2015. With Almaty a candidate city for the 2022 Winter Olympics, activists and athletes have intensively lobbied the International Olympic Committee to pressure the government of Kazakhstan to reject the legislation.

Outside the region, Russia has acquired partners willing to introduce the traditional-values agenda in international fora. On 27 September 2012, a resolution of the UN Human Rights Council cosponsored by Russia called for "a better understanding and appreciation of traditional values" to be applied in human-rights work. The vote was 25 for and 15 against, with 7 countries abstaining.[9] In a sharp criticism of the text, the EU affirmed that human rights are "universal and inalienable" while warning that traditional values are "inherently subjective and specific to a certain time and place." The EU's statement went on to worry that introducing "the concept of 'traditional values' into this discourse can result in a misleading interpretation of existing human rights norms, and undermine their universality."[10] Although emphasizing different goals, the counterterror, civilizational-diversity, and traditional-values agendas all question the feasibility or desirability of liberal democracy's universal aspirations. Basic changes in the international order over the last two decades have powered the rise of each of these sources of counternorms.

Goodbye NGOs, Hello Zombies

Nowhere is the contrast between the relatively democratization-friendly world of twenty years ago and today's harsher international environment more apparent than in the NGO realm. In the 1990s, academics and policy makers heralded the rise of NGOs. These independent actors in international politics, it was said, were achieving a new prominence and fueling a shift away from traditional state power. The most influential scholarly study of the topic claimed that NGOs regularly "boomeranged" around recalcitrant governments to effect positive change, exerting pressure via transnational networks that include other NGOs, international organizations, and like-minded states.[11] In hindsight, this celebratory account appears clearly premature. Such optimistic studies assumed that NGO campaigns and activities would enjoy a clear field indefinitely, while the severity and effectiveness of future state responses went unanticipated.

The turning point came after the so-called color revolutions that flared in the former USSR during the first half of the 2000s. In Georgia (2003), Ukraine (2004), and Kyrgyzstan (2005), street protests following flawed elections swept regimes from power. Experts still debate whether Western-funded NGOs played a decisive role. Whatever the case may be, a broad perception arose that Western democracy promoters were using NGOs as political weapons. "Color revolution" became a synonym for "foreign-sponsored regime change," and governments began to treat democracy monitors as potential security threats. Within eighteen months of the March 2005 "Tulip Revolution" in Kyrgyzstan, all five former Soviet Central Asian republics enacted restrictive NGO-registration laws. In 2011, the Arab Spring drew more attention to the role that foreign-funded civil society groups (and social media) might play in political unrest. Three years after that, the EuroMaidan protests in Ukraine brought down a Russian-backed president and again heightened the anxiety felt in certain quarters about the political weight of foreign-backed civil society groups.

In response, governments across the world have developed a "counter-revolutionary playbook" that targets NGOs and democracy monitors. The common charge is that they act on behalf of outside interests eager to influence domestic political outcomes. New legal restrictions limit NGOs' access to foreign funds and even stigmatize the groups as Trojan horses that covertly serve the West. In addition to the best-known cases in Eurasia and the Middle East, countries including Ecuador, Ethiopia, Hungary, India, Mexico, Pakistan, Sudan, Venezuela, Vietnam, and even Canada have moved over the last ten years to put a squeeze on the activities of foreign-funded NGOs within their borders. Measures range from outright bans on foreign funding (Eritrea, Saudi Arabia), to restrictions on foreign funding of political work, to burdensome mandates that force NGOs to secure government approval of any outside funding and to meet stringent reporting requirements.[12] Darin Christensen and Jeremy Weinstein's 2013 study of 98 countries found that 12 governments had prohibited the foreign funding of the third sector, while 38 had imposed restrictions on outside funding (20 of them since 2002).[13] Another recent academic survey identified 45 countries that have imposed laws restricting foreign funding of domestic NGOs since 1993, noting that 38 of them have adopted these restrictions since 2003.[14] Demonstration effects also seem to be important: Studies suggest that countries carefully pay attention to and emulate the normative practices of their neighbors.[15] Far from being a temporary measure, the clampdown on NGOs is a growing global trend.

Evidence from the latest crackdowns strongly suggests that these new restrictions are accomplishing their political objectives. In Russia, ground zero of the NGO backlash, a 2012 law required NGOs receiving outside funds to register as "foreign agents" on pain of fines. Few chose to register at first, so the law was amended to allow the Russian Justice Ministry to decree whether a group qualifies as independent or not. The ministry has since formally warned twenty groups that they must register, while at least six groups—including election watchdogs, legal societies, and LGBT organizations—chose to close rather than accept the stigmatizing label of "foreign agent."[16]

In the case of Ethiopia, a pioneering study exploring the effects of a restrictive 2009 NGO law found that 90 percent of domestic NGOs concerned with political or human-rights issues either folded or shifted to work in less contentious areas such as economic development or social services.[17] Governments have learned that they will face few international consequences for cracking down on NGOs, and that such "sovereignty-preserving" efforts have the encouragement of China, Russia, and other non-Western powers.

Even as they ramp up their repression of independent NGOs, governments have been promoting pseudo-NGOs and fake democracy monitors that emulate the form but not the substance of true civil society groups. The proliferation of government-organized nongovernmental organizations (GONGOs) has been especially striking: Unhappy with a civil society that independently monitors and challenges them, authorities have been busy building their own tame simulacrum of it that collaborates with power rather than criticizing it. In like manner, governments have begun funding youth movements, such as the Russian group Nashi, that stress themes of national pride and sovereignty.

The rise of what I call "zombie" election monitors offers another dramatic case in point. Traditionally, election monitoring has been the mission of a few skilled NGOs and international organizations such as the OSCE, acting through its Office for Democratic Institutions and Human Rights (ODIHR). These groups bring to their work extensive experience, technical expertise, and a code that lays out the best practices to be followed in observing and evaluating elections, including measures such as long-term monitoring. Over the last decade, many authoritarian governments and ruling parties have continued to avow their acceptance of external election observation as a norm, but have undercut it in practice by using "zombie" monitors. Zombie monitors try to look like democratic observers, but serve autocratic purposes by pretending that clearly flawed elections deserve clean bills of health.

Authoritarians have increasingly hired or deployed zombies on election days without regard to their expertise, competence, or credibility. Azerbaijan's 9 October 2013 presidential election appears to have marked a watershed in the practice—of the 42 invited organizations that were there to observe the elections, many had never been heard of before. The process ended with incumbent president Ilham Aliyev claiming a third term (he has been free to run indefinitely since engineering a 2009 constitutional change that erased term limits) on the basis of almost 85 percent of the vote. The process began with the national election commission accidentally releasing a "result"—before voting had even started—that showed Aliyev as the winner with nearly 73 percent. Of the reports that observer groups issued on the electoral process, only the ODIHR's was critical.[18]

It may be tempting to dismiss zombie monitors as laughably phony and hence powerless to undermine international standards with their bogus assessments, or to reverse general international impressions of an election's poor quality. Yet, critically, zombies are not meant to function as perfect substitutes for Western democratic watchdogs. Instead, their role is less ambitious, and thus easier to play: Regimes use zombies to confuse and distract, to sow uncertainty by promoting progovernment "narratives," and to boost the plausibility of government complaints that critical foreign observers are biased.[19] What is more, zombies are allowing authoritarians to attempt a gradual redefinition of the very purpose and role of outside election observation. Instead of being a neutral activity that evaluates the quality of electoral processes objectively and openly, even if this might "undermine" sovereignty, election observation becomes in authoritarian eyes a "sovereignty-enhancing" partnership between invited observers and the governments that summon them.

The New Authoritarian Regionalism

Another international development that has fostered the rise of counter-norms involves various regional organizations and the new legal frameworks and activities that they have been fostering. As had been the case with NGOs, scholars who studied regional organizations in the wake of the Cold War believed that on the whole they would assist democratic consolidation.[20] The expansion of the EU and its adoption of the strict Copenhagen criteria for membership spread an impression that deeper regional integration would reinforce democratic consolidation and institutional transformation. The EU standards, for instance, gave democrats in such then-aspirants as Slovakia and Romania a basis for criticizing the democratic shortcomings of their own governments. There was scholarly criticism of this view, but it stopped short of questioning the basic idea that regional organizations would by and large promote the diffusion of democratic norms.[21]

Such optimism now seems less warranted. Across Eurasia, the Middle East, Africa, and Latin America, new regional organizations are flourishing. Yet their political agendas seem to be drifting away from reaffirming democratic principles, and may even be veering toward new practices that serve to shield their authoritarian members from outside criticism of what they do at home. As Latin America expert Christopher Sabatini has observed regarding the Bolivarian Alliance for the Peoples of Our Americas (ALBA, founded in 2004) and the Union of South American Nations (UNASUR, founded in 2008), these new organizations rely on "anti-imperialist" sentiment plus what he calls "the vague basis of norms of regional solidarity."[22]

Of particular concern are the agreements and treaties that some regional organizations have been forging, often in the name of new norms of regional security, stability, or counterterrorism. These compacts are creating legal frameworks that could serve to institutionalize authoritarian and anticonstitutional practices. For instance, the SCO's 2009 Anti-Terrorism Treaty and the 2012 Joint Security Agreement of the Gulf Cooperation Council (GCC) give executive authorities and security services a number of extraterritorial powers that bypass traditional domestic legal checks and international norms. Each compact provides for a common blacklist of suspected terrorists and "extremists," and each allows any member state to extradite suspects to any other member state on the basis of a mere accusation, with no clear standards of evidence. The security services of member states, meanwhile, may conduct investigations on one another's territory, with information about suspects and targeted individuals to be shared upon request.[23] Not surprisingly, human-rights watchdogs have criticized both of these treaties for undermining political rights in member countries.[24] Kuwait's legislature delayed ratification of the GCC pact amid worries—voiced by lawmakers and civil society groups—that it would undermine the country's constitutional principles. After Kuwait finally ratified the pact in 2015, these concerns appeared justified as three prominent Kuwait activists were reportedly detained at the request of Saudi authorities.[25]

When not dreaming up agreements that embed authoritarian practices, regional organizations have been busy diluting democratic standards and incubating fresh "zombie monitors." In Eurasia, the Commonwealth of Independent States (CIS) Election Monitoring Observers (founded 2005) like to associate themselves with international standards and Western organizations such as the OSCE. In fact, however, the CIS observers have offered an assessment opposite to the ODIHR's in every regional election that both have observed save one—the 2010 balloting that made Viktor Yanukovych president of Ukraine. In Latin America, UNASUR wants its monitors to "accompany" host governments throughout the electoral process and to reach accommodation with the results. It does not expect monitors to assess either the political environment that precedes the voting or the conduct of the election itself.[26] And even the African Union, which in other ways has embodied democratic principles—it has a policy against according recognition to coups, for instance—has proven too accommodating in its assessments. Thus its observation team was quick to declare the Democratic Republic of the Congo's November 2011 presidential election a success even as EU and U.S. observers were reporting chaotic conditions and irregularities that had damaged the quality of the vote.[27]

Why do regional organizations so often fail to show firmness when upholding democratic standards? A major and perhaps surprising role in the failure is played by leading regional powers. States such as Brazil and South Africa are preoccupied with leveraging their newfound prominence in regional organizations to cement coveted status as regional bellwethers and "emerging" global powers. They seem to fear that criticizing neighboring governments will arouse unwanted resentment, while embattled authoritarians are practiced in the art of using appeals to regional solidarity to deflect international opprobrium. The 2015 assumption of the African Union's rotating presidency by Zimbabwe, for example, has given that country's nonagenarian strongman Robert Mugabe a welcome new platform from which to repeat his denunciations of "imperialists and colonialists."[28]

None of this means that regional organizations are playing a solely negative role, of course. On the contrary, groups such as the African Union and ASEAN in Southeast Asia openly reflect on democratic issues and conduct regular outreach to civil society. And yet the broader analytical point remains: Regional groups themselves have become institutional arenas where democratic norms are contested and counternorms introduced. Indeed, even the OSCE, long the embodiment of the 1975 Helsinki Accords' normative "human values" agenda, has come under siege as a group of Eurasian states led by Russia has proposed to reduce the ODIHR's budget and autonomy.

New Patrons and Providers

A third international trend that has reinforced the rise of counternorms is the advent of alternative providers of international public goods. Since the 2008 financial crisis, it has become commonplace to speak of the West's economic retrenchment and the rise of emerging powers as major players in the world economy. Although obituaries of the Western-led liberal economic order seem premature—overall world trade recovered by 2010, and in 2013 U.S. dollars constituted more than 60 percent of global reserve holdings and over 80 percent of foreign exchange—the one area where Western economic hegemony has markedly waned is that of providing development aid, including project finance, stabilization assistance, and concessionary loans.

Emerging donors, especially China and the Gulf states, have transformed the dynamics of international development lending. China now has the world's second-largest economy, smaller only than that of the United States (by some reckonings, China's may even have recently nosed into first place). Beijing's stock in trade is to offer packages that defy traditional distinctions between aid and investment, often accepting as security for its loans access to host-country energy resources, commodities, or other assets.

Whatever China's intentions, its influence as a political model is linked unavoidably to its growing economic engagement and international patronage. The availability of alternative donors who demand fewer democratic conditions and good-governance guarantees, makes it easier for state recipients throughout the developing world to reject Western funding if the prodemocratic "strings" attached to it are considered too constricting. The prestige of these economically successful authoritarians gives other leaders who are bent on deviating from liberal-democratic norms a plausible alternative to having to submit to liberal values and Western criticism. Thus Turkish president Recep Tayyip Erdoğan has repeatedly brought up the idea of dropping talks with the EU in order to seek membership in the SCO. That organization, he says, "is better and more powerful [than the EU], and we have common values with them."[29]

The rise of alternative patrons is transforming the development landscape. Over the last four years, China has lent more money in Latin America than have the World Bank and the Inter-American Development Bank combined. In Africa, China has doubled its development financing, going from US$10 billion lent from 2009 through 2012 to twice that amount for the period from January 2013 to February 2015.[30] Beijing has also become the leading lender to Central Asia, and is playing a major role in the Caribbean as well as the island states of the Pacific. Together with this, a shift from grants to loans secured by concessions has raised further concerns about repayment terms, political conditions, and the demands that Beijing might make on its debtors in the future.

In other cases, emerging donors have stepped in to aid countries not serviced by the Western-led aid community. Since the instability of the Arab Spring, the oil-rich Gulf states have sent tens of billions of dollars abroad, and now provide the lion's share of development aid to Egypt, Bangladesh, the Maldives, and Yemen. Other cases suggest that in postconflict settings, governments that have been shunned or sanctioned by the West can now readily find new patrons as alternatives to the liberal peace-building complex. After the Sinhalese-dominated Sri Lankan government launched its ruthless and successful 2009 military offensive against Tamil insurgents, it bypassed Western donors and their human-rights concerns by turning to China and India for postconflict assistance.[31] Angola, Sudan, and Tajikistan can also be seen as part of this growing new "illiberal" peace-building complex.

In 2014, Beijing strongly backed and indeed capitalized two new lending organizations in order to challenge the West's monopoly of control over official international financial institutions. The New Development Bank (or NDB, originally called the BRICS Development Bank) and the Asian Infrastructure Investment Bank (AIIB) are supposed to perform tasks resembling those of the World Bank and Asian Development Bank, with an emphasis on financing large-scale infrastructure projects in developing countries. Interestingly, while U.S. officials were cautiously supportive of the NDB, they publicly campaigned against the AIIB to the point of lobbying allies such as Australia to forgo membership. Yet U.S. geopolitical influence now appears weak as 53 states have joined, including France, Germany, and the United Kingdom as well as (after a change of mind) Australia. Whether these banks can truly devise workable lending practices without imposing Western-style oversight and conditions remains to be seen. Yet their political significance as alternative sources of international financing should not be underestimated.

Another former Western monopoly of the liberal order that has been broken is the field of global media. As the United States and other Western countries have continued to whittle down their presence in international news-gathering (few U.S. newspapers maintain permanent foreign bureaus or correspondents anymore), Russia and China have been pouring state funds into news and broadcasting operations. As of 2013, according to one report, China Central Television (CCTV) had set up seventy international bureaus, including twenty in Africa and a dozen in Latin America, with a plan to broadcast (in local languages) to regions and countries where China has made big investments.[32]

Russia has upped its international media presence by expanding the reach of its television channel Russia Today (now rebranded simply as RT), and by launching (in November 2014) a state-run multimedia outlet called Sputnik in 34 countries across five continents. Sputnik's stated goal is to counter "Western propaganda" worldwide.[33] Going forward alongside these efforts are the activities of global outlets such as Iran's Press TV, the Venezuelan-run Telesur consortium, and several Gulf broadcasters. Together, they pose a serious, amply funded challenge across large swaths of the world in covering news, setting journalistic standards, and editorializing about political events.

In the 1990s, the West still had a near-exclusive role as *the* provider of international funding and information the world over. Emerging donors and alternative patrons have changed that. In development assistance, in project finance, and in global media, emerging powers are displacing the West. The upshot of these trends is more contention over the normative foundations of the international order (with nonliberal voices having a bigger say than before), more authority for counternorms such as noninterference in countries' internal affairs, and more influence for various authoritarian alternatives to liberal democracy.

Handling the Shock of the New

As we have seen, rising new counternorms are threatening to straitjacket liberal democracy's power even as they chip away at its status as the most influential source of norms for global governance. The appearance of these counternorms is not adventitious, but has a basis in fundamental changes that have been altering the post–Cold War international order. Changes in the legal status and role of NGOs, the conversion of regional organizations into arenas of contestation, and the rise of alternative patrons have turned a world that was once relatively favorable to the spread of democratic norms into one where authoritarians can push back—and have learned to do so in innovative ways. Whatever the exact extent of worldwide democratic regression, it is clear that counternorms to liberal democracy have taken root and are helping authoritarians to retain power.

What can democracy advocates and prodemocratic policy makers do about all this? A key challenge is to disentangle, as much as possible, the issue of perceived Western political decline from the fate of liberal democracy.

The first need is to combat the rise of counterdemocratic practices embodied in new regional frameworks or the proliferation of zombies. Here, policy makers should concentrate on benchmarking these new phenomena against existing international standards or introducing new standards against which the credibility of such practices and frameworks must be tested. For example, a code of standards governing election observation does exist, and longstanding UN principles undergird it. Similarly, new regional treaties and agreements should not be passively accepted, but should instead be actively scrutinized in light of international human-rights laws and countries' commitments to such standards. Identifying best practices in election observation, news coverage, legal development, blacklisting, and data-sharing will be critical to stopping the "anything goes" thinking that is too often assumed to be a natural concomitant of multipolarity.

Moreover, diplomats and foreign-policy officials should reconsider how emerging powers can gain status by adopting, rather than rejecting, standards that respect good governance and democracy. Recent scholarship has shown that political practices such as gender quotas for legislatures tend to spread not on principled grounds, but rather because countries get the impression that adopting them is the "high-status" thing to do.[34] In view of this, liberal democracies should do all they can to reinscribe principles such as good governance, transparency, and respect for the due autonomy of civil society in the honor roll of "things that enhance a country's standing in the world." Appeals to national pride and prestige are likely to have more effect on emerging powers than will lectures about democratic shortcomings.

Finally, Western representatives charged with public diplomacy and regional engagement must resist the urge to decouple normative from geopolitical issues. If the West were to reduce its support for liberal norms and a rule-based international order for the sake of political expediency, it would only hasten the erosion of its own normative standing and emphasize that we are now in world of competitive patronage dynamics where the highest bidder wins. Instead, the onset of multipolarity, when it truly emerges, should be embraced with a clear sense of liberal democracy's purpose and unique standing in the universe of competing norms and counternorms. Without confidence in its own values, the West not only will continue to lose its global appeal, but will lose itself.

Notes

1. Larry Diamond, "Facing up to the Democratic Recession," *Journal of Democracy* 26 (January 2015): 141–55; Steven Levitsky and Lucan Way, "The Myth of the Democratic Recession," *Journal of Democracy* 26 (January 2015): 45–58.

2. See Kim Lane Scheppele's "Law in a Time of Emergency: States of Excep-

tion and the Temptations of 9/11," *University of Pennsylvania Journal of Constitutional Law* 6, no. 5 (2004): 1001–8, and her "The Migration of Anti-Constitutional Ideas: The Post-9/11 Globalization of Public Law and the International State of Emergency," in Sujit Choudhry, ed., *The Migration of Constitutional Ideas* (New York: Cambridge University Press, 2006).

3. Gavin Sullivan and Ben Hayes, "Blacklisted: Targeted Sanctions, Preemptive Security and Fundamental Rights," ECCHR Report, December 2010.

4. Alexander Cooley, *Great Games, Local Rules: The New Great Power Contest in Central Asia* (New York: Oxford University Press, 2012), ch. 6.

5. Fair Trials International, "Strengthening Respect for Human Rights, Strengthening Interpol," November 2013.

6. Thomas Ambrosio, "Catching the 'Shanghai Spirit': How the Shanghai Cooperation Organization Promotes Authoritarian Norms in Central Asia," *Europe-Asia Studies* 60 (October 2008): 1321–44.

7. David Lewis, "Who's Socialising Whom? Regional Organisations and Contested Norms in Central Asia," *Europe-Asia Studies* 64 (September 2012): 1219–37.

8. Alexander Lukin, "Eurasian Integration and the Clash of Values," *Survival* 56 (June 2014): 43–60.

9. See UN Human Rights Council, "Promoting Human Rights and Fundamental Freedoms Through a Better Understanding of Traditional Values of Humankind: Best Practices," Resolution A/HRC/RES/21/3, item no. A/HRC/21/L.2, 20 September 2012 (adopted on 27 September 2012), *www.ohchr.org/EN/HRBodies/HRC/RegularSessions/Session21/Pages/ResDecStat.aspx*.

10. See European Union Permanent Delegation to the United Nations Office and other international organisations in Geneva, "Contribution of the European Union: Traditional Values," Geneva, 15 February 2013, *www.ohchr.org/Documents/Issues/HRValues/EU.pdf*.

11. Margaret E. Keck and Kathryn Sikkink, *Activists Beyond Borders: Advocacy Networks in International Politics* (Ithaca: Cornell University Press, 1998).

12. Thomas Carothers and Saskia Brechenmacher, *Closing Space: Democracy and Human Rights Support Under Fire* (Washington, D.C.: Carnegie Endowment for International Peace, 2014).

13. Darin Christensen and Jeremy M. Weinstein, "Defunding Dissent: Restrictions on Aid to NGOs." *Journal of Democracy* 24 (April 2013): 77–91.

14. Kendra Dupuy, James Ron, and Aseem Prakash, "'Stop Meddling in My Country!'—Governments' Restrictions on Foreign Aid to Non-Governmental Organizations," working paper, University of Washington and University of Minnesota, 23 November 2014.

15. Beth A. Simmons, *Mobilizing for Human Rights: International Law in Domestic Politics* (Cambridge: Cambridge University Press, 2009).

16. Human Rights Watch, "Russia: Government Against Rights Groups," 28 May 2015.

17. Kendra Dupuy, James Ron, and Aseem Prakash, "Who Survived? Ethiopia's Regulatory Crackdown on Foreign-Funded NGOs," *Review of International Political Economy* 22, no.2 (2015): 419–56.

18. Christopher Walker and Alexander Cooley, "Vote of the Living Dead," *Foreign Policy.com,* 31 October 2013.

19. Judith Kelley, "The More the Merrier? The Effects of Having Multiple International Election Monitoring Organizations," *Perspectives on Politics* 7 (March 2009): 59–64.

20. Jon C. Pevehouse, *Democracy from Above: Regional Organizations and Democratization* (Cambridge: Cambridge University Press, 2005).

21. See Amitav Acharya's "How Ideas Spread: Whose Norms Matter? Norm Localization and Institutional Change in Asian Regionalism," *International Organization* 58 (Spring 2004): 239–75, and his "Norm Subsidiarity and Regional Orders: Sovereignty, Regionalism, and Rule-Making in the Third World," *International Studies Quarterly* 55 (March 2011): 95–123.

22. Christopher Sabatini, "Meaningless Multilateralism: In International Diplomacy, South America Chooses Quantity over Quality," *Foreign Affairs* (online), 8 August 2014.

23. Alexander Cooley, "League of Authoritarian Gentleman," *ForeignPolicy.com,* 30 January 2013.

24. Human Rights in China, "Counter-Terrorism and Human Rights: The Impact of the Shanghai Cooperation Organization," white paper, March 2011; and Human Rights Watch, "GCC: Joint Security Agreement Imperils Rights: Vaguely Worded Provisions Endanger Free Expression, Privacy," 27 April 2014.

25. Madawi Al-Rasheed, "Kuwaiti Activists Targeted Under GCC Security Pact," *Al Monitor,* 20 March 2015, *www.al-monitor.com/pulse/originals/2015/03/saudi-gcc-security-dissident-activism-detention-opposition.html.*

26. Sabatini, "Meaningless Multilateralism."

27. Judith Kelley, "Watching the Watchmen: The Role of Election Observers in Africa," *Think Africa Press,* 31 May 2013.

28. Sam Jones, "Robert Mugabe Assumes African Union Helm with Familiar Battle Cry," *Guardian,* 30 January 2015.

29. Emrullah Uslu, "Turkey Debates the SCO as an Alternative to the EU," *European Dialogue,* 8 February 2013.

30. See Global Economic Governance Initiative (Boston University), "Chinese Lending to LAC in 2014: Key Findings," Inter-American Dialogue, 27 February 2015, *http://chinaandlatinamerica.com/2015/02/27/chinese-lending-to-lac-in-2014-key-findings*; Yun Sun, "China's Aid to Africa: Monster or Messiah?" *Brookings East Asia Commentary,* no. 75, February 2014; and Charles Wolf Jr., Xiao Wang, and Eric Warner, *China's Foreign Aid and Government-Sponsored Investment Activities: Scale, Content, Destinations, and Implications* (Santa Monica: RAND, 2013).

31. David Lewis, "The Failure of a Liberal Peace: Sri Lanka's Counter-Insur-

gency in Global Perspective," *Conflict, Security and Development* 10 (November 2010): 647–71.

32. Anne Nelson, "CCTV's International Expansion: China's Grand Strategy for Media?" Center for International Media Assistance, National Endowment for Democracy, Washington, D.C., 22 October 2013.

33. Peter Pomerantsev and Michael Weiss, "The Menace of Unreality: How the Kremlin Weaponizes Information, Culture and Money," *The Interpreter* (a project of the Institute of Modern Russia, New York), 2014.

34. Ann E. Towns, *Women and States: Norms and Hierarchies in International Society* (Cambridge: Cambridge University Press, 2010).

CHAPTER EIGHT

Election Monitoring vs. Disinformation

PATRICK MERLOE

OVER THE LAST THIRTY YEARS, nonpartisan citizen election monitoring has spread to more than a hundred countries and involved millions of people. It is a tangible and sustained aspect of democratic development, and it poses a serious challenge to autocrats bent on electoral theft—a challenge that autocrats are devoting considerable resources to addressing.

The fountainhead example of monitoring by citizens is the work that the National Citizens' Movement for Free Elections (NAMFREL) did in stopping Ferdinand Marcos from stealing the 1986 presidential election in the Philippines. More than a half-million NAMFREL volunteers turned out to safeguard their fellow citizens' votes that year, and the group has monitored more than twenty national and other elections since. Inspired by NAMFREL and early efforts in Latin America, the Balkans, Africa, Eurasia, and the Middle East, citizen election-monitoring organizations and coalitions in scores of countries came together, often with help from the National Democratic Institute (NDI) and its programs in peer-to-peer experience-sharing and best-practices development. Many such organizations can now boast decades of hard-won experience in promoting accountability and citizen participation not only at election time but also when it comes to the conduct of other political processes, the activities of parliaments, the delivery of public services, and more. Citizen election monitoring is not only generally accepted today, it has enhanced democratic political culture in many countries.

Ties have grown across borders and spanned the globe. More than two-hundred citizen election-monitoring organizations from eighty-four countries, along with the regional networks that these groups have organized, belong to the Global Network of Domestic Election Monitors (GNDEM). All GNDEM members endorse the Declaration of Global Principles for Non-Partisan Election Observation and Monitoring by Citizen Organizations and its Code of Conduct, launched at the UN Secretariat in 2012. This document provides a professional and ethical basis for citizen organizations that wish to monitor their country's elections. Sixteen key international organizations support the declaration, providing international recognition for citizen election monitoring's critical role in promoting electoral integrity. Organizationally, GNDEM provides a means for credible citizen election-monitoring groups and regional networks to share knowledge, show solidarity, and create peer-to-peer accountability for their activities.

Although examples of international election observation can be found as far back as the middle of the nineteenth century, the practice became truly widespread much more recently, as the "third wave" of democratic transitions began washing over the globe after 1974. The collapse of the Iron Curtain and the fall of brutal one-party, military, or personal dictatorships across substantial swaths of the globe brought a rise in elections that is with us still. While most transitions produced a desire for genuine elections, in some countries ruling factions do not really want to abide by the people's will. However, even they feel obliged to allow voting of some sort if only for appearances' sake. In these regimes, fakery is often part of the electoral package. This places a crucial responsibility on election observers, domestic and international alike. The credibility with which they do their work has benefited from its integration with international human-rights fact-finding principles under the influence of the 1984 Guidelines for International Election Observing and related methods that some organizations have elaborated and shared.

As post–Cold War transitions advanced, the sanctioning of international election observation became a common practice of sovereign states. Although it is not yet universal, it is now widely recognized as central to the task of holding genuine elections in the developing world. An increasing number of traditional democracies have opened their own elections to international observation as well, which is further evidence of its becoming a norm. A wide variety of international election observers may be organized under the auspices of the UN or a number of other institutions. These include: regional and other intergovernmental organizations, associations of parliamentarians, international nongovernmental organizations, regional networks of citizen election-observation organizations, scholarly groups, delegations from political parties that have affinity with one or more of the parties that are competing, and diplomats accredited to the country holding the elections. Foreign governments also send observer delegations to elections.

Many elections are witnessed by a multiplicity of international observers, not all of whom operate with the same rigor, consider the crucial role of the election-related processes that come before and after the day or days of actual voting, or have the same level of commitment to political impartiality. This diversity can lead to international election-observation missions that issue differing views of the same election, sometimes resulting in confusion. Autocrats not only try to exploit such confusion but actively try to *create* it through a variety of tactics—and they have shown themselves willing to devote weighty resources and remarkable levels of ingenuity to these efforts.

Key election-observation organizations—each one known for politically impartial and rigorous observation activities—launched at the UN Secretariat in 2005 the Declaration of Principles for International Election Observation and its Code of Conduct (known collectively as the Declaration of Principles or DoP). Now endorsed by 49 intergovernmental and international nongovernmental organizations, the DoP has spawned an ongoing implementation process that focuses on boosting cooperation, knowledge-sharing, and peer accountability. Three UN General Assembly resolutions have recognized the DoP and its implementation process for making the practice of international election observation more consistent. That practice, however, is still well short of *fully* consistent, largely because there are so many international observers and their motives vary.

Observation findings by one or more of the DoP-endorsing organizations are likely to influence both the people of the country where the election was held and the international community. Not surprisingly, autocratic or other corrupt regimes will often strive to subvert credible international election observation in order to blunt its impact.

Shining a Light into Elections

Citizens have a right to genuine elections, and they have a right to know whether elections are genuine. The mere avowal by those in power that an election has been truly and fairly conducted and its votes properly counted requires blind-faith acceptance, and that is not a basis for *democratic* citizenship or genuine elections. In order to be confident of an election's authenticity, citizens must be able to see into the various processes that compose it.

As a practical matter, multitudes of citizens cannot be expected to inspect personally each aspect of an election's many complex and large-scale processes. These include the registration of voters and parties and the drawing of electoral-district boundaries as well as the final tabulation and publication of results, not to mention the adjudication of disputes and the regulations governing campaigning and its financing, the use of media and public resources, and so on. Instead, the "eyes" of the citizenry when it comes to elections are those who make this their mission: national and international journalists, citizen monitors, international observers, scholars who study electoral integrity, and the agents of electoral contestants. It is they who, to change the metaphor, shine a light into elections and their workings. All these light-shiners must in turn establish their credibility with the citizens, but that task can have meaning only when transparency is present. Fact-based analyses and relevant findings depend on the ability to witness processes and to access electoral data in a timely fashion.

Electoral transparency, in other words, is not a nicety. It is absolutely and inescapably fundamental to genuine elections. Just as citizens need enough accurate information to make an informed choice in voting, so do they require accurate information about the character of electoral processes in order to vest authority in governments that result from elections. Put another way, public confidence in elections is essential to public trust in government. Moreover, that trust is important for the governmental stability that elections are supposed to buttress.

The international community has a stake in electoral integrity for reasons of peace and security. Elections are meant to resolve peacefully the contest for state power, and dubious elections all too often become flashpoints for strife. The charters of the UN and regional organizations, along with other treaties and agreements, provide a foundation for election monitoring and describe a legitimate international interest in whether a country is meeting its obligations to respect and promote fundamental rights in this area.

Incumbent governments, with few exceptions, are duty-bound by their constitutions and solemn international commitments to deliver genuine elections to their citizens. Governments also have an obligation to protect and foster the right to seek, receive, and impart information (the elements of freedom of expression), which reinforces the requirement of electoral transparency.[1] This obligation holds whether those seeking to acquire and transmit information are journalists, citizen election monitors, agents of electoral contestants, scholars, or international election observers.

Another fundamental aspect of genuine elections that supports monitoring is the precept that every citizen has the right to take part in public affairs without discrimination or unreasonable restrictions.[2] This broad democratic principle reinforces the essential role of citizens in monitoring elections, whether as journalists, scholars, members of civic groups, or agents of electoral contestants. To close electoral processes and information to witnesses is to block participation. Election monitoring—and electoral credibility—thus depend on "open government" and "open government data" policies.[3] Governments that want to count as democratically legitimate must provide the transparency needed to verify electoral integrity and bolster public trust.

Some governments and ruling parties, however, may become bent on extending their power irrespective of the people's will. They will seek to manipulate electoral processes even as they deny transparency in order to avoid the stigma of illegitimacy. Blocking transparency is akin to a criminal cover-up. Witnesses must be avoided, prevented from testifying, or discredited. Distractions must be created and smokescreens generated to conceal the facts—in efforts to spread public confusion and make accountability less likely. We should expect authoritarians to be inventive when creating tactics for negating genuine elections while hiding what is really taking place. Their goal, after all, is not only to manipulate the electoral process, but to be able to claim legitimacy while doing so.

Disinformation and Subversion

When the UN General Assembly approved the Universal Declaration of Human Rights in 1948, the world had only a handful of democracies. Yet member states voted unanimously, with only eight abstentions, to adopt the Declaration, including Article 21's democratic precepts.[4] Since then, the number of democracies has soared, and there is now a widespread expectation that countries will hold genuine elections. There is also a general acceptance internationally that the participation of domestic and international election monitors is part of that norm.

Gaining the "democracy" label matters for a country's status in the world. So too, therefore, does the classification of a country's elections as genuine rather than phony. Zimbabwe, for instance, was suspended from the Commonwealth for holding violent, repressive elections in 2002, while Pakistan's 2007 suspension ended after its 2008 elections were deemed credible. Fiji was suspended from the Commonwealth in 2006 for failing to call elections and was reinstated after its 2014 elections were deemed credible.

Intergovernmental organizations beside the Commonwealth also regard the holding of genuine elections as obligatory.[5] The European Union, the United States, and other democracies take into account whether a country holds true or phony elections, albeit at times in a lamentably inconsistent way. When commenting publicly on elections, U.S., EU, and other officials often cite reports from credible monitors, as do major news outlets. Anyone seeking to distort or fake an electoral process, therefore, must worry about the findings of credible election monitors.

In recent years, a perception has spread that the West, driven by economic woes and terrorism fears, is placing less emphasis internationally on democracy and human rights. Whether or not staging sham elections has become more tempting as a result, autocratic and autocratic-leaning regimes still often go to considerable lengths to cover up their electoral corruption and dishonesty. These efforts at camouflage add up to a tacit admission by autocrats that they are obligated to hold genuine elections, and they know it.

The motives for manipulating electoral outcomes vary. Incumbents in one country may truly fear defeat in a free and fair polling. Incumbents in another may justifiably expect that they will win based on popularity or name recognition alone (especially if the opposition, civil society, and the media have all been stifled), but clientelism or some other corrupt feature of authoritarian rule may give them an incentive to pad their totals by dishonest means. In either case, successfully hiding the manipulation will require subverting credible election monitoring by national and international organizations as well as journalists.

As for the means of theft, elections can be stolen in many ways. Electoral processes are not one-day events. They include many components that occur over a long period of time and involve a wide array of governmental institutions and a range of rights and responsibilities. How the processes surrounding an election are conducted reflects something broader: the respect (or lack of it) that a government and those who are vying to control its powers have for the citizenry. Election monitoring, when credibly conducted, highlights both the positive and the negative—the good news and the bad about how an election was carried out—casting the electoral environment into higher relief in order to promote the cause of democratic accountability.

An election's integrity hinges on a diverse array of processes. These include, for example, the procedures that are used to document the birthplaces and residences of prospective voters and candidates, and also the larger-scale, data-intensive methods by which the accuracy of the voter registry is verified, the fairness of electoral-district boundaries is gauged, and the tabulation of results is checked for accuracy. The freedoms of political expression and organization must be secure. State-controlled media must remain impartial, the use of state financial and other resources must be politically neutral, and those charged with administering the elections must be not only impartial but competent. Law-enforcement and security forces must remain alert, effective, and outside the political fray so that parties and candidates can freely compete—and citizens freely vote—without fear of violence or retribution.

Electoral integrity also depends on courts and administrative complaint mechanisms that act in a timely, effective manner when election-related rights are infringed or electoral abuses committed. This illustrates how equality before the law and equal protection of the law are related to universal and equal suffrage. Removing barriers that keep women, young people, and other marginalized populations from taking part is at the core of genuine elections. Enfranchisement requires inclusion without discrimination or unreasonable restriction. Inclusion, transparency, and accountability underlie genuine elections, and indeed democratic governance more broadly.[6] Tampering with even one of these pillars of genuine democratic choice can be enough to turn an election into a sham. Election monitoring must therefore look to all of them, taking care lest autocrats distort, undermine, or counterfeit any of them.

Although no election can be perfect, positive indications across the range of election-related processes point to the presence of a democratic political dynamic, including respect for human rights and citizens' freedom to make political choices. Autocratic tactics and authoritarian governance can gut the genuineness of elections by reducing inclusiveness, transparency, and accountability, just as authoritarians can steal an election by falsifying results or—should fraud fall short—refusing to accept the voters' verdict.

Denials of access to election-related processes and the government-held data needed to assess their credibility are classic authoritarian stratagems.

Such moves typically coincide with efforts to disable and disempower journalists, civil society groups, and the political opposition. News outlets may be targeted for control, social media blocked, choruses of support for the tainted elections orchestrated, public-relations firms hired, and both domestic and international monitoring efforts attacked.

Credible Monitoring in the Crosshairs

Nonpartisan election monitoring by citizen organizations—when these groups are credible and enjoy proper support—assesses a country's electoral processes in a way that is both methodical and reliable. Such assessment efforts are conducted in local languages and with knowledge of a country's political culture. They can extend over the long electoral timeline while mobilizing and training the large numbers of people needed to scrutinize key processes. They can detect electoral manipulation or other deficiencies in elections, highlighting problems and promoting public confidence where warranted. Would-be election-fakers must outsmart, block, or otherwise subvert credible citizen election monitors. Others need to know how to distinguish credible, effective monitors from those who are feckless or biased.

Autocrats' tactics against citizen election monitors resemble those meant to weaken civil society more broadly. They include denying access to information and producing laws and regulations that run counter to the standard that rights are to be protected and promoted without discrimination or unreasonable restriction. Examples include laws concerning domestic nongovernmental organizations (NGOs) that make it impossible or very difficult to gain and maintain legal status, or that ban the monitoring of electoral and political processes. Foreign funding or even technical assistance to NGOs may be banned as well. Electoral regulations may be written or interpreted in ways that are intended to block NGOs from witnessing key processes or that limit the number of observers so that credible groups may be kept from entering polling stations or other facilities. Individual monitors may be hit with overly onerous qualification requirements, including accreditation fees or a demand that all prospective monitors report in person to the capital city or a handful of other places that are burdensome to reach—a ploy meant to stop the monitoring effort from covering the whole nation.

Abuse of law enforcement is another arrow in the authoritarians' quiver.

Offices may be raided under various pretexts, with NGO leaders, their staffs, and even relatives hauled in for questioning and put under unwarranted surveillance. Prosecutors' offices may be bent to the task as well, bringing cases under repressive NGO laws, tax laws, or even criminal libel laws. The personal and financial strains imposed by raids, interrogations, subpoenas, or even false imprisonments can disrupt monitoring efforts and deter citizens from joining them. False imprisonments of election monitors rank on an autocratic roll of shame alongside the illegitimate jailings of other human-rights advocates, independent journalists, and peaceful oppositionists.

The intimidation of credible monitors may begin with threats to have them fired from their jobs or to take away their children's scholarships, and can even escalate to physical violence. Monitors may find themselves being refused entrance to or kicked out of polling places or other facilities, with harassment at the hands of the regime's minions tossed in for good measure.

A thorough autocratic regime will accompany its street assaults with online and other electronic attacks. Telecommunications systems—including the Internet and social media—may be shut down at critical times to stop citizen monitors, journalists, and electoral contestants from making known their findings. A wise citizen-run monitoring group will brace itself for cyberattacks and other disruptions before, during, and after election day.

The spread of disinformation through state-run media both old and new is essential to authoritarian attempts to control the electoral narrative. Reports asserting the credibility of manipulated electoral processes will be broadcast in extended profusion while critical reports go unmentioned. Rumors and false accusations impeaching the motives, efficacy, and veracity of genuine monitors will also fly through these state-dominated channels.

The Rise of the Zombie Monitors

As citizen election monitoring has spread and become an accepted part of genuine elections, autocrats have begun to create phony election-monitoring organizations. Like state-run media and the government-organized nongovernmental organizations (GONGOs) that authoritarian regimes have set up to confuse and obscure the broader civil society environment, these "zombie" election-monitoring groups spin rosy but fake narratives about what are in fact manipulated election processes. All three—the state media, the GONGOs, and the zombie monitors—seek to obscure the findings of credible monitoring efforts with clouds of rumors and phony charges. As is the case with government-created shadow political parties and candidates, the bogus groups often assume names that are very similar to those of credible monitoring organizations.

Citizen election monitors encounter these abuses in countries ranging from Azerbaijan to Ethiopia and Egypt to Venezuela. As with similar measures used to weaken civil society organizations more generally and to suppress the media, the use of these tactics across numerous countries indicates that autocratic regimes are learning from one another.

Credible international observers may be targeted in some of the same ways as their local-citizen counterparts. Data denial is popular among autocrats even as open access to government data is becoming established practice. Thus both domestic and international monitoring groups may find themselves barred not only from entering facilities, but also from consulting census data, voter registries, maps of electoral-district boundaries and polling-place locations, or material on the workings of election-related technologies, such as voting machines. Refusing or failing at the timely release of polling-station vote counts and only announcing voting totals is a favorite means to hide fraud, while technology advances belie excuses for the denial.

Regimes may manipulate legal procedures to degrade observation efforts. Officials can "forget"—or openly refuse—to invite intergovernmental organizations to send international election-observation missions; can withhold accreditations from credible organizations; or can limit numbers so that people from such organizations are too thin on the ground to be effective. Or officials may move so slowly on necessary approvals that key electoral processes escape independent assessment. Sometimes the trick can be as simple as issuing invitations and promising accreditations—thereby *seeming* to cooperate with credible monitoring—only to have mysterious "visa delays" gum up the works.

Again, like credible domestic observers, credible international observers may be subjected to intimidation and threats of violence, perhaps as officials conspicuously "look the other way" rather than ensure the protection of law. International observers' impartiality and professionalism may be impugned by regime mouthpieces and rumor-mongers intent on confusing world and domestic opinion while distracting credible observers from their tasks. Other regime ploys may aim at creating conflicting characterizations of the election in domestic and world media.

One way to sow narratives that favor the ruling party and sap credible monitoring of its force is to invite "friendly" delegations to see the elections. Members of sibling political parties, affiliates of allied governments, and well-known individual supporters of the incumbents are used to fill the ranks of observers. The idea is to stage an election-observation mission that leans in favor of the ruling party at least enough to weaken prospects for a critical report.

Autocrats also sometimes work to capture or enfeeble otherwise credible observer missions by influencing their personnel appointments. "Mission-stacking" may not suffice to secure the fabrication of wholesale favorable findings, but autocrats can still hope that it might cause the watering-down of an unfavorable report or divert an observer mission into extended internal debates and departures from established election-observation principles.

Not quite rising to the level of attempting to manipulate observer missions but akin to it is the practice of having prominent but naïve foreigners—politicians including former members of the U.S. Congress and European Parliament, election commissioners, or other well-known figures—tour the country as the government's guests at election time. They witness positive (and carefully chosen) electoral developments, then offer public comments that receive heavy play in all state-run media. The term "zombie observers" was originally coined to describe such reputable but deceived individuals.

A regime that can afford public-relations firms can hire them to mount campaigns of disinformation and diversion. The methods can be as overt as major media advertisements (some governments favor full-color magazine or newspaper inserts printed on slick paper), or as subtle as quiet "charm offensives." These may feature personal visits by leaders and friends of the regime to Western capitals, behind-the-scenes lobbying, or the promotion of discourse about the country that does not dwell on the elections as such but focuses on how important the country and its stability are to Western economic or strategic interests.

Three Recent Cases

Three recent cases illustrate how election-rigging and cover-up tactics are being used. The first is that of Azerbaijan's October 2013 presidential election, which returned Ilham Aliyev to the presidency for a third five-year term with a reported 85 percent of the vote. The OSCE's Office for Democratic Institutions and Human Rights (ODIHR) was the only prominent international mission allowed to observe various election processes, though it observed election day together with the OSCE's Parliamentary Assembly (OSCE-PA). The Parliamentary Assembly of the Council of Europe (PACE) and a delegation from the European Parliament (EP) also observed, but only focused on the election day. Normally, those groups would join the OSCE bodies in a joint preliminary statement immediately following the election. This time, however, a split developed. The OSCE bodies focused on a sharp preelection crackdown (which undermined freedoms of expression, association, and assembly), as well as ballot-box stuffing and counting irregularities. The PACE and EP delegations presented positive findings.[7]

Aliyev's government apparently maneuvered to stack the PACE and EP delegations, and brought in sympathetic observers from friendly sources, including other ex-Soviet republics. In order to reinforce upbeat claims about the integrity of the balloting, the government orchestrated the presence of foreign election commissioners. They were shown selected polling stations and invited to comment publicly on what they saw. Public-relations firms in the pay of the Azerbaijani government also worked throughout the electoral period and beyond to paint a rosy picture.

At the same time, journalists and citizen observers had been targeted for intimidation. Azerbaijan's Election Monitoring and Democracy Studies Center (EMDS), a credible citizen election-observation organization and GNDEM member, had seen its overseas funding cut off. Then, following the election, the head of EMDS and two colleagues were hit with trumped-up charges of tax evasion, illegal business activities, and abuse of authority. An Azerbaijani court gave Anar Mammadli, the head of EMDS, five and a half years in prison, while Bashir Suleymanli and Elnur Mammadov got three and a half years each. Their real "crime" was having had the temerity to report truthfully on elections in their country. As of this writing in May 2015, Mammadli remains behind bars; Mammadov's sentence was suspended, and Suleymanli was released approximately ten months after his false conviction. Other human-rights defenders, journalists, bloggers, and more have landed in jail as the Aliyev regime has continued a broad crackdown on civil society and political opposition.

When Zimbabwe's government held July 2013 elections for the presidency and the bicameral Parliament—our second case—the only international observers allowed came from the African Union and the Southern Africa

Development Community (SADC). Zimbabwean authorities blocked U.S. and EU observation efforts, and President Robert Mugabe warned SADC observers that Zimbabwe would pull out of the SADC if it "decides to do stupid things."[8] (Zimbabwe had withdrawn from the Commonwealth after being suspended for the repressive 2002 elections.)

Although the 2013 polling proceeded more peacefully than had the bloody 2008 elections, opposition supporters were systematically disenfranchised in huge numbers by either being denied registration or being turned away on election day. The disenfranchisement and high incidence of "assisted voting" (that is, accompanying the voter to help mark the ballot) undermined the credibility of Mugabe's claim to a landslide 61 percent and his ruling party's lopsided majorities in the two houses of Parliament. Yet the SADC observers made positive pronouncements.[9] The head of the African Union delegation offered glowing comments to the press[10] in advance of the more nuanced official statement that came from the AU mission as a whole.[11] By contrast, the Zimbabwe Election Support Network (ZESN)—a credible citizen election-observation coalition and GNDEM member that mobilized 7,099 monitors on election day while keeping key processes under long-term study and assessment—had severe criticisms of the electoral process.[12] Echoing these strictures was the 80-member observer team from Botswana, which formed part of the SADC mission but put out its own statement contradicting the SADC's sunny findings.[13] The earlier and more positive statements overshadowed the ZESN and Botswanan criticisms, however—a testament to the Mugabe regime's grasp of how important it was to "seize control of the narrative" and get its story out first.

The third case is that of Venezuela, where credible election monitoring by international and citizen sources has been undermined at least since the 2008 regional elections. Citizen election observers who accept foreign funds face fines. The permitted number of citizen observers is limited, and the way in which credentials are distributed between what electoral authorities call "pro-*chavista*" and "pro-opposition" groups makes it extremely difficult for credible observers to deploy to the representative sample of polling stations that they must observe in order to perform sufficiently precise statistical analyses of electoral-process quality. The incumbent regime, meanwhile, makes a point of inviting friendly regional organizations such as the Council of Election Experts in Latin American (CEELA) and more recently the Union of South American Nations (UNASUR), with every expectation that they will make positive statements about the voting and the larger electoral process.[14] Between the regime's refusals, restrictions, and scheduling decisions, the OAS, the EU, and the Carter Center have all found themselves effectively blocked from observing Venezuelan elections.

When President Hugo Chávez died of cancer on 5 March 2013 without a permanent constitutional successor, the government organized the vote to replace him on April 14, leaving insufficient time for international organizations to arrive and mount observation missions. Foreign witnesses, individually and in small clusters, were present for the voting, which very narrowly favored Chávez's handpicked successor, interim president Nicolás Maduro. The opposition candidate, Henrique Capriles, demanded a full ballot audit, the implementation of which he later denounced as bogus. The small OAS delegation that was present for election day noted the official results and supported a full recount, while the UNASUR delegation saluted the democratic spirit of the polls and called for respecting the result.[15]

Piercing the Fog

It is important to identify the tactics that autocrats use to fog the electoral environment so that their subterfuges can be exposed and accurate electoral assessments can be seen clearly. Citizens, national and international journalists, international and domestic election monitors, diplomats, and others all have roles to play in this effort. Electoral contestants themselves must learn to defend electoral integrity by documenting abuses and using evidence-based approaches to seeking redress, just as electoral authorities need to assert independence and integrity. These efforts reinforce and advance the norms and standards for genuine elections, improving the efficacy and integrity of election competition, administration, and monitoring. They also support those facing autocratic hostility and pressure.

Promoting democratic norms is essential to countering authoritarian resurgence. As democratic electoral practices gain ground, autocratic tactics will become harder to hide. As most countries embrace wider transparency, including access to important election-related data, efforts to block witnesses and deny information will stand out in starker relief. As the beachhead of accountability expands, providing redress to those who have seen their election-related rights abridged and justice to the violators, impunity for autocratic abuses against candidates and voters will be broken down. As barriers to participation are leveled, autocratic techniques of disenfranchisement will be more easily countered. Making such advances takes time and must be approached in the unevenness of national circumstances.

Both citizen monitors and international observers will need to continue countering authoritarian learning with democratic learning and innovation. Methods must be improved: Manipulation takes place across a spectrum of electoral processes, so long-term monitoring and systematic counter-techniques must be employed. Credible international observers should take seriously constraints on their ability to perform tasks such as evaluating the quality of key processes that take place months before election day, or weighing the efficacy of certain electoral technologies. This highlights their need to improve cooperation with credible citizen monitors. Citizen election monitors, in turn, can benefit from cooperation with credible international observers, who can bring attention to their findings and help keep open their space to operate. Both international observers and citizen monitors should also seek out others—from civil society, the media, election authorities, and reform-minded sectors of officialdom—with whom relationships can be built to serve political impartiality and electoral integrity. Such multisided interaction is needed to pursue electoral and broader democratic development, including follow-up on observer recommendations.

Networks, regional and global, should be reinforced so that peer learning, the sharing of innovative techniques, peer-to-peer accountability, and solidarity actions can be further developed. This is particularly important for citizen election monitors, who operate in many countries and often cover electoral and political processes that extend beyond and between elections. Public communications efforts need improvement as well. Credible citizen monitors and international observers should concentrate on getting accurate findings to the public as quickly and responsibly as possible whether through various social media, infographics, videos, or other communications technologies. When it comes to countering false narratives, timing is critical.

Supporting those who work to prevent and expose authoritarian electoral maneuvers is essential. Citizen monitors in many countries can use direct help in the form of systematic monitoring methods and sophisticated communications techniques, as well as aid in making their organizations stronger. Global and regional peer networks have untold potential to provide such assistance and to build solidarity.

Media freedoms are essential to genuine elections, democracy, and countering rising authoritarianism. The media—broadly defined to include bloggers, citizen journalists, and social-media users as well as more traditional press outlets—provide a safeguard for electoral and governmental integrity when they operate ethically. The media's watchdog role makes them a part of credible election monitoring and gives them a responsibility to cover credible citizen monitors and international observers as well as to expose zombie and phony observers.

International and domestic media should learn how to distinguish credible citizen election monitors and international observers from GONGOs and zombies, and should report on the broader electoral context rather than just election day. Identifying organizations that endorse GNDEM's Declaration of Global Principles for citizen election monitors and those that endorse the Declaration of Principles for International Election Observation provides a fundamental starting point. Journalists, scholars, and others should "monitor the monitors" and document the dealings of phony election observers as well as the efforts of public-relations firms and lobbyists in major capitals to spread fog over authoritarian electoral theft. Proper information can cut through the fog of disinformation.

That information must be accurate and credible, and its circulation must be timely. Only then can the true nature of an election be illuminated. That is how public confidence is established and political volatility is reduced—it is also how chicanery is exposed.

The world's democratic actors, including governments, are being challenged. Authoritarians have made a priority of controlling the narrative concerning their elections—and more—by blocking or suppressing truth-tellers and fogging the scene with disinformation.

Do democratic activists and democracies have the resolve to cut through the fog by supporting real election monitoring and calling elections by their true character? Genuine stability, like democracy, is about much more than elections, but both depend on elections being credible.

Notes

1. See Universal Declaration of Human Rights (UDHR), Article 19 and International Covenant on Civil and Political Rights (ICCPR), Article 19.

2. See UDHR, Article 21 and ICCPR, Article 25.

3. See, for example, Open Government Guide, "Elections," *www.opengovguide.com/topics/elections*.

4. The abstentions came from the three USSR voters, Czechoslovakia, Poland, Saudi Arabia, South Africa, and Yugoslavia.

5. See the Inter-American Democratic Charter; the African Charter on Democracy, Elections and Governance; the OSCE's Copenhagen Document; and Article 25 of the ICCPR.

6. Patrick Merloe, "Human Rights—The Basis for Inclusiveness, Transparency, Accountability and Public Confidence in Elections," section 2 of "Promoting Legal Frameworks for Democratic Elections," NDI report, 30 September 2008, *www.ndi.org/files/2404_ww_elect_legalframeworks_093008-3.pdf*.

7. Compare OSCE International Election Observation Mission, "Republic of Azerbaijan—Presidential Election, 9 October 2013: Statement of Preliminary Findings and Conclusions," Baku, 10 October 2013 (*www.osce.org/odihr/elections/106901?download=true*) with Council of Europe Parliamentary Assembly, "Presidential Election in Azerbaijan: Joint Statement by PACE and EP Delegations," 10 October 2013 (*www.assembly.coe.int/nw/xml/News/NewsView-EN.asp?newsid=4699&lang=2&cat=31*).

8. See "Mugabe Threatens Sadc Pullout. . . Labels Lindiwe Zulu 'Street Woman,'" *News Day* (Harare), 6 July 2013, *www.newsday.co.zw/2013/07/06/mugabe-threatens-sadc-pullout-labels-lindiwe-zulu-street-woman*.

9. See the Preliminary Statement of the SADC Election Observation Mission to the Republic of Zimbabwe, 2 August 2013, *www.sadc.int/files/4313/7545/6616/FINAL_Preliminary_Statement_of_the_SADC_Election_Observer_Mission_to_the_July_31_2013_Zimbabwe_Harmonised_Elections_as_at1148_on__August_02_2013.pdf*.

10. "Zimbabwe Poll 'Free and Peaceful' Say Obasanjo and SADC," BBC News Africa, 2 August 2013, *www.bbc.com/news/world-africa-23546050*.

11. See AU observation mission's preliminary statement on Zimbabwe's 31 July 2013 elections, *http://pa.au.int/en/sites/default/files/Final%20Copy%20Preliminary%20Statement%20ZImbabwe%202013.pdf*.

12. See the Zimbabwe Election Support Network's report on Zimbabwe's 31 July 2013 elections, *http://263chat.com/wp-content/uploads/2014/10/ZESN-2013-Advance-Harmonised-Election-Report.pdf*.

13. See "Statement from Botswana SADC Parliamentary Observer Team," 9 August 2013, *www.safpi.org/news/article/2013/statement-botswana-sadc-parliamentary-observer-team*. The Botswanan government's 5 August 2013 statement is at *www.sokwanele.com/thisiszimbabwe/statement-government-botswana-2013-election-republic-zimbabwe/05082013*.

14. "International Observers in Venezuelan Election Report Their Findings from Yesterday," 15 April 2013, *www.democraticunderground.com/110813210*.

15. See Organization of American States, "Insulza Salutes Civic Spirit of Venezuelans and Supports Recount Proposals," press release, 15 April 2013 and "Declaración de la Misión Electoral de la UNASUR," 15 April 2013.

CHAPTER NINE

The Leninist Roots of Civil Society Repression

ANNE APPLEBAUM

IN 1947, STEFAN JĘDRYCHOWSKI, a communist veteran, member of the Polish Politburo, and minister in the government, wrote a memo somewhat pompously titled "Notes on Anglo-Saxon Propaganda." He had many complaints—about the influence of British and U.S. news services in Poland, and about foreign fashions and films. But his most sustained attack was on Polska YMCA, the Polish section of the Young Men's Christian Association. Founded in Warsaw in 1923 and later banned by Hitler, Polska YMCA had restarted itself in April 1945 with some help from the international YMCA in Geneva, as well as a good deal of local enthusiasm.

The YMCA in Warsaw was avowedly apolitical. Its main tasks in Poland were to distribute foreign aid—clothes, books, and food—and to provide activities and classes for young people. Jędrychowski suspected ulterior motives, however. The YMCA's propaganda, he wrote, was conducted "carefully . . . avoiding direct political accents," which of course made it more dangerous. He recommended that the minister for state security conduct a financial audit of the organization and monitor carefully which publications were being made available and which kinds of courses were being taught. After two years of watching, the communist authorities finally decided that they had had enough. They declared the YMCA a "tool of bourgeois-fascism" and dissolved it. With bizarre Orwellian fury, communist youth activists descended on the club with hammers and smashed all the jazz records, and the building was given to something called the League of Soldiers' Friends, a state-run organization.

The reconstruction of Polska YMCA in the immediate postwar period was a classic example of what is nowadays called "civil society," a phenomenon that has gone by other names in the past. In the eighteenth century, philosophers first began to identify the importance of organizations such as guilds, clubs, and unions that functioned apart from the institutions of the state. Edmund Burke wrote admiringly of the "little platoons"—the small social organizations from which, he believed, public spirit arose. In the nineteenth century, Alexis de Tocqueville wrote equally enthusiastically of the "associations" that "Americans of all ages, all conditions, and all dispositions constantly form." He concluded that they helped to ward off dictatorship: "If men are to remain civilized or to become so, the art of associating together must grow and improve." More recently, Robert Putnam has redefined the same phenomenon as "social capital" and concluded that voluntary organizations lie at the heart of what we call "community."

But in the early part of the twentieth century, the small group of revolutionaries who became the Russian Bolsheviks developed an alternative theory of civil society. Burke, Tocqueville, and even Russian intellectuals believed that civil society was fundamental to democracy; Lenin believed that the destruction of civil society was crucial to totalitarian dictatorship. As historian Stuart Finkel has explained, Lenin believed that "the public sphere in a socialist society should be unitary and univocal," and dismissed the "bourgeois" notion of open discussion. Accordingly, the Bolsheviks regarded all independent associations, trade unions, and guilds as "separatist" or "caste" divisions within society. As for bourgeois political parties, these were meaningless. Lenin wrote, "The names of parties, both in Europe and in Russia, are often chosen purely for purposes of advertisement, the 'programs' of parties are more often than not written with the sole purpose of defrauding the public."[1] In fact, the Bolsheviks disliked independent organizations for the same reason that Burke and Tocqueville admired them: because they gave people the power to control their own lives, because they encouraged independent thought, and because they made people more critical of state power.

In this as in so many other spheres, the Bolsheviks applied their theory to reality as soon as they could. In the wake of the Russian Revolution, they created what was probably the first political party ever to have as one of its explicit goals the destruction of any institution not directly created by, and not loyal to, itself. In the Soviet Union, even completely apolitical organizations were banned, because Lenin believed that all organizations were inherently political: If they were not openly political, then they were secretly political.

From that assumption, it also followed that no organized group was above suspicion. Associations that claimed to be interested in soccer or chess might well be "fronts" for something more sinister. The St. Petersburg academic Dmitri Likhachev—later Russia's most celebrated literary critic—was arrested in 1928 because he belonged to a philosophic discussion circle whose members greeted one another in ancient Greek. While in prison, Likhachev encountered the head of the Petrograd Boy Scouts, an organization that later would be considered highly dubious in Eastern Europe as well.

This profound suspicion of civil society was central to Bolshevik thinking, far more so than is usually acknowledged. Finkel points out that even as the Soviet leadership was experimenting with economic freedom in the 1920s (during Lenin's "New Economic Plan"), the systematic destruction of literary, philosophical, and spiritual societies continued unabated. Even for orthodox Marxists, free trade was preferable to free association, including the free association of apolitical sporting or cultural groups. This was true under Lenin's rule, under Stalin's rule, under Khrushchev's rule, and under Brezhnev's rule. Although many other things changed over the course of Soviet history, the persecution of civil society continued after Stalin's death, well into the 1970s and 1980s.

The East European communists inherited this paranoia, whether because they had observed it and acquired it for themselves during their many visits to the Soviet Union, or because their colleagues in the secret police had acquired it during their training, or in some cases because the Soviet generals and ambassadors in their countries at the end of the war gave them explicit instructions to be paranoid. In a few cases, Soviet authorities in Eastern Europe directly ordered local communists to ban particular organizations or types of organizations. In postwar East Germany, for example, they outlawed hiking groups.

As in postrevolutionary Russia, the political persecution of civic activists in communist Eastern Europe not only preceded the persecution of actual politicians, it also took precedence over other Soviet and communist goals. Even in the years between 1945 and 1948, when elections were still theoretically free in Hungary and when Poland still had a legal opposition party, certain kinds of civic associations were already under threat. In Germany, Soviet commanders made no attempt to ban religious services or religious ceremonies in the first months of occupation, but they often objected strongly to church-group meetings, religious evenings, and even organized religious and charitable associations that met outside the church in restaurants or other public spaces. Private trade remained legal in many places in the late 1940s and early 1950s, even as members of Catholic youth groups were arrested and persecuted.

In the postwar era, other countries influenced by Bolshevik doctrine adopted some of the same policies. Communist China and North Korea are the two most obvious examples, and indeed they might be said to have equaled or exceeded the Bolshevik mania for destroying independent organizations. Perhaps less obviously, several Arab dictatorships, including those in Libya and Iraq, followed similar policies. Muammar al-Qadhafi was so fanatical about destroying civil society that he blocked even the creation of a single state political party, preferring to govern alone. The absence of alternative associations is one important reason for the rise of radical Islam in the wake of the Arab Spring: In many countries, the mosque had for many years been the only functioning independent institution.

From Repression Springs Dissent

In a very real sense, the complete repression of civil society made the Soviet Union, its colonies, and its imitators unique. Although Hitler may have had similar aspirations, he was not in power long enough to destroy all of Germany's civic institutions. The Bolsheviks and their followers, by contrast, had plenty of time to eliminate not only opposition political parties and private enterprise, but all kinds of youth groups, sports clubs, educational societies, and more—and to move them all beneath the umbrella of the state.

In the end, the Bolsheviks' thoroughness may have been one of their most important mistakes. For Lenin did not see that by attempting to control every aspect of society, totalitarian regimes would eventually turn every aspect of society into a potential source of dissent. The state had dictated high daily quotas for the workers—and so an East German workers' strike against bad working conditions in 1953 mushroomed quickly into a protest against the state. The state had dictated what artists could paint or writers could write—and so an artist or writer who painted or wrote something different automatically became a political dissident. The state had dictated that no one could form independent organizations—and so anybody who founded one, however anodyne, became an opponent of the regime.

And when large numbers of people joined an independent organization—as when some ten-million Poles joined the Solidarity trade union in 1981, for example—the regime's very existence was suddenly at stake.

Over time, some political opponents of the communist regimes came to understand that this was an inherent weakness of Soviet-style totalitarianism. In his brilliant 1978 essay "The Power of the Powerless," Czech dissident Václav Havel famously urged his countrymen to discard false and meaningless jargon and to "live in truth"—in other words, to speak and act as if the regime did not exist. More to the point, he also called upon his countrymen to take advantage of their rulers' obsession with total control. If the state wanted to monopolize every sphere of human activity, he wrote, then every thinking citizen should work to preserve the "independent life of society," which he defined as including "everything from self-education and thinking about the world, through free creative activity and its communication to others, to the most varied, free, and civic attitudes, including instances of independent social self-organization."

In due course, some version of this "independent life of society"—"civil society"—began to flourish in many unusual ways. Hungarians joined academic discussion clubs. Czechs created jazz bands. Poles organized underground Scout troops and, eventually, independent trade unions. Everywhere, people played rock music, organized poetry readings, set up clandestine businesses, held underground philosophy seminars, sold black-market meat, and went to church. They also told jokes, which were often very subversive indeed. In a different kind of society, these activities would have been considered apolitical, and even in Eastern Europe they did not necessarily constitute "opposition" as such. But they gave people control over some aspects of their own lives—and, in practice, gave them what they felt were spheres of freedom and independence from the state.

At times, they also had a very profound impact on politics. In 1956, tiny Hungarian academic-discussion groups slowly grew larger, became public meetings, and eventually led to the Hungarian Revolution. In 1980, Solidarity briefly won the legal right to exist before it was crushed a year and a half later by martial law. And then in 1989, East German Protestant groups and independent activists organized a series of marches in Leipzig that helped to precipitate the fall of the Berlin Wall.

After communism had come to an end, it once again became possible to speak freely and to organize freely in the countries of Central and Eastern

Europe. But in many places this was easier said than done: The private, civic, social, and charitable institutions through which citizens had once channeled their independent intellectual, political, benevolent, or athletic initiatives no longer existed. Neither did the legal system to support them. Much has been written about the loss of the work ethic in communist Europe and the absence of stock markets and capitalist institutions. But by 1989, the habits, customs, laws, and even etiquette associated with everything from the culture of a responsible newsroom to the organization of annual charity balls also had been missing from much of the Soviet Union for seventy years, and from Central Europe for forty. They were no easier to replace.

Worse, some part of the population in virtually all the former Soviet-bloc countries was, at least to start with, actively opposed to their revival. In 1989, the notion of a newspaper that would publish articles critical of the government was bizarre, even suspect, to many ex-Soviet citizens. The very thought of a school organized according to a different philosophy from state schools seemed strange. The idea that a charity could be funded entirely by private people was, to many, unacceptable and even suspicious: What would be the motives of the people who contributed? Political parties engaging in uncontrolled debate presented the most terrifying prospect of all. The spectacle of people disagreeing in public, sometimes even shouting at each other, seemed disruptive, divisive, and even dangerous.

It is also true that, in the absence of both the state and civil society, words such as "freedom" sometimes seemed like empty slogans. You might be free to spend your time as you wanted, but the local state-run football club had collapsed for lack of funding, nothing had replaced it, and your community had forgotten how to organize football teams on its own. You might be free to engage in politics, but political parties and organizations were weak, corrupt, and poorly organized. You might feel outraged about the poverty around you, but you no longer knew how to raise money to help.

With time, of course, many citizens of former communist states adjusted to the new realities, grew accustomed to the idea of individual liberty, and enthusiastically began to rebuild civil society. Others, however, did not. Across the region, the size of these two groups still varies a great deal, depending on a particular country's history and culture. Indeed, their relative weight is extremely important: In the postcommunist world, citizens' attitudes toward civil society have, to a surprising extent, helped to determine the political situation of their countries. In Poland, "illegal" civil society had flourished during the last two decades of communism, spawning not only the Solidarity trade union but dozens of other independent organizations: artists' and writers' groups, church organizations, even an underground Scouting movement. By 1989, Poles not only were ready to legalize civic organizations, they already had some experience running them.

In Russia, by contrast, where the right to freedom of association had been repressed for seventy years—and had been very limited even before that—ordinary people were more cautious about the idea of free civic institutions. Worse, the men who came to power in the early 2000s, after the short Yeltsin interregnum, were once again blatantly hostile to them. The Putin presidency's crusade against the very notion of independent civil society in Russia has reflected, in part, the return to power of the old KGB, an institution whose primary goal was the destruction of all independent organizations inside the USSR. In the course of their training, all these men would have learned that events cannot be allowed just to happen, they must be manipulated; that markets cannot be genuinely open, they must be managed from behind the scenes; that elections cannot be unpredictable, they must be planned in advance. By the same token, they also were taught that organizations that they do not control are by definition hostile.

Putin himself had personal experience with the danger posed to an authoritarian state by independent groups. As a young KGB officer in Dresden in 1989, he witnessed mass street protests and the ransacking of the headquarters of the Stasi, the East German secret police. And he is not alone. Most of the people who now surround him were trained and educated inside the same system, and most appear to think the same way.

Perhaps unsurprisingly, the return of the KGB to power has been marked by the slow but systematic elimination of all kinds of independent groups and organizations from Russian society. In November 2012, the Russian Duma passed a law that, in effect, required any organization receiving any Western funding to register as a "foreign agent"—in other words, an agent of espionage. Spot checks and audits of a huge range of groups, including those working in education and healthcare, have led many to close their offices or move them outside Russia. Among the more than fifty organizations forced to register as foreign agents are Memorial, an organization dedicated both to human rights and to preserving the history of Stalinism, and the Dynasty Foundation, a Russian-funded charity that supports math and science. Dynasty's Russian founder and sole funder had said earlier in the year that he would stop financing the organization if the foreign-agent designation was not lifted, and in July the organization's board decided to close it.

A more recent law gives the Russian state the right to shut down "undesirable" foreign organizations of any kind. Among the groups mentioned as possible targets are Human Rights Watch and Amnesty International. Under the law, Russian organizations known to "cooperate" with "undesirable" foreign organizations can also be fined or punished.

Russian society, long unaccustomed to participating in civic organizations, will now be further discouraged from doing so by fear. Very soon, it may become difficult to found, run, or join an independent organization of any kind at all in Russia; the only "legitimate" organizations will be run by the state. As long as Russia is ruled by people who have not abandoned this element of Bolshevik thinking, that is how it is likely to remain.

The question now is whether other postcommunist societies—and indeed the many other societies heavily influenced by Soviet ideology—will take a similar route. Most of the Central European and Baltic countries that made it into the European Union seem likely to maintain the right to organize freely (although Hungarian prime minister Viktor Orbán has fulminated against the existence of some independent organizations in Hungary that receive money from abroad). The civic sector is also very strong in Ukraine, drawing on pre-Soviet Ukrainian traditions of self-help and peasant organizations.

But in Belarus, Central Asia, China, Cuba, parts of Africa, and much of the Arab world, those in power remain attached to the old Bolshevik idea that independent civic institutions are a threat to the state. There is an irony here, for in their most important goals, the Bolsheviks failed. They never did succeed in carrying out an international communist revolution, their economic theories have been discredited, and central planning is no more. But Lenin's narrower ideas about civil society live on in places as varied as Beijing, Cairo, Havana, Minsk, Pyongyang, and Tashkent—proving, perhaps, that they were always the most potent and dangerous of all.

Notes

1. V. I. Lenin, quoted in *The Communist Party of the Soviet Union (Bolsheviks) Is the Leading and Guiding Force of Soviet Society* (Moscow: Foreign Languages Publishing House, 1951).

CHAPTER TEN

Civil Society Under Assault

DOUGLAS RUTZEN

T WENTY YEARS AGO, the world was in the midst of an "associational revolution."[1] Civil society organizations (CSOs) enjoyed a mostly positive reputation within the international community, gained from their important contributions to health, education, culture, economic development, and a host of other objectives beneficial to the public. Political theorists, meanwhile, associated civil society with social justice, as exemplified by the U.S. civil-rights movement, the Central European dissident movements, and South Africa's anti-apartheid movement.

With the fall of the Berlin Wall, the rise of the Internet, and the renaissance of civil society, many observers at the close of the twentieth century saw political, technological, and social developments interweaving to give rise to an era of civic empowerment. Reflecting this era, the UN General Assembly adopted in September 2000 the Millennium Declaration. Among its other provisions, the declaration trumpeted the importance of human rights and the value of "non-governmental organizations and civil society, in general."

A year later, the global zeitgeist began to change. After the 9/11 terrorist attacks, discourse shifted away from an emphasis on human rights and the positive contributions of civil society. U.S. president George W. Bush launched the War on Terror, and CSOs became an immediate target. "Just to show you how insidious these terrorists are," Bush stated in his September 2001 remarks on the executive order freezing assets of terrorist and other organizations, "they oftentimes use nice-sounding, non-governmental organizations as fronts for their activities. . . . We intend to deal with them, just like we intend to deal with others who aid and abet terrorist organizations."[2] Shortly thereafter, Bush launched the Freedom Agenda, which included support for civil society as a key component. Because of the association of civil society with both terrorism and the Freedom Agenda, governments around the world became increasingly concerned about CSOs, particularly organizations that received international assistance.

This concern heightened after the so-called color revolutions. The 2003 Rose Revolution in Georgia roused Russia, but the turning point was the 2004 Orange Revolution in Ukraine. Russian president Vladimir Putin viewed Ukraine as a battleground in the contest for geopolitical influence between Russia and the West. The Orange Revolution also caught the attention of other world leaders. As protesters flooded the streets of Kyiv, Belarus's President Alyaksandr Lukashenka famously warned, "There will not be any rose, orange, or banana revolutions in our country."[3] During the same period, Zimbabwe's parliament adopted a law restricting CSOs. Soon thereafter, Belarus enacted legislation restricting the freedoms of association and assembly. If there was a global associational *revolution* in 1994, by 2004 the global associational *counterrevolution* had begun.

Also contributing to this shift was the dwindling appetite for civil society support in countries that had undergone political transformations during the 1980s and 1990s. Years had passed, and these governments no longer considered themselves to be "in transition." Rather, they had transitioned as far as they were inclined to go, and were now focused on consolidating governmental institutions and state power. This was particularly true in "semi-authoritarian" or "hybrid" regimes that held elections but had little interest in the rule of law, human rights, and other aspects of pluralistic democracy.

All this led numerous states to begin imposing restrictions on CSOs. Governments were able to coat these new constraints with a veneer of political theory. Those with autocratic tendencies touted variants of Putin's theory of "managed democracy," which seamlessly morphed into notions of "managed civil society." Two models emerged in these countries: In some, CSOs were given latitude to operate, provided that they stayed away from politics. In others, the government sought to coopt CSOs and to shut down groups that resisted, particularly those that received international funding.

The trend toward restricting CSOs also gained momentum from international efforts to improve the performance of foreign aid. In March 2005, ninety countries endorsed the Paris Declaration on Aid Effectiveness, which incorporated the concepts of "host-country ownership" (soon to be

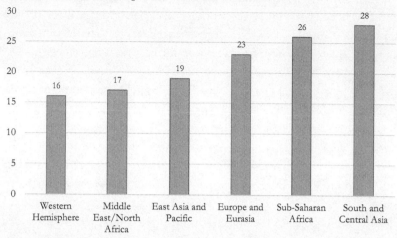

interpreted as "host-government ownership") and "alignment of aid with partner countries' priorities." Shortly thereafter, a number of governments introduced restrictive measures regulating international funding that covered not only bilateral aid but also cross-border philanthropy.

As a result of these and other factors, civic space quickly contracted. According to data from the International Center for Not-for-Profit Law (ICNL), between 2004 and 2010 more than fifty countries considered or enacted measures restricting civil society. These restrictions were grounded in concerns about terrorism, foreign interference in political affairs, and aid effectiveness. These issues, coupled with the longstanding debate about the accountability and transparency of CSOs, provided governments with a potent cocktail of justifications to rationalize restrictions.

The Arab Spring, which began in late 2010, set off a second wave of legislative constraints. Once again, governments around the world took notice of these mass movements and initiated measures to restrict civil society in the hopes of preventing similar uprisings on their own soil. Since 2012, more than 120 laws constraining the freedoms of association or assembly have been proposed or enacted in 60 countries. This trend is consistent with the continuing decline in democracy worldwide. *Freedom in the World 2015* reveals that 2014 was the ninth consecutive year of a global decline in freedom. As the Figure above (based on ICNL's tracking data) shows, the restrictions of association and assembly, while more common in certain regions, is a global phenomenon.

Of these initiatives, approximately half could be called "framework" legislation: They constrain the incorporation, registration, operation, and general lifecycle of CSOs. Roughly 19 percent restrict the freedom of assembly. The greatest uptick, however, has been in restrictions on international funding, which now account for 35 percent of all restrictive measures.

The many legal and regulatory measures used by governments to curtail international funding include 1) requiring prior government approval for the receipt of international funding; 2) enacting "foreign-agents" legislation to stigmatize internationally funded CSOs; 3) capping the amount of international funding that a CSO is allowed to receive; 4) requiring international funding to be routed through government-controlled entities; 5) restricting activities that can be undertaken with international funding; 6) prohibiting CSOs from receiving international funding from specific donors; 7) constraining international funding through the overly broad application of anti–money laundering and counterterrorism measures; 8) taxing the receipt of international funding; 9) imposing onerous reporting requirements on the receipt of international funding; and 10) using defamation, treason, and other laws to bring criminal charges against recipients of international funding.

Darin Christensen and Jeremy M. Weinstein assessed the scale and scope of such restrictions as well as "the factors that account for variation in the incidence of foreign-funding restrictions" in 2013.[4] I seek to build on this scholarly foundation by categorizing the various restrictions on CSOs, summarizing justifications for those restrictions, and analyzing such restrictions under international law.

Government Justifications

The justifications that governments use for enacting restrictions on CSOs fall into four broad categories: 1) protecting state sovereignty; 2) promoting transparency and accountability in the civil society sector; 3) enhancing aid effectiveness and coordination; and 4) pursuing national-security, counterterrorism, and anti–money laundering objectives.

STATE SOVEREIGNTY. Some governments invoke state sovereignty as a justification to restrict international funding. For example, in justifying the

Russian foreign-agents law, Vladimir Putin stated, "The only purpose of this law after all was to ensure that foreign organisations representing outside interests, not those of the Russian state, would not intervene in our domestic affairs. This is something that no self-respecting country can accept."[5] Similarly, in July 2014 Hungarian prime minister Viktor Orbán lauded the establishment of a parliamentary committee to monitor civil society organizations: "We're not dealing with civil society members but paid political activists who are trying to help foreign interests here. . . . It's good that a parliamentary committee has been set up to monitor the influence of foreign monitors" on CSOs.[6] In Egypt, 43 CSO staff members were charged in 2012 with "establishing unlicenced chapters of international organisations and accepting foreign funding to finance these groups in a manner that breached the Egyptian state's sovereignty."[7] Egyptian officials claimed that the CSOs were contributing to international interference in the country's domestic political affairs.[8]

Some governments claim that foreigners are seeking not only to meddle in domestic political affairs, but actually to destabilize their countries or otherwise promote regime change. Accordingly, these governments argue that restrictions on international funding are necessary to thwart such efforts. In June 2015, for example, Pakistani authorities ordered Save the Children to leave the country, claiming that the aid organization was involved in "anti-Pakistan activities" and was "working against the country."[9] Although the decision was reversed days later, the interior minister warned, "Local NGOs that use foreign help and foreign funding to implement a foreign agenda in Pakistan should be scared. We will not allow them to work here whatever connections they enjoy, regardless of the outcry."[10] While Russia's foreign-agents law was pending in parliament, one of its drafters stated, "There is so much evidence about regime change in Yugoslavia, now in Libya, Egypt, Tunisia, in Kosovo—that's what happens in the world, some governments are working to change regimes in other countries. Russian democracy needs to be protected from outside influences."[11] In July 2014, the vice-chairman of the China Research Institute of China-Russia Relations argued that China should "learn from Russia" and enact a foreign-agents law "so as to block the way for the infiltration of external forces and eliminate the possibilities of a Color Revolution."[12]

TRANSPARENCY AND ACCOUNTABILITY. Another justification commonly invoked by governments to regulate and restrict the flow of foreign funds is the importance of upholding the integrity of CSOs by promoting transparency and accountability through government regulation. Consider, for example, the following responses by government delegations to a UN Human Rights Council panel on the promotion and protection of civil society held in March 2014: Ethiopia, on behalf of the African Group, stated, "Domestic law regulation consistent with the international obligations of States should be put in place to ensure that the exercise of the right to freedom of expression, assembly and association fully respects the rights of others and ensures the independence, accountability and transparency of civil society"; and India, on behalf of the Like Minded Group, stated, "The advocacy for civil society should be tempered by the need for responsibility, openness and transparency and accountability of civil society organizations." Kyrgyzstan has used this same argument to justify its proposed foreign-agents law. The explanatory note to the draft law claims that it "has been developed for purposes of ensuring openness, publicity, [and] transparency for non-profit organizations."[13]

Aid effectiveness and coordination. A global movement advocating greater effectiveness of international development assistance has steadily been gaining strength. Strategies for achieving such improvement include promoting "host-country ownership" and harmonizing development assistance.[14] Some states, however, have interpreted host-country ownership to mean host-*government* ownership, and have otherwise exploited the aid-effectiveness campaign to justify constraints on international funding.

For example, in July 2014 Nepal's government released its Development Cooperation Policy, which requires development partners to channel all assistance through the Ministry of Finance, rather than directly to CSOs. The Ministry of Finance stated that this was necessary in order to maximize aid efficiency: "Both the Government and the development partners are aware of the fact that the effectiveness can only be enhanced if the ownership of aid funded projects lies with the recipient government."[15] That same month, Sri Lanka's Finance and Planning Ministry issued a public notice requiring CSOs to receive government approval of international funding. The ministry justified the move by claiming that projects financed with international funding were "outside the government budget undermining the national development programmes."[16] The year before, Egypt's government had similarly argued that government coordination of aid was necessary in order to mitigate the negative effects of having multiple CSOs at work in the country.[17]

NATIONAL SECURITY, COUNTERTERRORISM, AND ANTI–MONEY LAUNDERING. Governments sometimes invoke national security, counterterrorism, and anti–money laundering aims in order to justify imposing restrictions on international funding, including cross-border philanthropy. China's government defended draft legislation restricting international funding by insisting that the law was intended to safeguard China's "national security and social stability." Azerbaijan's government, meanwhile, justified amendments relating to the registration of foreign grants by claiming that the amendments were meant "to enforce international obligations of the Republic of Azerbaijan in the area of combating money-laundering."[18] And in the British Virgin Islands, CSOs with more than five employees are required by law to appoint a designated Money Laundering Reporting Officer and submit to audit requirements not imposed on businesses. These burdens were supposedly based on the intergovernmental Financial Action Task Force's recommendation on nonprofit organizations and counterterrorism.

The International Legal Framework

International norms and laws provide a framework for the protection of civil society, while also allowing for exceptions that permit national governments to enact restrictions under certain circumstances and adhering to specified conditions.

Global norms. Article 22 of the International Covenant on Civil and Political Rights (ICCPR) states, "Everyone shall have the right to freedom of association with others." According to Maina Kiai, UN Special Rapporteur (UNSR) on the rights to freedom of peaceful assembly and of association, "The right to freedom of association not only includes the ability of individuals or legal entities to form and join an association but also to seek, receive and use resources—human, material and financial—from domestic, foreign and international sources."

The UN Declaration on Human Rights Defenders similarly states that access to resources is a self-standing right: "Everyone has the right, individually and in association with others, to solicit, receive and utilize resources for the express purpose of promoting and protecting human rights and fundamental freedoms through peaceful means." Furthermore, according to the UN High Commissioner for Human Rights, this right specifically encompasses "the receipt of funds from abroad."[19]

Regional and bilateral commitments to protect international funding. International funding for civil society is also protected at the regional level. Take, for example, the Council of Europe Recommendation on the Legal Status of NGOs, which states, "NGOs should be free to solicit and receive funding—cash or in-kind donations—not only from public bodies in their own state but also from institutional or individual donors, another state or multilateral agencies." Likewise, according to the Inter-American Commission on Human Rights, "states should allow and facilitate human rights organizations' access to foreign funds in the context of international cooperation, in transparent conditions."[20]

Many jurisdictions also have concluded bilateral investment treaties that help to protect the free flow of capital across borders. Some treaties, such as the U.S. treaties with Kazakhstan and Kyrgyzstan, respectively, expressly extend investment-treaty protections to organizations not "organized for pecuniary gain." The letters from the White House transmitting these treaties to the U.S. Senate explicitly state that they cover "charitable and nonprofit entities."[21]

Restrictions permitted under international law. International law allows a government to restrict access to resources if three conditions are met: The restriction is 1) prescribed by law; 2) in pursuance of one or more legitimate aims; and 3) "necessary in a democratic society" to achieve those aims.[22]

1) *Prescribed by law.* The first condition requires restrictions to have a formal basis in law. This means that "restrictions on the right to freedom of association are only valid if they had been introduced by law (through an act of Parliament or an equivalent unwritten norm of common law), and are not permissible if introduced through Government decrees or other similar administrative orders."[23] Yet the aforementioned Nepalese and Sri Lankan policies affecting foreign assistance to CSOs were based on executive actions and not "introduced by law (through an act of Parliament or an equivalent unwritten norm of common law)." Thus they seem to violate the "prescribed by law" standard required under both the Council of Europe's Convention for the Protection of Human Rights and Fundamental Freedoms and the ICCPR.

Moreover, according to international law, restrictions must be "'prescribed by law,' which implies that the law must be accessible and its provisions must be formulated with sufficient precision."[24] In other words, a provision must be sufficiently precise for an individual or NGO to understand whether or not its intended conduct would constitute a violation of law. This requirement helps to limit the scope of permissible restrictions. For example, some laws ban the funding of organizations that cause "social anxiety," have a "political nature," or have "implied ideological conditions." Because these terms are undefined and provide little guidance to individuals or organizations about what is and is not prohibited, however, it can be reasonably argued that they fail the "prescribed by law" requirement.

2) *Legitimate aims.* The second condition requires that restrictions must advance at least one legitimate aim—specifically, national security or public safety; public order; the protection of public health or morals; or the protection of the rights and freedoms of others. This provides a useful lens through which to analyze the various justifications that governments use to defend constraints on civil society. As noted above, some governments have cited the enhancement of "aid effectiveness" as a reason for imposing restrictions on CSOs. But, as a UNSR report states, aid effectiveness "is not listed as a legitimate ground for restrictions." Similarly, "the protection of State sovereignty is not listed as a legitimate interest in the [ICCPR]," and "States cannot refer to additional grounds . . . to restrict the right to freedom of association."[25]

Of course, assertions of national security or public safety may, in certain circumstances, constitute a legitimate aim. Under the Siracusa Principles on the Limitation and Derogation Provisions in the ICCPR, however, assertions of national security must be construed restrictively "to justify measures limiting certain rights only when they are taken to protect the existence of the nation or its territorial integrity or political independence against force or threat of force." In addition, a state may not use "national security as a justification for measures aimed at suppressing opposition . . . or at perpetrating repressive practices against its population."[26] This includes defaming or stigmatizing foreign-funded groups by accusing them of "treason" or "promoting regime change."[27]

3) *Necessary in a democratic society.* In a 2012 report, UNSR Maina Kiai wrote that "longstanding jurisprudence asserts that democratic societies only exist where 'pluralism, tolerance and broad-mindedness' are in place," and "minority or dissenting views or beliefs are respected."[28] Accordingly, unless a restriction is "necessary in a democratic society," it violates international law even if the government is able to articulate a legitimate aim. Elaborating on this point, the Guiding Principles of Freedom of Association of the OSCE's Office for Democratic Institutions and Human Rights states that the necessity requirement does not have "the flexibility of terms such as 'useful' or 'convenient': instead, the term means that there must be a 'pressing social need' for the interference."[29]

A 2013 UNSR report notes that governments frequently justify constraints with a rhetorically appealing term such as "sovereignty," "counterterrorism," or "accountability and transparency," which upon inspection proves to be merely "a pretext to constrain dissenting views or independent civil society" in violation of international law. With regard to counterterrorism efforts, the report states, "In order to meet the proportionality and necessity test, restrictive measures must be the least intrusive means to achieve the desired objective and be limited to the associations falling within the clearly identified aspects characterizing terrorism only. They must not target all civil society associations." With regard to the aid-effectiveness justification, the report concludes that "deliberate misinterpretations by Governments of ownership or harmonization principles to require associations to align themselves with Governments' priorities contradict one of the most important aspects of freedom of association, namely that individuals can freely associate for any legal purpose."[30] But as one civil society representative in China told the *Washington Post,* "The target is not the money, it is the NGOs themselves. The government wants to control NGOs by controlling their money."[31]

Several recent studies examining constraints on international funding and the political environments in which they arise support the UNSR's assertions. One study found that in most countries where political opposition is unhindered and voting is conducted in a "free and fair" manner, international funding restrictions generally are not imposed on CSOs. By contrast, in countries where election manipulation takes place, governments tend to restrict CSO access to foreign support, fearing that well-funded CSOs could contribute to their defeat at the polls.[32] In other words, vulnerable regimes hoping to cling to power sometimes restrict international funding in order to weaken the opposition.

After the fall of the Berlin Wall, many countries saw the importance of defending civil society. Today, however, many countries are defunding civil society. Using all sorts of pretexts, governments that feel threatened by such organizations impose restrictions on them. These governments are able to do so in part because the cornerstone concepts of civil society are still being developed, debated, and—at times—violently contested. The outcome of this debate will shape the future of civil society for decades to come.

Notes

The author expresses his appreciation to Brittany Grabel for her research support.

1. Lester Salamon, "The Rise of the Nonprofit Sector," *Foreign Affairs* 74 (July–August 1994), *www.foreignaffairs.com/articles/50105/lester-m-salamon/the-rise-of-the-nonprofit-sector*.

2. George W. Bush, "President Freezes Terrorists' Assets," Remarks on Executive Order, U.S. Department of State Archive, 24 September 2001, *http://2001-2009.state.gov/s/ct/rls/rm/2001/5041.htm*.

3. Nick Paton Walsh, "Europe's 'Last Dictator' Defies Calls for Change," *Guardian*, 5 May 2005, *www.theguardian.com/world/2005/may/06/russia.nickpatonwalsh*.

4. Darin Christensen and Jeremy M. Weinstein, "Defunding Dissent: Restrictions on Aid to NGOs," *Journal of Democracy* 24 (April 2013): 83.

5. President of Russia, remarks at "Meeting of Council for Civil Society and Human Rights," 12 November 2012, *http://eng.kremlin.ru/news/4613*.

6. Zoltan Simon, "Orban Says He Seeks to End Liberal Democracy in Hungary," *Bloomberg News*, 28 July 2014, *www.bloomberg.com/news/2014-07-28/orban-says-he-seeks-to-end-liberal-democracy-in-hungary.html*.

7. Agence France Press, "Egypt Says Working to End NGO Row: McCain," AlterNet, *www.alternet.org/rss/breaking_news/804643/ egypt_says_working_to_end_ngo_row%3A_mccain.*

8. Josh Levs and Saad Abedine, "Egypt Sentences American NGO Workers to Jail," CNN, 4 June 2013, *www.cnn.com/2013/06/04/world/africa/egypt-ngos/ index.html.*

9. Irfan Haider, "'Save the Children' Ordered to Leave Pakistan: Officials," *DAWN,* 12 June 2015, *www.dawn.com/news/1187601.*

10. "Pakistan Orders Save the Children to Leave Country," BBC, June 12, 2015, *www.bbc.com/news/world-asia-33105128.*

11. "Russian Parliament Gives First Approval to NGO Bill," BBC, 6 July 2012, *www.bbc.com/news/world-europe-18732949.*

12. Simon Denyer, "China Taking the Putin Approach to Democracy," *Washington Post,* 1 October 2014, A7.

13. "Statement by Ethiopia on Behalf of the African Group at the 25th Session of the Human Rights Council on the Panel Discussion on the Importance of the Promotion and Protection of Civil Society Space," 11 March 2014; "Joint Statement: India on Behalf of Like-Minded Countries," 11 March 2014; and Explanatory Note, Law of the Kyrgyz Republic on Amendments to Some Legislative Acts of the Kyrgyz Republic (on file with the author).

14. See the Aid Effectiveness Agenda of the Paris Declaration (2005), the Accra Agenda for Action (2008), and the Busan Partnership for Effective Development Co-operation (2011).

15. Government of Nepal, Ministry of Finance, "Development Cooperation Policy, 2014," unofficial translation, *www.mof.gov.np/uploads/document/file/ DCP_English_20140707120230_20140721083326.pdf.*

16. Government of Sri Lanka, Ministry of Finance and Planning, "Notice to all Government Officials, Civil Society Organizations, and General Public," 15 July 2014, published in several news sources, including *Colombo Telegraph, www.colombotelegraph.com/wp-content/uploads/2014/07/Be-alert-Notice-by- ERD-Final-English.pdf;* see also "No Foreign Funds Without Approval: Ministry," *Daily Mirror* (Colombo), 22 July 2014, *www.dailymirror.lk/50038/tech.*

17. "Clustered ID with the WG on HR and Transnational Corporations and the SR on The Rights to Freedom of Assembly and Association: Intervention delivered by the Permanent Delegation of Egypt," 30 May 2013.

18. Justus Wanga, "NGOs Lose Licences over Terrorism Claim," *Daily Nation,* 27 May 27, 2015, *www.nation.co.ke/news/NGOs-lose-licences- over-terrorism-claim/-/1056/2731888/-/3g9vonz/-/index.html;* Simon Denyer, "NGOs in China Fear Clampdown as Xi Jinping Plans New Security Controls," *Guardian,* 30 March 2015, *www.theguardian.com/world/2015/mar/30/ngos- china-fear-security-clampdown;* Charity and Security Network, "How the FATF Is Used to Justify Laws That Harm Civil Society, Freedom of Association and Expression," Charity and Security Network, 16 May 2013.

19. Maina Kiai, "Report of the Special Rapporteur on the Rights to Freedom of Peaceful Assembly and of Association," UN Doc. A/HRC/23/39, 24 April 2013, para. 8, *http://freeassembly.net/wp-content/uploads/2013/04/A. HRC_.23.39_EN-funding-report-April-2013.pdf*; UN General Assembly, "Declaration on the Right and Responsibility of Individuals, Groups and Organs of Society to Promote and Protect Universally Recognized Human Rights and Fundamental Freedoms," UN Res. 53/144, Article 13, *www.un.org/Docs/asp/ ws.asp?m=A/RES/53/144*; and "Declaration on Human Rights Defenders," UN OHCHR, *www.ohchr.org/EN/Issues/SRHRDefenders/Pages/Declaration.aspx*.

20. Council of Europe, "Recommendation CM/Rec (2007)145 of the Committee of Ministers to Member States on the Legal Status of Non-Governmental Organisations in Europe," adopted 10 October 2007, Article 50, *https://wcd. coe.int/ViewDoc.jsp?id=1194609*; and Inter-American Commission on Human Rights, *Report on the Situation of Human Rights Defenders in the Americas*, 7 March 2006, Recommendation 19, *www.icnl.org/research/resources/assembly/ oas-human-rights-report.pdf*.

21. U.S.-Kazakh Bilateral Investment Treaty, Article 1(b); U.S.-Kyrgyz Bilateral Investment Treaty, Article 1(b). See also Luke Eric Peterson and Nick Gallus, "International Investment Treaty Protection of Not-for-Profit Organizations," *International Journal of Not-for-Profit Law* 10 (December 2007), *www. icnl.org/research/journal/vol10iss1/art_1.htm*. For letters of transmittal, see White House to Senate, "Kazakhstan Bilateral Investment Treaty," 7 September 1993, *www.state.gov/documents/organization/43566.pdf* and White House to Senate, "Kyrgyzstan Bilateral Investment Treaty," 7 September 1993, *www.state. gov/documents/organization/43567.pdf*.

22. Council of Europe, Convention for the Protection of Human Rights and Fundamental Freedoms as Amended by Protocols No. 11 and No. 14, Rome, 4 November 1950, Article 11, *http://conventions.coe.int/Treaty/en/Treaties/ Html/005.htm*; and UN High Commissioner for Human Rights, International Covenant on Civil and Political Rights (ICCPR), adopted and opened for signature, ratification and accession by General Assembly resolution 2200A (XXI) of 16 December 1966, entry into force 23 March 1976, Article 22, *www.ohchr.org/ en/professionalinterest/pages/ccpr.aspx*.

23. UN Special Rapporteur on the Situation of Human Rights Defenders, "Commentary to the Declaration on the Right and Responsibility of Individuals, Groups and Organs of Society to Promote and Protect Universally Recognized Human Rights and Fundamental Freedoms," July 2011, 44, *www.ohchr.org/ Documents/Issues/Defenders/CommentarytoDeclarationondefendersJuly2011.pdf*.

24. Maina Kiai, "Report of the Special Rapporteur on the Rights to Freedom of Peaceful Assembly and of Association," UN Doc. A/HRC/20/27, 21 May 2012, para. 16, *http://freeassembly.net/wp-content/uploads/2013/10/A-HRC-20-27_en-annual-report-May-2012.pdf*.

25. Kiai, "Report of the Special Rapporteur," 24 April 2013, para. 30.

26. See UN Economic and Social Council, UN Sub-Commission on Prevention of Discrimination and Protection of Minorities, Siracusa Principles on the Limitation and Derogation of Provisions in the International Covenant on Civil and Political Rights, Annex, UN Doc. E/CN.4/1985/4 (1984)], *http://www1.umn.edu/humanrts/instree/siracusaprinciples.html.*

27. Kiai, "Report of the Special Rapporteur," 24 April 2013, para. 27.

28. Maina Kiai, "Report of the Special Rapporteur," 21 May 2012, para. 17 and para. 84(a).

29. OSCE/Office for Democratic Institutions and Human Rights (ODIHR), *Key Guiding Principles of Freedom of Association with an Emphasis on Non-Governmental Organizations*, para. 5

30. Kiai, "Report of the Special Rapporteur," 24 April 2013, para. 23 and para. 41.

31. Simon Denyer, "China Taking the Putin Approach to Democracy," *Washington Post,* 1 October 2014, A7.

32. Christensen and Weinstein, "Defunding Dissent," 81.

CHAPTER ELEVEN

The Kremlin's Information War

PETER POMERANTSEV

"IF STALIN WAS 80 percent violence and 20 percent propaganda," Russian journalism professor Igor Yakovenko once told me, "then Putin is 80 percent propaganda and 20 percent violence." Media are crucial to Vladimir Putin's rule. When he was first appointed prime minister in the late 1990s, Putin was considered by many to be a bland nobody with few political prospects. But after a war in Chechnya and a massive TV-makeover that recast him as a strong military leader, Putin managed to win the 2000 presidential election and later cement his hold on power. One of his first moves after becoming president was to capture television and put it under his direct control. Russia's media moguls—both those who had supported Putin's rise and those who had opposed him—were arrested or forced into exile.

Russian television had begun spinning political pseudorealities as early as 1996, when oligarchs such as Vladimir Gusinsky and Boris Berezovsky helped to keep President Boris Yeltsin in power by broadcasting claims that the candidates running against him were part of a fascist-communist menace. Yet for most of the 1990s, Russia's oligarchs opposed one another, creating a sort of perverse system of checks and balances among the various campaigns of disinformation. With power centralized under Putin, however, the Kremlin could run both television and politics like one vast scripted reality show.

At the center of the show was the president himself: Putin bare-chested, riding on a horse; Putin stroking tigers; Putin in leather, riding a Harley. The staged images of Putin as B-movie hunk were used to cultivate his image as superhero-czar and to set him above the fray of real politics (a regular set piece on Russian news has Putin scolding government ministers and regional governors for failing the country). From 1999 to 2011, the man running this show was Vladislav Surkov. Officially the deputy head of the presidential administration, Surkov was actually in charge of everything from the arts to religion to political parties and civil society. Every Friday, Surkov met with the heads of the major news channels to tell them what the week's main stories should be and which political figures would be allowed on television.

This system has only become more stringent since the start of the war with Ukraine in 2014. According to "Messages of Russian TV: Monitoring Report 2015," an EU-funded study of Russian news channels conducted by NGOs from seven countries, the president and government receive mainly positive or neutral coverage from Kremlin-controlled channels, while opposition members are covered only rarely and usually negatively. The study reports that in March 2015 almost 32 percent of Channel One's coverage was devoted to Ukraine, compared to just 12.7 percent devoted to domestic politics, 4 percent to the economy, and 1.3 percent to social issues.[1]

Television news has thus become grand theater, juxtaposing the "chaos in Ukraine" with Putin-guaranteed stability in Russia. Russian news has featured fake television items that were later exposed by journalists—for example, staged interviews with Russian "victims" (who were really actors) of alleged atrocities by Ukrainian "fascists,"[2] and an invented tale about a child being crucified by Ukrainian forces.[3] A leading Russia media-studies professor told a European Endowment for Democracy project funded by the Dutch and Latvian governments that "the Kremlin has blurred the line between fact and fiction" with such efforts, "making news and current affairs [seem] like an engaging, sensationalist drama."

Surkov and his successors have run domestic politics much as they have television, turning the political process into pure spectacle. Surkov even had direct telephone lines to "opposition" politicians, telling them what to say and where and when to say it—always with the goal of making Putin look better by contrast. The Russian parliament thus became a place of choreographed speechmaking: "The Duma is not a place for debate," Duma speaker Boris Gryzlov declared in 2003. Surkov likewise controlled civil society, creating tame NGOs, cultivating liberal elites, and even sponsoring radical modern-art festivals, while simultaneously fostering nationalist youth movements such as Nashi that beat up modern-art curators and labeled liberals as traitors. This strategy gave the Kremlin ownership of all forms of discourse, allowing it to spin them to its own advantage and ultimately to render them toothless and absurd.

Under Surkov's successor, Vyaceshlav Volodin, the discourse has been ratcheted up: Liberals are now described as a dangerous "fifth column," and the imperialist far right has been mobilized as a violent avant-garde. But the Kremlin still guides all the narratives, allowing it to frame any argument in the way that best suits its needs at any given time, for any given situation. Thus political talk shows regularly feature nationalists attacking Kremlin-sanctioned liberals. This is what Andrew Wilson calls the "highly developed industry of political manipulation," which in the post-Soviet world is commonly known as "political technology."[4]

Are Russians buying the Kremlin's narrative? This might be the wrong question. As Václav Havel wrote in "The Power of the Powerless," the Soviet bloc was not sustained by fervent belief in the system, but by acquiescence in a common discourse that coopted the population—a case of propaganda signaling what was "correct" behavior rather than achieving ideological indoctrination. Likewise, the point of Putin's "managed democracy" is not to convince anyone that Russian democracy is real, but to send a message to the population about how they should behave. Russia watchers are often puzzled by a seeming contradiction: Why does Putin, who is extremely popular, rig elections, when he would most likely win them anyway? Would he not gain more credibility by staging a closely fought runoff, "proving" that he was democratically elected? As Ivan Krastev and Stephen Holmes explain, these questions misunderstand the role of presidential elections in Russia.[5] Their purpose is to burnish the image of Putin as untouchable, an image that would only be tarnished by serious competition.

The Kremlin wants to show that it has total control over the script. This principle is also behind the regime's use of show trials. The trials of independent-minded oligarch Mikhail Khodorkovsky and opposition leader Alexei Navalny both were characterized by absurdity—Khodorkovsky was accused of having stolen oil from himself, and Navalny allegedly took part in corrupt business deals from which he made no profit. In both cases, the sentencing judge used the testimony of *defense* witnesses as proof of guilt. But this absurdity is the point—the Kremlin can say "black is white" and "white is black," and no one can contradict it.

The underlying goal of the Kremlin's propaganda is to engender cynicism in the population. Cynicism is useful to the state: When people stop trusting any institutions or having any firmly held values, they can easily accept a conspiratorial vision of the world. The state-television channels actively encourage such a vision—for example, by finding the hidden hand of the CIA behind all the world's prodemocracy movements. In showing that democracy is so easily manipulated, that everyone and everything is for sale, the Kremlin is dashing people's hopes for the possibility of an alternative politics while simultaneously insisting that the West is just as corrupt as Russia.

The Kremlin peddles conspiracy theories to get this point across. Particularly noteworthy in this regard is RTR's weekly news show *Vesti Nedeli,* hosted by Dmitry Kiselev, head of the new Rossiya Sevodnya (Russia Today) news agency.[6] On the show, Kiselev offers a mash-up of truths assembled and interpreted in ways that rewrite reality: For example, a Swedish children's TV show about sex education must be a sign that Europe is mired in sexual perversion; and the fact that Navalny spent time at Yale must mean that he is working for the United States. Similarly, the online videos "Why America Needs a Big War in Europe" and "What Awaits Russia If Putin Puts Troops in Ukraine" purportedly reveal baroque conspiracies in which the Russian nationalists who are agitating for war in Ukraine turn out to be working for the West, which wants Russia to be pulled into war in the Donbas.[7] This is not classic "agitational propaganda"; rather, it aims at producing apathy, distrust, and a vague sense of paranoia.

A final key element in the regime's continued control is corruption, which helps to keep the current vertical governing structure intact. By doling out financial favors and preferential treatment, the president keeps his cronies and other oligarchs in line. Preparations for the Sochi Olympics, which straddled the presidencies of Dmitri Medvedev and Putin, provide a good example. While Medvedev was president, "his" oligarchs were granted the top positions and won the most lucrative contracts. When Putin became president again in 2012, Medvedev's people were pushed out and Putin's oligarchs reclaimed the favors and top spots.

Courting the Left and the Right

The Kremlin uses this mix of political technology, fluid ideology, and corruption not only domestically but also in managing foreign relations. During the Cold War, the Kremlin cultivated ties mainly with ideologically similar leftist groups. Today, the Kremlin forges alliances with and funds groups on both the left and the right: European right-wing nationalists are seduced by Russia's anti-EU message; Europe's far left is enticed by the prospect of fighting U.S. hegemony; and U.S. religious conservatives are attracted to the Kremlin's stance against homosexuality. The Kremlin's fluid use of ideology allows it to ally with an array of actors and to promote a range of principles that foster divisions within the West.

The Kremlin retains deep institutional ties to former and current communist parties throughout Eastern Europe. Ukraine even banned its communist party, believing it to be a proxy for the Kremlin. The Left party (Die Linke) in Germany also has been outspoken in its defense of Russian positions. According to NATO, Russia has also managed to manipulate green movements by funding European ecological groups whose antifracking agendas coincide with the Kremlin's desire to keep Europe dependent on Russian gas.[8] Yet at home, the Kremlin is clamping down on anticapitalist leftist groups and arresting ecological activists.

On the right, the Kremlin has built alliances with radical social conservatives and anti-EU nationalists. Right-wing political figures and groups on both sides of the Atlantic—from U.S. conservative columnist Patrick Buchanan to French right-nationalist leader Marine Le Pen (whose party has received funds from Moscow[9]), to Britain's anti-EU politician Nigel Farage, to Hungary's anti-Semitic Jobbik party, to the U.S.-based anti-LGBT coalition World Congress of Families—have proclaimed their admiration for Putin, in turn receiving plenty of airtime on Russian-controlled airwaves.[10] Far-right activists, white supremacists, neo-Nazis, and anti-Semites from across Europe and the United States have appeared with Kremlin-connected ideologues at conferences in Europe, while Kremlin advisors have presented lectures to European and U.S. far-right parties in Yalta.[11]

In addition to ideological appeals, the Kremlin also wields financial incentives to draw in allies. For example, Jörg Haider, the now-deceased leader of the far-right Freedom Party of Austria, once accepted €900,000 in return for helping Russian businessmen to secure their residency permits. According to Anton Shekhovtsov, "Putin's Russia cooperates with European far right parties partly because the latter help Russian political and business elites worm into the West economically, politically and socially, and . . . for them, the far right's racism and ultra-conservatism are less important [than its] corruptibility."[12]

Shekhovtsov also notes that the financial transactions do not necessarily need to be direct bribes. Businesspeople associated with far-right movements can also be given preferential treatment when dealing in Russia in return for their political support. For example, one of the first European businessmen to do business in Crimea after its annexation by Russia was Frenchman Philippe de Villiers, leader of the Euroskeptic party Movement for France, who will build theme parks in Moscow and Crimea.[13] According to Shekhovtsov, Putin's cooperation with Europe's far right is driven only by the desire to achieve his economic and political aims, not by ideological kinship.[14]

Despite its relative weakness, the Kremlin has learned the art of what Nicu Popescu and Mark Leonard call "asymmetric interdependence"—advancing Russia's interests by making other states reliant on its money, markets, and trade. Energy is often the Kremlin's trump card. A Swedish Defense Agency study found that, between 1992 and 2006, Russia cut off energy to countries in Central and Eastern Europe 55 times. Officially, Russia claimed these cutoffs were caused by technical problems. Yet they almost always happened when there was an election that Russia wanted to influence or an energy deal that it wanted to promote.[15]

Controlling the Message

Russia's international television broadcaster, RT, provides an international forum for uniting the various groups that the Kremlin works with. According to its own statistics, the channel now reaches 600 million people globally and 3 million hotel rooms across the world. It boasts of having a billion hits online, making it one of YouTube's most popular news channels. It has an enormous budget (believed to be more than US$300 million), and broadcasts in Arabic, English, German, and Spanish. Although RT's actual viewership is far lower than what it claims and its billion hits are not necessarily for political programs,[16] the channel's programming is worth examining for what it reveals about the Kremlin's overall thinking.

Programming about Russia makes up only a small part of RT's output. Its schedule focuses on what it calls "other" or "unreported" news, which is the network's special niche. WikiLeaks founder Julian Assange has had a show on RT, as has left-wing Scottish politician George Galloway. Leftist U.S. political theorist and linguist Noam Chomsky is a frequent guest. The channel devotes generous attention to 9/11 conspiracy theories, and it won an Emmy for its reporting on the Occupy Movement in the United States. RT regularly features figures from the right, such as UKIP's Nigel Farage. Some of RT's right-wing "experts" have ties to extremist or fringe groups that would make them *personae non gratae* on other channels. For example, Holocaust denier Ryan Dawson has appeared on RT as a "human-rights activist," and neo-Nazi Manuel Ochsenreiter as a "Middle East analyst."[17] Nevertheless, RT is not uniformly "antihegemonic." It also welcomes establishment figures such as former CNN host Larry King, who at one time had a show on RT and was widely featured in its advertisements.

Viewers that first come to RT for its anti-Western slant are then fed other programming that strays beyond even the wildest "opinion" television. Recently, Spanish-language RT featured a report that considered whether the United States engineered the Ebola outbreak[18]—a modern echo of 1980s Soviet *dezinformatsiya* about the CIA being behind the AIDS epidemic. RT contributors have called Ukraine's government a right-wing junta and claimed that Ukrainian nationalists are threatening Jews.

The channel edited an interview with Misha Kapustin, the rabbi of Simferopol in Crimea, in a way that gave the impression that he was leaving Crimea because of a wave of anti-Semitism from Ukrainian nationalists. In fact, Kapustin has condemned Russia's actions in the region, encourages Western sanctions against Russia, and told the *Times of Israel* that he was actually leaving Crimea because of Russian aggression. "There is no imminent danger to Jews in Crimea," the heads of the Ukrainian Jewish Committee said in a public statement; "the situation is being manipulated by the Russian government to make the world believe they are protecting us."[19] It is not just RT that spreads such disinformation. As Adrian Chen reported in the *New York Times,* the Kremlin uses "troll farms" and bots to create and spread fake stories online—for example, that there were Ebola outbreaks in the United States and ISIS attacks on U.S. towns.[20]

In and of themselves, such disinformation campaigns may seem farcical.

Indeed, if their aim is to build classic soft power, which is all about attractiveness and trust, then they are surely counterproductive (Putin's approval rating has been falling in Western countries since the conflict in Ukraine began). But if their aim is less to convince and persuade and more to muddle the information space and sow doubt and confusion, then perhaps these efforts are succeeding in terms of Russia's vision of "information-psychological" warfare.

According to retired Rear Admiral Vladimir Pirumov, former head of the Directorate for Electronic Warfare of Russia's Main Naval Staff, information war means "securing national policy objectives both in peacetime and in wartime through means and techniques of influencing the information resources of the opposing side." The enemy's information systems are not the only targets of information warfare; it also aims to influence the psyches of enemy populations through "disinformation (deception), manipulation (situational or societal), propaganda (conversion, separation, demoralization, desertion, captivity), lobbying, crisis control and blackmail."[21]

Russia's Disinformation Campaigns

The 2011 edition of the "Information-Psychological War Operations" handbook instructs intelligence officer trainees to act like "invisible radiation," where "the population doesn't even feel it is being acted upon." Latvian scholar Janis Berzins, writing on the future of Russian warfare, foresees a move from "direct clashes to contactless war," from "war in the physical environment to a war in the human consciousness and in cyberspace." The weapons in this contactless, perpetual war might be TV channels, energy companies, banks, Internet trolls, Russian expatriate groups that can incite unrest abroad—in other words, a "combination of political, economic, information, technological, and ecological campaigns."[22]

For an example of how this might work, we can look at what happened in Estonia in 2007. Ethnic Russians—the vast majority of whom are descendants of people forcibly moved there by Stalin to break Estonian nationhood—account for roughly 25 percent of Estonia's population. After the collapse of the Soviet Union, Estonia enacted a law requiring residents who arrived after 1946 and their descendants to pass Estonian-language tests to gain full citizenship. The ethnic Russian population did not see themselves as colonizers, however, and resented this requirement. They watch Russian TV, which broadcasts the official Russian line that Estonia had "voluntarily" given up its independence in 1944.

Every year in Tallinn, Russian nationalists and war veterans would meet at the statue of the Bronze Soldier, commemorating the Soviet victory in World War II. They would sing Soviet songs and drape the statue in Soviet flags. Some Estonians, however, considered the statue to be a symbol of Soviet occupation and took offense. Estonian nationalists began to organize countermarches, and one writer threatened to blow the statue up. In March 2007, the Estonian parliament voted to move the statue to a military cemetery.

Russian media and politicians went into overdrive. "Estonian leaders collaborate with fascism!" exclaimed the mayor of Moscow. "The removal of the statue is a fascist orgy," argued the Russian Communist Party. "The situation is despicable," claimed Russia's foreign minister. Russian media nicknamed the country "eSStonia," signaling that the country was dominated by Nazi sympathizers, and ethnic Russians camped out to protect the Bronze Soldier.

On the night of April 26, ethnic-Russian crowds started throwing Molotov cocktails at police. Riots broke out, there was mass looting, and one man died. Russian media claimed that he was killed by police (he was not). They also spread rumors that some Russians had been beaten to death at the ferry port, while others were tortured and fed psychotropic substances during interrogation. On April 27, Estonian government, newspaper, and bank employees arrived at work to find their computer systems down as a result of the largest cyberattack in history. Estonia was disabled.

Today, many Estonians are convinced that the media coverage, rioting, and cyberattacks were coordinated from Moscow, although this cannot be proven. "Patriotic hackers" with links to Kremlin youth groups and Russian MPs took credit for the attacks, but claimed to be working independently. Ethnic-Russian NGOs in Estonia claimed to have planned the protests. When I interviewed Estonian president Toomas Ilves last year, he said, "Sometimes we wonder whether the point of the attacks [was] to make us sound paranoid and unreliable to our NATO allies, and thus undermine trust in the alliance."

The aims of such information operations are often opaque, as they are designed to produce second- and third-order effects. This strategy has kept the Estonians forever guessing at the Kremlin's real intentions: "When Russian politicians make threats about being able to conquer Estonia, does that mean they would ever invade?" asks President Ilves's former security advisor Iivi Masso. "Are they just trying to demoralize us," he wonders, "or do they want Western journalists to quote them, which will send a signal to the markets that we're unsafe," causing investments to plummet?

It is not just in Russia's near abroad, or even just in Europe, that Russia's information war is being waged. In October 2014, Putin and Argentina's President Cristina Fernández de Kirchner inked a deal to have RT news broadcast in Spanish on Argentine television. "Our peoples can communicate without any intermediaries," Kirchner said in a joint video conference with Putin, claiming that national media (that is, the media critical of her government) and international media do not show the *true* Argentina or *true* Russia. Putin echoed this statement, noting that "the rapid progress of electronic media has made news reporting enormously important and turned it into a formidable weapon that enables public opinion manipulations."[23] RT's partnerships are not limited to Latin America. For example, the channel has also been pooling stories with Syrian state television, including a report of Syrian rebels gassing themselves in order to fake a chemical attack by President Bashar al-Assad's forces.

It is hard to say how effective the Kremlin's approach is—or indeed even what its goals are. But another reason that the Kremlin's thinking deserves attention and analysis is the fact that other neoauthoritarian regimes are adopting similar approaches. China's use of the media to control its citizens, for example, has become increasingly supple. And just as the Kremlin's use of ideology is fluid, so too is that of the ruling Chinese "Communist" Party (CCP). Today's CCP manages to champion both Confucius and communism, and to support the Shanghai stock market while praising Maoist propaganda songs. Moreover, China's propaganda, like Russia's, is as much about signaling as it is indoctrination.[24] As a U.S. government report concludes, China's information tactics are "guided . . . by the belief that whose story wins is more important than whose army wins."[25]

The Kremlin's current strategy for keeping control—manipulating all facets of the political process, adopting whatever ideological stance is expedient for a given situation, and buying loyalty with money and favors—has created a cynical citizenry, shaped by propaganda and conspiracy theories, that is bereft of hope. It also leaves Russia's international adversaries and allies alike uncertain of what to expect. Increasingly, illiberal regimes across the world are adopting similar strategies and uniting to create global networks of pseudorealities. The world's liberal democracies must rise to the challenge by finding ways to counter these false narratives with true ones.

Notes

1. Memo 98 et al., "Messages of Russian TV: Monitoring Report 2015" (2015), *http://eap-csf.eu/assets/files/Monitoring%20report_Russian%20TV.pdf.*

2. Paul Gregory, "Russian TV Propagandists Caught Red-Handed: Same Guy, Three Different People (Spy, Bystander, Heroic Surgeon)," *Forbes*, 12 April 2014; Lucy Crossley, "The 'Aggrieved Housewife,' the 'Soldier's Mother' and the 'Kiev Resident': Did Russian Television 'Use Actress to Portray Five Different Women' As It Reported Normal Ukrainians Backed Kremlin," *Daily Mail*, 5 March 2014.

3. "Refugee from Slovyansk Remembers How the Young Son and Wife of a Rebel Were Executed Before Her Eyes" (in Russian), Channel 1, 12 July 2014, *www.1tv.ru/news/other/262978.*

4. Andrew Wilson, "'Political Technology': Why Is It Alive and Flourishing in the Former USSR?" *OpenDemocracy,* 17 June 2011, *www.opendemocracy.net/od-russia/andrew-wilson/political-technology-why-is-it-alive-and-flourishing-in-former-ussr.*

5. Ivan Krastev and Stephen Holmes, "An Autopsy of Managed Democracy," *Journal of Democracy* 23 (July 2012): 33–45.

6. Joshua Yaffa, "Dmitry Kiselev Is Redefining the Art of Russian Propaganda," *New Republic,* 1 July 2014, *www.newrepublic.com/article/118438/dmitry-kiselev-putins-favorite-tv-host-russias-top-propogandist.*

7. See *www.youtube.com/watch?v=ifoeXbIprnw* and *www.youtube.com/watch?v=9cQ2ddv4qQU,* respectively.

8. Sam Jones, Guy Chazan, and Christian Oliver, "Nato Claims Moscow Funding Anti-Fracking Groups," *Financial Times,* 19 June 2014.

9. See John Lichfield, "€40m of Russian Cash Will Allow Marine Le Pen's Front National to Take Advantage of Rivals' Woes in Upcoming Regional and Presidential Elections," *Independent* (London), 27 November 2014, *www.independent.co.uk/news/world/europe/40m-of-russian-cash-will-allow-marine-le-pens-front-national-to-take-advantage-of-rivals-woes-in-upcoming-regional-and-presidential-elections-9888509.html.*

10. For more on the European right, see Dalibor Rohac, "Europe's Neo-

reaction Is Scarier Than You Think," 6 August 2014, The Umlaut blog, *http://theumlaut.com/2014/08/06/europes-neoreaction-is-scarier-than-you-think/?utm_content=bufferebof7&utm_medium=social&utm_source=twitter.com&utm_campaign=buffer.*

11. Tom Porter, "Putin Nationalist to Appear with US White Supremacists at Far-Right Conference," 31 August 2014, *www.ibtimes.co.uk/putin-follower-appear-us-white-supremacists-far-right-conference-1463350*; and Robert Beckhusen, "As Russia Invades Ukraine, the Kremlin's Far Right Allies Meet in Yalta," 31 August 2014, *https://medium.com/war-is-boring/as-russia-invades-ukraine-the-kremlins-far-right-allies-meet-in-yalta-94a30929c35.*

12. Anton Shekhovtsov, "Freedom Party of Austria," personal blog, 20 June 2014, *http://anton-shekhovtsov.blogspot.co.uk/2014/06/freedom-party-of-austria-far-right.html.*

13. "French Politician to Build Historic Amusement Park in Crimea," *Moscow Times,* 15 August 2015, *www.themoscowtimes.com/article/505178.html*

14. Anton Shekhovtsov, "The Kremlin's Marriage of Convenience with the European Far Right," *OpenDemocracy,* 28 April 2014, *www.opendemocracy.net/od-russia/anton-shekhovtsov/kremlin%E2%80%99s-marriage-of-convenience-with-european-far-right.*

15. Mark Leonard and Nicu Popescu, "A Power Audit of EU-Russia Relations," EFCR Policy Paper, 7 November 2007.

16. See Robert Orttung, Elizabeth Nelson, and Anthony Livshen, "How Russia Today Is Using YouTube," *Washington Post,* Monkey Cage blog, 23 March 2015, *www.washingtonpost.com/blogs/monkey-cage/wp/2015/03/23/how-russia-today-is-using-youtube.*

17. Adam Holland, "Ryan Dawson, RT's 'Human Rights Activist,' A Holocaust Denier Who's Friends With Hate Criminals," *Interpreter,* 10 June 2014, *www.interpretermag.com/ryan-dawson-rts-human-rights-activist-a-holocaust-denier-whos-friends-with-hate-criminals*; and Holland, "*RT's Manuel Ochsenreiter*: The Neo-Nazi Representing Germany on Russian TV News," *Interpreter,* 21 March 2014, *www.interpretermag.com/rts-manuel-ochsenreiter.*

18. Karen Méndez, "Centro de investigación biológica de EE.UU. Fort Detrick, ¿detrás del brote de ébola?" RT, 7 August 2014, *http://actualidad.rt.com/actualidad/view/136298-centro-investigacion-biologica-eeuu-fort-detrick-brote-ebola.*

19. "Junta Government in Kiev Trigger for Mine That Will Explode Sooner or Later," RT OpEdge, 26 April 2014, *http://rt.com/op-edge/155112-washington-policy-europe-ukraine*; "Pushed to Leave," RT, 15 March 2014, *http://rt.com/news/jews-jewish-ukraine-nationalist-106/*; Victor Davidoff, "Putin's Fabricated Anti-Semitism in Ukraine," *Moscow Times,* 13 April 2014, *www.themoscowtimes.com/opinion/article/putin-s-fabricated-anti-semitism-in-ukraine/497950.html*; Amanda Borschel-Dan, "Crimea's Sole Rabbi Advises Jews 'Not to Become Targets,'" *Times of Israel,* 2 March 2014, *www.timesofisrael.com/crimeas-sole-rabbi-advises-jews-not-to-become-targets*; and

Daniel K. Eisenbud, "Ukrainian Jewish Committee: Russian Claims of Anti-Semitism in Crimea Are Lies, Propaganda," *Jerusalem Post,* 3 October 2014, *www.jpost.com/International/Ukrainian-Jewish-Committee-Russian-claims-of-anti-Semitism-in-Crimea-are-lies-propaganda-344828*

20. Adrian Chen, "The Agency," *New York Times,* 2 June 2015, *www.nytimes.com/2015/06/07/magazine/the-agency.html.*

21. V.S. Pirumov, *Informatsionnoe Protivoborstvo* (Moscow, 2010), quoted in Timothy L. Thomas, *Recasting the Red Star* (Fort Leavenworth, Kan.: FMSO, 2011), 158.

22. Janis Berzinš, "The New Generation of Russian Warfare," *Aspen Review* (Central Europe), no. 3 (2014): 63–67.

23. "Russia Today TV Channel Starts Broadcasting in Argentina: Vladimir Putin and President of the Argentine Republic Cristina Fernandez de Kirchner Launched Russia Today TV Channel's Spanish-Language Broadcasts on Argentina's National Television via TV Linkup," transcript, 9 October 2014, *http://en.kremlin.ru/events/president/transcripts/46762.*

24. For more on China's propaganda efforts, see Anne-Marie Brady's essay "China's Foreign Propaganda Machine" in this volume.

25. *China: The Three Warfares,* prepared by Stefan Halper for Andy Marshall, Office of the Secretary of Defense, Washington, D.C., May 2013, 31.

CHAPTER TWELVE

China's Foreign Propaganda Machine

ANNE-MARIE BRADY

T HE PEOPLE'S REPUBLIC OF CHINA (PRC) has long suffered from a poor international image and weak "soft power." The country's negative image has hindered international acceptance of its rise as a global great power. Because the ruling Chinese Communist Party (CCP) wants China to "gain face" (*yao mianzi*) in the international arena, it has in recent years invested heavily in boosting the country's international approval rating.

The CCP believes that the outside world has a distorted view of contemporary China due to its misrepresentation in Western media. Liu Qibao, head of the CCP's Central Propaganda Department, argued in a lengthy May 2014 article in *Guangming Daily,* "There are always some people who wear colored glasses to see China. They view the country through the lenses of 'China threat theory,' 'resource plundering theory,' or 'China collapse theory.'"[1] Indeed, a 2015 Gallup poll found that 50 percent of U.S. respondents had a "very" or "mostly" unfavorable view of China. In the same survey, two-fifths agreed that China's economic power posed a critical threat. This is not a new development. For most of Gallup's forty years of polling, U.S. respondents have expressed a negative view of China.[2]

The CCP has long regarded persuasion and information management as top government priorities. It devotes considerable resources to them, and it has an extensive bureaucracy in place to carry out propaganda initiatives. (In CCP usage, the word "propaganda" or *xuanchuan* is not negative.) Traditional media and publishing are only one aspect of foreign-propaganda work. China has learned from Western countries also to incorporate public diplomacy, cultural diplomacy, electronic games, and social media into public-opinion management.

The CCP Central Committee Foreign Propaganda Group, whose members are CCP senior cadres and leaders of the country's foreign-aimed media outlets, sets China's foreign-propaganda agenda. The CCP Central Office of Foreign Propaganda (OFP), more commonly known as the State Council Information Office (SCIO), oversees the country's external propaganda, guiding the foreign-propaganda activities of the multiple government offices whose portfolios touch on foreign matters. The OFP-SCIO is also in charge of "clarifying and refuting" any stories that are forbidden from being covered in China but which have been reported on in foreign media. The SCIO's Fifth Office (better known as the State Council Internet Information Office) is in charge of policing the Chinese Internet.

China's foreign cultural diplomacy, meanwhile, falls under the purview of the Ministries of Culture and Education and includes initiatives such as cultural exchanges designed to dispel prejudices about China while fostering warm feelings toward the country. Beijing has been promoting the study of Chinese internationally since the late 1980s, hoping that people who study the language will be more sympathetic to Chinese perspectives.[3] In 2004, China began opening Confucius Institutes, which teach Chinese language and culture in universities all over the world. As of 2015, there were 1,086 Confucius Institutes and classrooms worldwide. Confucius Institutes must follow Chinese law as well as the law of the host country;[4] this means that their employees cannot be members of Falun Gong or supporters of independence for Taiwan, Xinjiang, or Tibet.

The scale and range of China's current annual investment in foreign-propaganda activities is so great that it would be impossible to come up with an accurate total budget. International reports have cited figures ranging from US$7 billion to $10 billion,[5] but these numbers include only the subsidies given to media targeted at non-Chinese foreigners. The Chinese government funds propaganda activities in a variety of ways. In 1992, China imposed a 3 percent "propaganda-industry tax" (*xuanchuan shiye fei*) on all profit-making enterprises in the public sphere. The funds are used to subsidize propaganda activities that are not commercially profitable. In addition to national-level propaganda efforts, each Chinese province has a budget for promoting itself to the outside world.

Two Target Audiences

China's foreign-propaganda activities target two broad groups: Overseas Chinese and non-Chinese foreigners. The Taiwanese are considered a subcategory of Overseas Chinese. Chinese embassy officials around the world mobilize pro-PRC elements among Overseas Chinese and non-Chinese elites within each country, while isolating and opposing those who promote Taiwanese independence and any others whom the CCP regards as being "anti-China."

China's propaganda work aimed at Overseas Chinese has three main goals: to neutralize antagonism toward the regime among Overseas Chinese, to increase their antipathy toward anti-CCP forces (both within China and in exile), and to encourage Overseas Chinese to invest in China.[6] China's propaganda efforts have been remarkably successful in fostering positive public opinion among Overseas Chinese, especially new migrants, and marginalizing opposition groups within Chinese expatriate communities.

Propaganda targeting Overseas Chinese flows through numerous media channels. These include local (foreign) Chinese-language newspapers, radio, and television abroad, as well as state-owned China Central Television (CCTV), which broadcasts a channel (CCTV-4) aimed specifically at Overseas Chinese. China's Xinhua News Service provides free content to Chinese-language news sources outside of China, ensuring that Beijing's perspectives prevail in the Chinese diaspora. Over the last decade, the Internet has become increasingly useful in building support for China among Overseas Chinese. PRC-based websites are now the leading source of Chinese-language and China-related news for Overseas Chinese.

The Taiwan Affairs Office, an agency within the State Council, coordinates with other relevant bodies to oversee China's Taiwan-related propaganda activities and agencies. The PRC has invested heavily in Mainland-based television stations, websites, newspapers, and radio stations that specifically target a Taiwanese audience. Beijing's efforts are aimed at shaping both domestic and global public opinion on Taiwan-related matters, and at curtailing Taiwan's global political and commercial influence. These efforts have been extremely successful.[7]

For the last twenty years, the main goal of propaganda aimed at non-Chinese foreigners has been to raise awareness of China's social, economic, and political stability, and the nation's incredible economic growth.

Although China's efforts at publicizing the strength of its economy have paid off, the country's efforts to shift Western perceptions about China's politics have fared much worse.

China promotes its messages abroad through a variety of media, including PRC-based outlets such as *China Daily, Beijing Review,* CCTV, China Radio International, the online version of *People's Daily* (which appears in a number of languages), China.org (the main Internet portal for China's foreign propaganda), and the Foreign Languages Press.

The CCP's efforts to shape a positive international image include two longstanding approaches. The first is known as "using foreign strength to promote China" (*liyong waili wei wo xuanchuan*). Beijing forges close partnerships of mutual advantage with highly prominent foreign figures who can bring commercial or political advantages to China—people such as former U.S. secretary of state Henry Kissinger or former British prime minister Tony Blair.[8] Every country now has some prominent figures whom the CCP has designated "friends of China." Modern friends of China are frequently asked by Chinese news outlets to write positive articles for the Chinese media and to participate in events to support China's soft-power initiatives. The government also regularly treats foreign delegations of "prominent persons" to all-expenses-paid tours of China, in hopes that participants will promote Chinese viewpoints when they return home.

The other long-used approach is called "borrowing foreign newspapers" (*jieyong haiwai baokan*).[9] In the past, this referred to official propagandists' efforts to cultivate good relationships with foreign journalists considered to be politically friendly to China. In the mid-2000s, this practice expanded to include placing China's own news articles in leading foreign newspapers. For example, once a month the *Washington Post* publishes a paid supplement from *China Daily*. Similarly, CCTV and China Radio International place programming on non–Chinese-language foreign television and radio stations. In the Mao era, this strategy was also known as "borrowing a boat to go out on the ocean."

In 2000, CCTV launched the satellite channel CCTV 9, aimed at English-speaking foreigners. In 2004, it began broadcasting in French and Spanish as well, and was relaunched as CCTV International. The station was intended to be the Chinese equivalent of CNN—a global media presence with 24-hour news coverage. Although the state granted CCTV International substantial resources, it was less generous in granting the channel editorial independence, which undermined its effectiveness.

In early 2009, Beijing announced that it would invest ¥45 billion (roughly US$7.25 billion) into its main media outlets in order to strengthen its international news coverage and global presence. As part of this campaign, known as "big propaganda" (*da waixuan*), Xinhua News Service increased its number of overseas bureaus from 100 to 186. That same year, the *Global Times* (a popular tabloid with an international focus owned by *People's Daily*) launched an English-language edition. CCTV International also began broadcasting in Arabic and Russian, and in 2010 rebranded itself as CCTV News. China's massive investment in these media attracted considerable international interest and debate. But this strategy is now widely regarded by Chinese mass-communication experts as a failure. If foreign audiences know that a piece of information comes from an official Chinese media source, they are likely to interpret it as "propaganda" rather than "news."

Changes Under Xi Jinping

Under Jiang Zemin (1989–2002) and Hu Jintao (2002–12), China stepped up its foreign-propaganda activities, going to great lengths to boost the country's image abroad. In the Jiang Zemin era, especially after 1992, foreign propaganda focused primarily on promoting the Chinese economy and encouraging further foreign investment and trade.[10] In the Hu Jintao era, building "soft power" was the primary goal, but China's international image still did not markedly improve. In fact, as Gallup surveys show, it actually deteriorated during these years.

In November 2012, Xi Jinping became general secretary of the CCP. Compared to all his recent predecessors, Xi has concentrated an unprecedented degree of power in his hands. He has used this power to push through a number of significant changes to China's foreign policy, including ramping up efforts to influence foreign audiences. In a speech at the August 2013 National Meeting on Propaganda and Thought Work, Xi stated that, in response to shifting global dynamics, "China should spread new ideas and new perspectives to emerging and developing states." He also stressed the need for China "to strengthen media coverage . . . use innovative outreach methods . . . tell a good Chinese story, and promote China's views internationally."[11]

At a January 2014 meeting, Xi pushed to increase spending on promoting Chinese culture abroad in order to expand China's soft power. Xi told members of the CCP Politburo that "China should be portrayed as a civilized country featuring a rich history, ethnic unity, and cultural diversity, and as an Eastern power with good government, a developed economy, cultural prosperity, national unity, and beautiful scenery." He added, "China should also be known as a responsible country that advocates peace and development, safeguards international fairness and justice, makes a positive contribution to humanity, and as a socialist country which is open and friendly to the world, full of hope and vitality."[12]

On 8 August 2014, Xi launched China's new media-management strategy. He said that China would create a "new-type mainstream media" (*xinxing zhuliu meiti*) that is "powerful, influential, and credible." In Xi's new-type media strategy, mergers and acquisitions are key means for influencing foreign public opinion, and traditional and new media are integrated into a multiplatform approach. In a departure from the Hu era, the expansion of media and foreign propaganda will be funded by forming huge media conglomerates and further commercializing media endeavors.[13] Chinese state media already receive few subsidies; since the 1990s, most of them have been required to make a profit while following CCP propaganda guidelines. Their privileged place in the Chinese market has made state media extremely lucrative. The new changes under Xi, which will give them further economic freedom, can only make them more profitable.

Since Xi's announcement of the new direction, China's foreign-propaganda efforts have taken on a new level of assertiveness, confidence, and ambition. There are several new themes now dominating China's foreign-propaganda work: "tell a good Chinese story," the "Chinese Dream," and "rich country, strong military."

A key goal of contemporary Chinese foreign propaganda is to "tell a good Chinese story" (*jiang yige hao Zhongguo gushi*). In essence, this means promoting a selective version of traditional Chinese culture to global audiences. The Confucius Institutes, Chinese cultural centers, and festivals are the primary vehicles for this type of propaganda.

Foreign propaganda that focuses on promoting the "Chinese Dream" tends to highlight opportunities for economic cooperation, with an emphasis on partnership and development. One such opportunity is China's New Silk Road initiative (*yilu, yidai*). According to Peng Guangqian, deputy secretary general of China's National Security Council, the country's New Silk Road policies are "beyond ideology." In contrast to the confrontational policies of the Cold War years, the New Silk Road policies are focused on economic cooperation. They are also aimed at setting new norms in international relations, with the goal of creating a mutually beneficial "community of interests" and "community of destiny" that will help to put an end not only to the bullying of weak states by strong ones, but to "all the other political and economic inequalities of the old order."[14]

The last major theme of Xi-era foreign propaganda is "rich country, strong military" (*fuguo, qiangbing*). China's military propaganda, which takes a hard line in Chinese, adopts a softer approach in English and other foreign languages. It is issued by authorized spokespersons from the People's Liberation Army, and their messages are aimed at both domestic and foreign audiences. In Chinese, military propaganda focuses on China's preparedness to fight to defend its interests. In other languages, propaganda emphasizes China's desire for a peaceful rise to international power and influence.[15]

Expanding China's Cultural Influence

China currently intends to further expand the numbers of Confucius Institutes and classrooms worldwide and to increase the number of scholarships and research programs offered by the Confucius Institutes. The government is also dedicating massive funds to the establishment of fifty more international cultural centers by 2020, and has plans to showcase Chinese literature, art, music, and film internationally. The country is intensifying its promotion of the "Chinese New Year" (rather than the Lunar New Year), organizing 900 events in 119 countries in 2015, as compared to just 65 events in 42 countries in 2010.[16]

China has also announced that it will make a sizeable investment in think tanks both in China and abroad,[17] establishing a hundred new ones over the next few years. In 2015, China launched its first foreign think tank, the Washington D.C.–based Institute for China-America Studies, which focuses heavily on maritime affairs and U.S.-China cooperation. It is funded by China's National Institute for South China Sea Studies. Henry Kissinger participated in the think tank's inaugural conference.[18]

During the last two years, *China Daily, Beijing Review,* CCTV International, Xinhua, and China Radio International have continued to expand and are increasingly "localizing" (*bentuhua*)—that is, employing large numbers of foreign media professionals while retaining editorial control. CCTV News has opened up major branches in Washington and Nairobi. The channel's broadcasts now rotate among its Beijing headquarters and its Washington and Nairobi studios. The new programming has high production values. As in the past, however, China-related stories must comply with the dictates of the CCP's Office for Foreign Propaganda. CCTV News has produced some thought-provoking coverage of international events since its rebranding, but when it comes to China-related reporting, the emphasis is still on "positive propaganda" (*zhengmian xuanchuan*). By refusing to deal with political controversy in China, the station's programming often fails to meet standards of newsworthiness. Its lack of critical coverage of the massive chemical explosion in Tianjin in August 2015 is a case in point.

Another part of Xi's new-type media strategy is to partner with foreign media to create pro-China films and documentaries. In 2015, one such joint venture, the Chinese-Korean documentary series "Super China," was a hit on Korean television.[19] Chinese companies with close ties to Beijing are now investing in Hollywood films. As a result, some recent Hollywood films (for example, the 2015 movie *Trainwreck*) have added pro-China references,[20] while others (such as the 2013 film *Iron Man 3*) have deleted plot elements that might have offended CCP political sensitivities.

A key change under Xi is that foreign-propaganda activities are increasingly conducted as business transactions. According to propaganda chief Liu Qibao, "Experience has shown that it is better when China's cultural products are 'sold out' rather than 'sent out.'"[21] China's state-owned cultural organizations therefore plan to make strategic acquisitions of relevant Western cultural enterprises. Punning on the saying "to borrow a boat to go out on to the ocean," Liu humorously refers to this as "buying a boat."

All these developments are happening as the Xi administration cracks down on political dissent and wages a harsh anticorruption campaign. The government has likewise been enacting stricter controls on the media, civil society, students, intellectuals, and government officials, thereby putting more pressure on Chinese citizens with connections abroad to toe the party line and "sing with one voice" when speaking to outsiders. Xi is trying to tighten the information environment in China in order to bolster CCP legitimacy, and influencing how China is promoted and perceived internationally is part of this strategy.

To date, China's considerable efforts to modernize its foreign-propaganda apparatus have only been partly successful in shifting international public opinion. On the one hand, CCP efforts to raise global awareness of the country's economic transformation have been very effective, as have its efforts to shape the discourse on Taiwan. China's perspective is now faithfully relayed in most Overseas Chinese media. On the other hand, as polls and other research show, CCP efforts to improve non-Chinese foreigners' perceptions of China's domestic politics and role on the international stage have so far largely failed to sway these audiences. In the long run, the new strategy of "buying a boat"—taking over Western cultural and media outlets—may turn out to be the most effective way of improving China's "international face" and constraining international debate about China-related issues.

Notes

1. Liu Qibao, "Vigorously Promote Chinese Culture to the World" (in Chinese), *Guangming Daily,* 22 May 2014, *http://epaper.gmw.cn/gmrb/html/2014-05/22/nw.D110000gmrb_20140522_1-03.htm.*

2. Jeffrey M. Jones, "Americans See China's Economic Power as Diminished Threat," Gallup, 26 February 2015, *www.gallup.com/poll/181733/americans-china-economic-power-diminished-threat.aspx.*

3. Zhu Muzhi, "Ba duiwai xuanchuan gongzuo tigao yibu," 22 June 1986, *Zhu Muzhi lun duiwai xuanchuan* [Zhu Muzhi discusses foreign propaganda] (Beijing: Wuzhou chuanbo chubanshe, 1995), 71.

4. See Li Changchun's 24 April 2007 statement on the international promotion of Chinese language, Xinhua, 25 April 2007, *http://news.xinhuanet.com/politics/2007-04/24/content_6022792.htm*; Confucius Institute Online, *www.chinesecio.com/m/cio_wci/*; and "Confucius Institute Constitution and By-Laws," *http://english.hanban.org/node_7880.htm.*

5. Halley C. Dale, Ariel Cohen, and Janice A. Smith, "Challenging America:

How Russia, China, and Other Countries Use Public Diplomacy to Compete with the U.S.," Heritage Foundation Backgrounder #2698, 21 June 2012, *www. heritage.org/research/reports/2012/06/challenging-america-how-russia-china-and-other-countries-use-public-diplomacy-to-compete-with-the-us*; David Shambaugh, "China's Soft Power Push: The Search for Respect," *Foreign Affairs* 94 (July–August 2015): 99–107, *www.foreignaffairs.com/articles/china/2015-06-16/ china-s-soft-power-push*.

6. Su Jinsong, "The Use of Overseas China Media in 'Big Propaganda'" (in Chinese), *People's Daily*, 9 April 2014, *http://media.people.com.cn/n/2014/0409/ c383351-24862187.html*.

7. See Anne-Marie Brady, "Unifying the Ancestral Land: The CCP's 'Taiwan' Frames," *China Quarterly* 222 (September 2015): 787–806.

8. Anne-Marie Brady, *Making the Foreign Serve China: Managing Foreigners in the People's Republic* (Lanham, Md.: Rowman and Littlefield, 2003), 195.

9. "The Place of 'Borrowing' in Foreign Propaganda" (in Chinese), *Fujian jixie*, 6 March 2012, *http://jx.fjsen.com/2012-03/06/content_8097318_29.htm*.

10. Zhongyang xuanchuanbu bangongting, *Dang de xuanchuan gongzuo wenjian xuanbian* [Selected articles on CCP propaganda], vol. 4 (Beijing:, Zhong gong zhongyang dangxiao chubanshe [CCP Party School Publishers, 1994], 1815–16.

11. "Xi Jinping: Tell a Good Story of China" (in Chinese), Xinhua, 20 August 2013, *http://news.xinhuanet.com/video/2013-08/20/c_125210825.htm*.

12. "Xi Jinping: Constructing a Socialist Cultural Great Power and Improving Cultural Soft Power," *People's Daily*, 1 January 2014, *http://cpc.people.com. cn/n/2014/0101/c64094-23995307.html*.

13. On the multiplatform approach, see *http://media.people.com.cn/ GB/22114/387950/*; on commercialization, see Zhang Ye, "SMG Looks to Establish Giant Media Group" (in Chinese), *Global Times*, 4 September 2014, *www. globaltimes.cn/content/879871.shtml*.

14. Peng Guangqian, "China's Silk Road Strategic Concept and the Reconstruction of the International Order" (in Chinese), Xinhua, 9 January 2015, *www.taiwan.cn/xwzx/gj/201501/t20150109_8645599.htm*.

15. "Foreign Media Worries That Tensions in the South China Sea Are Out of Control is Harmful to Sino-U.S. Relations" (in Chinese), Cankaoxiaoxiwang, 27 May 2015, *www.kaixian.tv/gd/2015/0527/1078841.html*; and Peng Guangqian, "A Chinese General's View as to Whether China Is a Challenge to America," *Huffington Post*, 10 November 2014, *www.huffingtonpost.com/peng-guangqian-/china-america-challenge_b_6107744.html*.

16. Julie Makinen, "Beijing Uses Chinese New Year to Push China's Soft Power," *Los Angeles Times*, 18 February 2015, *www.latimes.com/world/asia/ la-fg-china-new-year-20150218-story.html#page=1*.

17. "Guanyu jiaqiang Zhongguo tese xinxing zhiku jianshe de yijian" [Suggestions on the strengthening of the new think tank construction with Chinese

characteristics], Xinhua, 21 January 2015, *http://news.xinhuanet.com/zgjx/2015-01/21/c_133934292.htm.*

18. See the Institute for China-America Studies website, *http://chinaus-icas.org/*; for inaugural conference, see *www.youtube.com/watch?v=Tr56AifU9r0.*

19. "Documentary on China a Hit in South Korea," ChinaCulture.org, 17 February 2015, *www.chinaculture.org/2015-02/17/content_601143.htm.*

20. In the 2015 movie *Trainwreck*, when actor John Cena is asked to "talk dirty" by Amy Schumer, he says in Chinese, "China is a very important country" (*Zhongguo shi yige hen zhongyao de guojia*).

21. Liu Qibao, "Vigorously Promote Chinese Culture to the World."

CHAPTER THIRTEEN

Cyberspace Under Siege

RON DEIBERT

ECEMBER 2014 MARKED the fourth anniversary of the Arab Spring. Beginning in December 2010, Arab peoples seized the attention of the world by taking to the Internet and the streets to press for change. They toppled regimes once thought immovable, including that of Egyptian dictator Hosni Mubarak. Four years later, not only is Cairo's Tahrir Square empty of protesters, but the Egyptian army is back in charge. Invoking the familiar mantras of antiterrorism and cybersecurity, Egypt's new president, General Abdel Fattah al-Sisi, has imposed a suite of information controls.[1] Bloggers have been arrested and websites blocked; suspicions of mass surveillance cluster around an ominous-sounding new "High Council of Cyber Crime." The very technologies that many heralded as "tools of liberation" four years ago are now being used to stifle dissent and squeeze civil society. The aftermath of the Arab Spring is looking more like a cold winter, and a potent example of resurgent authoritarianism in cyberspace.

Authoritarianism means state constraints on legitimate democratic political participation, rule by emotion and fear, repression of civil society, and the concentration of executive power in the hands of an unaccountable elite. At its most extreme, it encompasses totalitarian states such as North Korea, but it also includes a large number of weak states and "competitive authoritarian" regimes.[2] Once assumed to be incompatible with today's fast-paced media environment, authoritarian systems of rule are showing not only resilience, but a capacity for *resurgence*. Far from being made obsolete by the Internet, authoritarian regimes are now actively shaping cyberspace to their own strategic advantage. This shaping includes technological, legal, extralegal, and other targeted information controls. It also includes regional and bilateral cooperation, the promotion of international norms friendly to authoritarianism, and the sharing of "best" practices and technologies.

The development of several generations of information controls has resulted in a tightening grip on cyberspace within sovereign territorial boundaries. A major impetus behind these controls is the growing imperative to implement cybersecurity and antiterror measures, which often have the effect of strengthening the state at the expense of human rights and civil society. In the short term, the disclosures by Edward Snowden concerning surveillance carried out by the U.S. National Security Agency (NSA) and its allies must also be cited as a factor that has contributed, even if unintentionally, to the authoritarian resurgence.

Liberal democrats have wrung their hands a good deal lately as they have watched authoritarian regimes use international organizations to promote norms that favor domestic information controls. Yet events in regional, bilateral, and other contexts where authoritarians learn from and cooperate with one another have mattered even more. Moreover, with regard to surveillance, censorship, and targeted digital espionage, commercial developments and their spinoffs have been key. Any thinking about how best to counter resurgent authoritarianism in cyberspace must reckon with this reality.

Mention authoritarian controls over cyberspace, and people often think of major Internet disruptions such as Egypt's shutdown in late January and early February 2011, or China's so-called Great Firewall. These are noteworthy, to be sure, but they do not capture the full gamut of cyberspace controls. Over time, authoritarians have developed an arsenal that extends from technical measures, laws, policies, and regulations, to more covert and offensive techniques such as targeted malware attacks and campaigns to coopt social media. Subtler and thus more likely to be effective than blunt-force tactics such as shutdowns, these measures reveal a considerable degree of learning. Cyberspace authoritarianism, in other words, has evolved over at least three generations of information controls.[3]

First-generation controls tend to be "defensive," and involve erecting national cyberborders that limit citizens' access to information from abroad. The archetypal example is the Great Firewall of China, a system for filtering keywords and URLs to control what computer users within the country can see on the Internet. Although few countries have matched the Great Firewall (Iran, Pakistan, Saudi Arabia, Bahrain, Yemen, and Vietnam have come the closest), first-generation controls are common. Indeed, Internet filtering of one sort or another is now normal even in democracies.

Where countries vary is in terms of the content targeted for blocking and the transparency of filtering practices. Some countries, including Canada, the United Kingdom, and the United States, block content related to the sexual exploitation of children as well as content that infringes copyrights. Other countries focus primarily on guarding religious sensitivities. Since September 2012, Pakistan has been blocking all of YouTube over a video, titled "Innocence of Muslims," that Pakistani authorities deem blasphemous.[4] A growing number of countries are blocking access to political and security-related content, especially content posted by opposition and human-rights groups, insurgents, "extremists," or "terrorists." Those last two terms are in quotation marks because in some places, such as the Gulf states, they are defined so broadly that content is blocked which in most other countries would fall within the bounds of legitimate expression.

National-level Internet filtering is notoriously crude. Errors and inconsistencies are common. One Citizen Lab study found that Blue Coat (a U.S. software widely used to automate national filtering systems) mistakenly blocked hundreds of nonpornographic websites.[5] Another Citizen Lab study found that Oman residents were blocked from a Bollywood-related website not because it was banned in Oman, but because of upstream filtering in India, the pass-through country for a portion of Oman's Internet traffic.[6] In Indonesia, Internet-censorship rules are applied at the level of Internet Service Providers (ISPs). The country has more than three-hundred of these; what you can see online has much to do with which one you use.[7] As censorship extends into social media and applications, inconsistencies bloom, as is famously the case in China. In some countries, a user cannot see the filtering, which displays as a "network error." Although relatively easy to bypass and document,[8] first-generation controls have won enough acceptance to have opened the door to more expansive measures.

Second-generation controls are best thought of as deepening and extending information controls into society through laws, regulations, or requirements that force the private sector to do the state's bidding by policing privately owned and operated networks according to the state's demands. Second-generation controls can now be found in every region of the world, and their number is growing. Turkey is passing new laws, on the pretext of protecting national security and fighting cybercrime, that will expand wiretapping and other surveillance and detention powers while allowing the state to censor websites without a court order. Ethiopia charged six bloggers from the Zone 9 group and three independent journalists with terrorism and treason after they covered political issues. Thailand is considering new cybercrime laws that would grant authorities the right to access emails, telephone records, computers, and postal mail without needing prior court approval. Under reimposed martial law, Egypt has tightened regulations on demonstrations and arrested prominent bloggers, including Arab Spring icon Alaa Abd El Fattah. Saudi blogger Raif Badawi is looking at ten years in jail and 950 remaining lashes (he received the first fifty lashes in January 2015) for criticizing Saudi clerics online. Tunisia passed broad reforms after the Arab Spring, but even there a blogger has been arrested under an obscure older law for "defaming the military" and "insulting military commanders" on Facebook. Between 2008 and March 2015 (when the Supreme Court struck it down), India had a law that banned "menacing" or "offensive" social-media posts. In 2012, Renu Srinavasan of Mumbai found herself arrested merely for hitting the "like" button below a friend's Facebook post. In Singapore, blogger and LGBT activist Alex Au was fined in March 2015 for criticizing how a pair of court cases was handled.

Second-generation controls also include various forms of "baked-in" surveillance, censorship, and "backdoor" functionalities that governments, wielding their licensing authority, require manufacturers and service providers to build into their products. Under new antiterrorism laws, Beijing recently announced that it would require companies offering services in China to turn over encryption keys for state inspection and build into all systems backdoors open to police and security agencies. Existing regulations already require social-media companies to survey and censor their own networks. Citizen Lab has documented that many chat applications popular in China come preconfigured with censorship and surveillance capabilities.[9] For many years, the Russian government has required telecommunications companies and ISPs to be "SORM-compliant"—SORM is the Russian acronym for the surveillance system that directs copies of all electronic communications to local security offices for archiving and inspection. In like fashion, India's Central Monitoring System gives the government direct access to the country's telecommunications networks. Agents can listen in on broadband phone calls, SMS messages, and email traffic, while all call-data records are archived and analyzed. In Indonesia, where BlackBerry smartphones remain popular, the government has repeatedly pressured Canada-based BlackBerry Limited to comply with "lawful-access" demands, even threatening to ban the company's services unless BlackBerry agreed to host data on servers in the country. Similar demands have come from India, Saudi Arabia, and the United Arab Emirates. The company has even agreed to bring Indian technicians to Canada for special surveillance training.[10]

Also spreading are new laws that ban security and anonymizing tools, including software that permits users to bypass first-generation blocks. Iran has arrested those who distribute circumvention tools, and it has throttled Internet traffic to frustrate users trying to connect to popular circumvention and anonymizer tools such as Psiphon and Tor. Belarus and Russia have both recently proposed making Tor and similar tools illegal. China has banned virtual private networks (VPNs) nationwide—the latest in a long line of such bans—despite the difficulties that this causes for business. Pakistan has banned encryption since 2011, although its widespread use in financial and other communications inside the country suggests that enforcement is lax. The United Arab Emirates has banned VPNs, and police there have stressed that individuals caught using them may be charged with violating the country's harsh cybercrime laws.

Second-generation controls include finer-grained registration and identification requirements that tie people to specific accounts or devices, or even require citizens to obtain government permission before using the Internet. Pakistan has outlawed the sale of prepaid SIM cards and demands that all citizens register their SIM cards using biometric identification technology. The Thai military junta has extended such registration rules to cover free WiFi accounts as well. China has imposed real-name registration policies on Internet and social-media accounts, and companies have dutifully deleted tens of thousands of accounts that could not be authenticated. Chinese users must also commit to respect the seven "baselines," including "laws and regulations, the Socialist system, the national interest, citizens' lawful rights and interests public order, morals, and the veracity of information."[11]

By expanding the reach of laws and broad regulations, second-generation controls narrow the space left free for civil society, and subject the once "wild frontier" of the Internet to growing regulation. While enforcement may be uneven, in country after country these laws hang like dark clouds over civil society, creating a climate of uncertainty and fear.

Authoritarians on the Offensive

Third-generation controls are the hardest to document, but may be the most effective. They involve surveillance, targeted espionage, and other types of covert disruptions in cyberspace. While first-generation controls are defensive and second-generation controls probe deeper into society, third-generation controls are *offensive*. The best known of these are the targeted cyberespionage campaigns that emanate from China. Although Chinese spying on businesses and governments draws most of the news reports, Beijing uses the same tactics to target human-rights, prodemocracy, and independence movements outside China. A recent four-year comparative study by Citizen Lab and ten participating NGOs found that those groups suffered the same persistent China-based digital attacks as governments and Fortune 500 companies.[12] The study also found that targeted espionage campaigns can have severe consequences including disruptions of civil society and threats to liberty. At the very least, persistent cyberespionage attacks breed self-censorship and undermine the networking advantages that civil society might otherwise reap from digital media. Another Citizen Lab report found that China has employed a new attack tool, called "The Great Cannon," which can redirect the website requests of unwitting foreign users into denial-of-service attacks or replace web requests with malicious software.[13]

While other states may not be able to match China's cyberespionage or online-attack capabilities, they do have options. Some might buy off-the-shelf espionage "solutions" from Western companies such as the United Kingdom's Gamma Group or Italy's Hacking Team—each of which Citizen Lab research has linked to dozens of authoritarian-government clients.[14] In Syria, which is currently the site of a multisided, no-holds-barred regional war, security services and extremist groups such as ISIS are borrowing cybercriminals' targeted-attack techniques, downloading crude but effective tradecraft from open sources and then using it to infiltrate opposition groups, often with deadly results.[15] The capacity to mount targeted digital attacks is proving particularly attractive to regimes that face persistent insurgencies, popular protests, or other standing security challenges. As these techniques become more widely used and known, they create a chilling effect: Even without particular evidence, activists may avoid digital communication for fear that they are being monitored.

Third-generation controls also include efforts to aim crowdsourced antagonism at political foes. Governments recruit "electronic armies" that can use the very social media employed by popular opposition movements to discredit and intimidate those who dare to criticize the state.[16] Such online swarms are meant to make orchestrated denunciations of opponents look like spontaneous popular expressions. If the activities of its electronic armies come under legal question or result in excesses, a regime can hide behind "plausible deniability." Examples of progovernment e-warriors include Venezuela's *chavista* "communicational guerrillas," the Egyptian Cyber Army, the pro-Assad Syrian Electronic Army, the pro-Putin bloggers of Russia, Kenya's "director of digital media" Dennis Itumbi plus his bloggers, Saudi Arabia's antipornography "ethical hackers," and China's notorious "fifty-centers," so called because they are allegedly paid that much for each progovernment comment or status update they post.

Other guises under which third-generation controls may travel include not only targeted attacks on Internet users but wholesale disruptions of cyberspace. Typically scheduled to cluster before and during major political events such as elections, anniversaries, and public demonstrations, "just-in-time" disruptions can be as severe as total Internet blackouts. More common, however, are selective disruptions. In Tajikistan, SMS services went down for several days leading up to planned opposition rallies in October 2014. The government blamed technical errors; others saw the hand of the state at work.[17] Pakistan blocked all mobile services in its capital, Islamabad, for part of the day on 23 March 2015 in order to shield national-day parades from improvised explosive devices.[18] During the 2014 prodemocracy demonstrations in Hong Kong, China closed access to the photo-sharing site Instagram. Telecommunications companies in the Democratic Republic of Congo were ordered to shut down all mobile and SMS communications in response to antigovernment protests. Bangladesh ordered a ban on the popular smartphone messaging application Viber in January 2015, after it was linked to demonstrations.

To these three generations, we might add a fourth. This comes in the form of a more assertive authoritarianism at the international level. For years, governments that favor greater sovereign control over cyberspace have sought to assert their preferences—despite at times stiff resistance—in forums such as the International Telecommunication Union (ITU), the Internet Governance Forum (IGF), the United Nations (UN), and the Internet Corporation for Assigned Names and Numbers (ICANN).[19] Although there is no simple division of "camps," observers tend to group countries broadly into those that prefer a more open Internet and a limited role for states and those that prefer a state-led form of governance, probably under UN auspices.

The United States, the United Kingdom, Europe, and the Asian democracies line up most often behind openness, while China, Iran, Russia, Saudi Arabia, and various other nondemocracies fall into the latter group. A large number of emerging-market countries, led by Brazil, India, and Indonesia, are "swing states" that can go either way. Battle lines between these opposing views were becoming sharper around the time of the December 2012 World Congress on Information Technology (WCIT) in Dubai—an event that many worried would mark the fall of Internet governance into UN (and thus state) hands. But the WCIT process stalled, and lobbying by the United States and its allies (plus Internet companies such as Google) played a role in preventing fears of a state-dominated Internet from coming true.

If recent proposals on international cybersecurity submitted to the UN by China, Russia, and their allies tell us anything, future rounds of the cybergovernance forums may be less straightforward than what transpired at Dubai. In January 2015, the Beijing- and Moscow-led Shanghai Cooperation Organization (SCO) submitted a draft "International Code of Conduct for Information Security" to the UN. This document reaffirms many of the same principles as the ill-fated WCIT Treaty, including greater state control over cyberspace.

Such proposals will surely raise the ire of those in the "Internet freedom" camp, who will then marshal their resources to lobby against their adoption. But will wins for Internet freedom in high-level international venues (assuming that such wins are in the cards) do anything to stop local and regional trends toward greater government control of the online world? Writing their preferred language into international statements may please Internet-freedom advocates, but what if such language merely serves to gloss over a ground-level reality of more rather than less state cyberauthority?

It is important to understand the driving forces behind resurgent authoritarianism in cyberspace if we are to comprehend fully the challenges ahead, the broader prospects facing human rights and democracy promotion worldwide, and the reasons to suspect that the authoritarian resurgence in cyberspace will continue.

A major driver of this resurgence has been and likely will continue to be the growing impetus worldwide to adopt cybersecurity and antiterror policies. As societies come to depend ever more heavily on networked digital information, keeping it secure has become an ever-higher state priority. Data breaches and cyberespionage attacks—including massive thefts of intellectual property—are growing in number. While the cybersecurity realm is replete with self-serving rhetoric and threat inflation, the sum total of concerns means that dealing with cybercrime has now become an unavoidable state imperative. For example, the U.S. intelligence community's official 2015 "Worldwide Threat Assessment" put cyberattacks first on the list of dangers to U.S. national security.[20]

It is crucial to note how laws and policies in the area of cybersecurity are combining and interacting with those in the antiterror realm. Violent extremists have been active online at least since the early days of al-Qaeda several decades ago. More recently, the rise of the Islamic State and its gruesome use of social media for publicity and recruitment have spurred a new sense of urgency. The Islamic State atrocities recorded in viral beheading videos are joined by (to list a few) terror attacks such as the Mumbai assault in India (November 2008); the Boston Marathon bombings (April 2013); the Westgate Mall shootings in Kenya (September 2013); the Ottawa Parliament shooting (October 2014); the *Charlie Hebdo* and related attacks in Paris (January 2015); repeated deadly assaults on Shia mosques in Pakistan (most recently in February 2015); and the depredations of Nigeria's Boko Haram.

Horrors such as these underline the value of being able to identify, in timely fashion amid the wilderness of cyberspace, those bent on violence *before* they strike. The interest of public-safety officials in data-mining and other high-tech surveillance and analytical techniques is natural and understandable. But as expansive laws are rapidly passed and state-security services (alongside the private companies that work for and with them) garner vast new powers and resources, checks and balances that protect civil liberties and guard against the abuse of power can be easily forgotten. The adoption by liberal democracies of sweeping cybercrime and antiterror measures without checks and balances cannot help but lend legitimacy and normative support to similar steps taken by authoritarian states. The headlong rush to guard against extremism and terrorism worldwide, in other words, could end up providing the biggest boost to resurgent authoritarianism.

Regional Security Cooperation as a Factor

While international cyberspace conferences attract attention, often overlooked are regional security forums. The latter are the places where cybersecurity coordination happens. They are focused sites of learning and norm promotion where ideas, technologies, and "best" practices are exchanged. Even countries that are otherwise rivals can and do agree and cooperate within the context of such security forums.

The SCO, to name one prominent regional group, boasts a well-developed normative framework that calls upon its member states to combat the "three evils" of terrorism, separatism, and extremism. The upshot has been information controls designed to bolster regime stability against opposition groups and the claims of restive ethnic minorities. The SCO recently held joint military exercises in order to teach its forces how to counter Internet-enabled opposition of the sort that elsewhere has led to "color revolutions." The Chinese official who directs the SCO's "Regional Anti-Terrorist Structure" (RATS) told the UN Counter-Terrorism Committee that RATS had "collected and distributed to its Member States intelligence information regarding the use of the Internet by terrorist groups active in the region to promote their ideas."[21]

Such information may include intelligence on individuals involved in what international human-rights law considers legitimate political expression. Another Eurasian regional security organization in which Russia plays a leading role, the Collective Security Treaty Organization

(CSTO), has announced that it will be creating an "international center to combat cyber threats."[22] Both the SCO and the CSTO are venues where commercial platforms for both mass and targeted surveillance are sold, shared, and exchanged. The telecommunications systems and ISPs in each of the five Central Asian republics are all "SORM-compliant"—ready to copy all data routinely to security services, just as in Russia. The SCO and CSTO typically carry out most of their deliberations behind closed doors and release no disclosures in English, meaning that much of what they do escapes the attention of Western observers and civil society groups.

The regional cybersecurity coordination undertaken by the Gulf Cooperation Council (GCC) offers another example. In 2014, the GCC approved a long-awaited plan to form a joint police force, with headquarters in Abu Dhabi. While the fights against drug dealing and money laundering are to be among the tasks of this Gulf Interpol, the new force will also have the mission of battling cybercrime. In the Gulf monarchies, however, online offenses are defined broadly and include posting items that can be taken as critical of royal persons, ruling families, or the Muslim religion. These kingdoms and emirates have long records of suppressing dissent and even arresting one another's political opponents. Whatever its other law-enforcement functions, the GCC version of Interpol is all too likely to become a regional tool for suppressing protest and rooting out expressions of discontent.

"Flying under the radar," with little flash, few reporters taking notice, and lots of closed meetings carried on in local languages by like-minded officials from neighboring authoritarian states, organizations concerned with regional governance and security attract far less attention than UN conferences that seem poised to unleash dramatic Web takeovers which may never materialize. Yet it is in these obscure regional corners that the key norms of cyberspace controls may be taking shape and taking hold.

The Cybersecurity Market as a Factor

A third driving factor has to do with the rapid growth of digital connectivity in the global South and among the populations of authoritarian regimes, weak states, and flawed democracies. In Indonesia the number of Internet users increases each month by a stunning 800,000. In 2000, Nigeria had fewer than a quarter-million Internet users; today, it has 68 million. The Internet-penetration rate in Cambodia rose a staggering 414 percent from January 2014 to January 2015 alone. By the end of 2014, the number of mobile-connected devices exceeded the number of people on Earth. Cisco Systems estimates that by 2019, there will be nearly 1.5 mobile devices per living human. The same report predicts that the steepest rates of growth in mobile-data traffic will be found in the Middle East and Africa.[23]

Booming digital technology is good for economic growth, but it also creates security and governance pressure points that authoritarian regimes can squeeze. We have seen how social media and the like can mobilize masses of people instantly on behalf of various causes (prodemocratic ones included). Yet many of the very same technologies can also be used as tools of control. Mobile devices, with their portability, low cost, and light physical-infrastructure requirements, are how citizens in the developing world connect. These handheld marvels allow people to do a wealth of things that they could hardly have dreamt of doing before. Yet all mobile devices and their dozens of installed applications emit reams of highly detailed information about peoples' movements, social relationships, habits, and even thoughts— data that sophisticated agencies can use in any number of ways to spy, to track, to manipulate, to deceive, to extort, to influence, and to target.

The market for digital spyware described earlier needs to be seen not only as a source of material and technology for countries who demand them, but as an active *shaper* of those countries' preferences, practices, and policies. This is not to say that companies are persuading policy makers regarding what governments should do. Rather, companies and the services that they offer can open up possibilities for solutions, be they deep-packet inspection, content filtering, cellphone tracking, "big-data" analytics, or targeted spyware. SkyLock, a cellphone-tracking solution sold by Verint Systems of Melville, New York, purports to offer governments "a cost-effective, new approach to obtaining global location information concerning known targets." Company brochures obtained by the *Washington Post* include "screen shots of maps depicting location tracking in what appears to be Mexico, Nigeria, South Africa, Brazil, Congo, the United Arab Emirates, Zimbabwe, and several other countries."[24]

Large industry trade fairs where these systems are sold are also crucial sites for learning and information exchange. The best known of these, the Intelligence Support Systems (ISS) events, are run by TeleStrategies,

Incorporated, of McLean, Virginia. Dubbed the "Wiretappers' Ball" by critics, ISS events are exclusive conventions with registration fees high enough to exclude most attendees other than governments and their agencies. As one recent study noted, ISS serves to connect registrants with surveillance-technology vendors, and provides training in the latest industry practices and equipment.[25] The March 2014 ISS event in Dubai featured one session on "Mobile Location, Surveillance and Signal Intercept Product Training" and another that promised to teach attendees how to achieve "unrivaled attack capabilities and total resistance to detection, quarantine and removal by any endpoint security technology."[26] Major corporate vendors of lawful-access, targeted-surveillance, and data-analytic solutions are fixtures at ISS meetings and use them to gather clients.

As cybersecurity demands grow, so will this market. Authoritarian policy makers looking to channel industrial development and employment opportunities into paths that reinforce state control can be expected to support local innovation. Already, schools of engineering, computer science, and data-processing are widely seen in the developing world as viable paths to employment and economic sustainability, and within those fields cybersecurity is now a major driving force. In Malaysia, for example, the British defense contractor BAE Systems agreed to underwrite a degree-granting academic program in cybersecurity in partial fulfillment of its "defense offsets" obligation.[27] India's new "National Cyber Security Policy" lays out an ambitious strategy for training a new generation of experts in, among other things, the fine points of "ethical hacking." The goal is to give India an electronic army of high-tech specialists a half-million strong. In a world where "Big Brother" and "Big Data" share so many of the same needs, the political economy of cybersecurity must be singled out as a major driver of resurgent authoritarianism in cyberspace.

Edward Snowden as a Factor

Since June 2013, barely a month has gone by without new revelations concerning U.S. and allied spying—revelations that flow from the disclosures made by former NSA contractor Edward Snowden. The disclosures fill in the picture of a remarkable effort to marshal extraordinary capacities for information control across the entire spectrum of cyberspace. The Snowden revelations will continue to fuel an important public debate about the proper balance to be struck between liberty and security.

While the value of Snowden's disclosures in helping to start a long-needed discussion is undeniable, the revelations have also had unintended consequences for resurgent authoritarianism and cyberspace. First, they have served to deflect attention away from authoritarian-regime cyberespionage campaigns such as China's. Before Snowden fled to Hong Kong, U.S. diplomacy was taking an aggressive stand against cyberespionage. Individuals in the pay of the Chinese military and allegedly linked to Chinese cyberespionage were finding themselves under indictment. Since Snowden, the pressure on China has eased. Beijing, Moscow, and others have found it easy to complain loudly about a double standard supposedly favoring the United States while they rationalize their own actions as "normal" great-power behavior and congratulate themselves for correcting the imbalance that they say has beset cyberspace for too long.

Second, the disclosures have created an atmosphere of suspicion around Western governments' intentions and raised questions about the legitimacy of the "Internet Freedom" agenda backed by the United States and its allies. Since the Snowden disclosures—revealing top-secret exploitation and disruption programs that in some respects are indistinguishable from those that Washington and its allies have routinely condemned—the rhetoric of the Internet Freedom coalition has rung rather hollow. In February 2015, it even came out that British, Canadian, and U.S. signals-intelligence agencies had been "piggybacking" on China-based cyberespionage campaigns—stealing data from Chinese hackers who had not properly secured their own command-and-control networks.[28]

Third, the disclosures have opened up foreign investment opportunities for IT companies that used to run afoul of national-security concerns. Before Snowden, rumors of hidden "backdoors" in Chinese-made technology such as Huawei routers put a damper on that company's sales. Then it came out that the United States and allied governments had been compelling (legally or otherwise) U.S.-based tech companies to do precisely what many had feared China was doing—namely, installing secret backdoors. So now Western companies have a "Huawei" problem of their own, and Huawei no longer looks so bad.

In the longer term, the Snowden disclosures may have the salutary effect of educating a large number of citizens about mass surveillance. In the nearer term, however, the revelations have handed countries other than the United States and its allies an opportunity for the self-interested promotion of local IT wares under the convenient rhetorical guise of striking a blow for "technological sovereignty" and bypassing U.S. information controls.

There was a time when authoritarian regimes seemed like slow-footed, technologically challenged dinosaurs whom the Information Age was sure to put on a path toward ultimate extinction. That time is no more—these regimes have proven themselves surprisingly (and dismayingly) light-footed and adaptable. National-level information controls are now deeply entrenched and growing. Authoritarian regimes are becoming more active and assertive, sharing norms, technologies, and "best" practices with one another as they look to shape cyberspace in ways that legitimize their national interests and domestic goals.

Sadly, prospects for halting these trends anytime soon look bleak. As resurgent authoritarianism in cyberspace increases, civil society will struggle: A web of ever more fine-grained information controls tightens the grip of unaccountable elites. Given the comprehensive range of information controls outlined here, and their interlocking sources deep within societies, economies, and political systems, it is clear that an equally comprehensive approach to the problem is required. Those who seek to promote human rights and democracy through cyberspace will err gravely if they stick to high-profile "Internet Freedom" conferences or investments in "secure apps" and digital training. No amount of rhetoric or technological development alone will solve a problem whose roots run this deep and cut across the borders of so many regions and countries.

What we need is a patient, multipronged, and well-grounded approach across numerous spheres, with engagement in a variety of venues. Researchers, investigative journalists, and others must learn to pay more attention to developments in regional security settings and obscure trade fairs. The long-term goal should be to open these venues to greater civil society participation and public accountability so that considerations of human rights and privacy are at least raised, even if not immediately respected.

The private sector now gathers and retains staggering mountains of data about countless millions of people. It is no longer enough for states to conduct themselves according to the principles of transparency, accountability, and oversight that democracy prizes; the companies that own and operate cyberspace—and that often come under tremendous pressure from states—must do so as well. Export controls and "smart sanctions" that target rights-offending technologies without infringing on academic freedom can play a role. A highly distributed, independent, and powerful system of cyberspace verification should be built on a global scale that monitors for rights violations, dual-use technologies, targeted malware attacks, and privacy breaches. A model for such a system might be found in traditional arms-control verification regimes such as the one administered by the Organization for the Prohibition of Chemical Weapons. Or it might come from the research of academic groups such as Citizen Lab, or the setup of national computer emergency-response teams (CERTs) once these are freed from their current subordination to parochial national-security concerns.[29] However it is ultimately constituted, there needs to be a system for monitoring cyberspace rights and freedoms that is globally distributed and independent of governments and the private sector.

Finally, we need models of cyberspace security that can show us how to prevent disruptions or threats to life and property without sacrificing liberties and rights. Internet-freedom advocates must reckon with the realization that a free, open, and secure cyberspace will materialize only within a framework of democratic oversight, public accountability, transparent checks and balances, and the rule of law. For individuals living under authoritarianism's heavy hand, achieving such lofty goals must sound like a distant dream. Yet for those who reside in affluent countries, especially ones where these principles have lost ground to antiterror measures and mass-surveillance programs, fighting for them should loom as an urgent priority and a practically achievable first step on the road to remediation.

Notes

The author wishes to thank Sarah McKune, Helmi Noman, Irene Poetranto, and John Scott Railton of Citizen Lab for comments and research assistance that they provided in the preparation of this essay.

1. Sam Kimball, "After the Arab Spring, Surveillance in Egypt Intensifies," *Intercept*, 9 March 2015, *https://firstlook.org/theintercept/2015/03/09/arab-spring-surveillance-egypt-intensifies*.

2. Steven Levitsky and Lucan A. Way, "The Rise of Competitive Authoritarianism," *Journal of Democracy* 13 (April 2002): 51–65.

3. Ronald Deibert and Rafal Rohozinski, "Beyond Denial: Introducing Next Generation Information Access Controls," *http://access.opennet.net/wp-content/uploads/2011/12/accesscontrolled-chapter-1.pdf*. Note that the "generations" of controls are not assumed to be strictly chronological: Governments can skip generations, and several generations can exist together. Rather, they are a useful heuristic device for understanding the evolution of information controls.

4. "YouTube to Remain Blocked 'Indefinitely' in Pakistan: Officials," *Dawn* (Islamabad), 8 February 2015, *www.dawn.com/news/1162139*.

5. Bennett Haselton, "Blue Coat Errors: Sites Miscategorized as 'Pornography,'" Citizen Lab, 10 March 2014, *https://citizenlab.org/2014/03/blue-coat-errors-sites-miscategorized-pornography*.

6. "Routing Gone Wild: Documenting Upstream Filtering in Oman via India," Citizen Lab, 12 July 2012, *https://citizenlab.org/2012/07/routing-gone-wild*.

7. "IGF 2013: Islands of Control, Island of Resistance: Monitoring the 2013 Indonesian IGF (Foreword)," Citizen Lab, 20 January 2014, *www.citizenlab.org/briefs/29-igf-indonesia/29-igf-indonesia.pdf*.

8. Masashi Crete-Nishihata, Ronald J. Deibert, and Adam Senft, "Not by Technical Means Alone: The Multidisciplinary Challenge of Studying Information Controls," *IEEE Internet Computing* 17 (May–June 2013): 34–41.

9. See *https://china-chats.net*.

10. Amol Sharma, "RIM Facility Helps India in Surveillance Efforts," *Wall Street Journal*, 28 October 2011.

11. Rogier Creemers, "New Internet Rules Reflect China's 'Intent to Target Individuals Online,'" *Deutsche Welle*, 2 March 2015.

12. Citizen Lab, "Communities @ Risk: Targeted Digital Threats Against Civil Society," 11 November 2014, *https://targetedthreats.net*.

13. Bill Marczak et al., "China's Great Cannon," Citizen Lab, 10 April 2015, *https://citizenlab.org/2015/04/chinas-great-cannon*.

14. "For Their Eyes Only: The Commercialization of Digital Spying," Citizen Lab, 30 April 2013, *https://citizenlab.org/2013/04/for-their-eyes-only-2*.

15. "Malware Attack Targeting Syrian ISIS Critics," Citizen Lab, 18 December 2014, *https://citizenlab.org/2014/12/malware-attack-targeting-syrian-isis-critics*.

16. Seva Gunitzky, "Corrupting the Cyber-Commons: Social Media as a Tool of Autocratic Stability," *Perspectives on Politics* 13 (March 2015): 42–54.

17. RFE/RL Tajik Service, "SMS Services Down in Tajikistan After Protest Calls," *Radio Free Europe/Radio Liberty*, 10 October 2014, *www.rferl.org/content/tajikistan-sms-internet-group-24-quvatov-phone-message-blockage-dushanbe/26630390.html*.

18. See "No Mobile Phone Services on March 23 in Islamabad," *Daily Capital* (Islamabad), 22 March 2015, *http://dailycapital.pk/mobile-phone-services-to-remain-blocked-on-march-23*.

19. Ronald J. Deibert and Masashi Crete-Nishihata, "Global Governance and the Spread of Cyberspace Controls," *Global Governance* 18 (2012): 339–61, *http://citizenlab.org/cybernorms2012/governance.pdf*.

20. See James R. Clapper, "Statement for the Record Worldwide Threat Assessment of the US Intelligence Community," Senate Armed Services Committee, 26 February 2015, *www.dni.gov/files/documents/Unclassified_2015_ATA_SFR_-_SASC_FINAL.pdf*.

21. See "Counter-Terrorism Committee Welcomes Close Cooperation with the Regional Anti-Terrorist Structure of the Shanghai Cooperation Organization," 24 October 2014, *www.un.org/en/sc/ctc/news/2014-10-24_cted_shangha-icoop.html*.

22. See Joshua Kucera, "SCO, CSTO Increasing Efforts Against Internet Threats," The Bug Pit, 16 June 2014, *www.eurasianet.org/node/68591*.

23. See Cisco, "Cisco Visual Networking Index: Global Mobile Data Traffic Forecast Update 2014–2019," white paper, 3 February 2015, *www.cisco.com/c/en/us/solutions/collateral/service-provider/visual-networking-index-vni/white_paper_c11-520862.html*.

24. Craig Timberg, "For Sale: Systems That Can Secretly Track Where Cellphone Users Go Around the Globe," *Washington Post*, 24 August 2014.

25. Collin Anderson, "Monitoring the Lines: Sanctions and Human Rights Policy Considerations of TeleStrategies ISS World Seminars," 31 July 2014, *http://cda.io/notes/monitoring-the-lines*.

26. Anderson, "Monitoring the Lines."

27. See Jon Grevatt, "BAE Systems Announces Funding of Malaysian Cyber Degree Programme," IHS Jane's 360, 5 March 2015, *www.janes.com/article/49778/bae-systems-announces-funding-of-malaysian-cyber-degree-programme*.

28. Colin Freeze, "Canadian Agencies Use Data Stolen by Foreign Hackers, Memo Reveals" *Globe and Mail* (Toronto), 6 February 2015.

29. For one proposal along these lines, see Duncan Hollis and Tim Maurer, "A Red Cross for Cyberspace," *Time*, 18 February 2015.

CHAPTER FOURTEEN

Dealing with the Authoritarian Resurgence

CHRISTOPHER WALKER

SINCE THE END of the Cold War, the democratic West has accorded particular prominence to the idea of integrating nondemocratic regimes into the liberal international order. For political leaders and analysts in the United States and Europe, integration has been a dominant foreign-policy organizing concept, serving as the West's strategic lodestar over the past quarter century. The democracies' central assumption has been that patient engagement with authoritarian states would yield clear mutual benefits. By embracing such regimes and encouraging their integration into the global economic system and key political institutions, Western powers hoped to coax the autocracies toward meaningful political reform, leading them eventually to become more like the democracies. Even the tougher cases for democratization, such as Russia and China, were expected slowly but inevitably to liberalize politically as their economies grew and their middle classes developed.

But in an unanticipated twist, the authoritarian regimes, both large and small, have turned the tables on the democracies. Rather than reforming, most of these repressive regimes have deepened their authoritarianism. And now they are turning it outward. Although the leading authoritarian regimes are today integrated in many ways into the global system, they have not become more like the democracies; rather, they have developed policies and practices aimed at blocking democracy's advance. Exploiting globalization and the opportunities presented by integration with the West, these states have set out to undermine the very institutions and arenas that welcomed them.

Today, authoritarian regimes are projecting power beyond their borders. They are targeting crucial democratic institutions, including elections and the media. They use deep economic and business ties to export corrupt practices and insinuate themselves into the politics of democracies, both new and established. They are influencing international public opinion and investing heavily in their own instruments of "soft power" in order to compete with democracy in the realm of ideas.

In 2014, the National Endowment for Democracy's International Forum for Democratic Studies launched a two-year initiative on resurgent authoritarianism, from which this essay and others in this volume come. The project found that regimes in countries as diverse as China, Russia, Venezuela, and even archrivals Iran and Saudi Arabia, despite disagreeing on many issues, broadly share the objective of containing the spread of democracy. Moreover, these regimes are capitalizing on the benefits of integration to pursue this goal both domestically and internationally.

One area in which the rise of authoritarian power has been highly visible is geopolitics. China has been exerting its influence more forcefully in the South China Sea, for example, flexing its muscles with an island-building spree in the Spratly Island chain and generally adopting a more assertive military profile in the region. Russia, although seen by some as enfeebled, has pushed into high gear a policy of disruption: Within a span of eighteen months, it has annexed Crimea, invaded Ukraine, and plowed significant new military resources into the Middle East. Russian airstrikes in Syria, begun in September 2015 on behalf of Bashar al-Assad's brutal regime, caught the West off guard, as did the Kremlin's military forays into Crimea and other parts of Ukraine in 2014. Iran, meanwhile, has upped its activities in Afghanistan, Iraq, and Lebanon. Augmenting its existing presence in Syria, Iran sent ground troops into the country in October 2015, side by side with Russia in a show of solidarity. Saudi Arabia, for its part, has undertaken a months-long bombing campaign in Yemen in an effort to contest rival Iran in a region beset with power vacuums.

The Authoritarian Toolkit

The willingness of these illiberal regimes to use military power is one sign of the changing international environment. But it is their development of so-called soft power that is the most conspicuous aspect of the new authoritarianism. The term *soft power* is a rather uncomfortable fit for these efforts, however, as none measures up to Joseph Nye's conception of such power that emphasized states' capacity to attract others by the legitimacy of their "policies and the values that underlie them."[1] Even the China model, which has attracted any number of authoritarian governments and even some Western analysts, is fraught with problems. Yet that has not stopped the leading authoritarian governments from hijacking the concept of soft power as part of a broad assault on democracy and its values.

Through authoritarian learning (for example, by adapting or mimicking democratic forms) and by exploiting the opportunities presented by globalization, authoritarian trendsetters have created a modern antidemocratic toolkit that in many ways serves as the mirror image of democratic soft power. Its contents include government-organized nongovernmental organizations (GONGOs), "zombie" election monitoring, foreign aid and investment, and both traditional- and new-media enterprises.

The leading authoritarian governments have established a wide constellation of regime-friendly GONGOs, including think tanks and policy institutes that operate at home and abroad. Some of these groups are benign, but many operate with the aim of subverting authentic debate, either by spreading regime messages in a nontransparent way or by crowding out authentic voices. "Zombie" election monitoring, which allows authoritarian regimes to manipulate the integrity of the election process, is a related innovation. In terms of aid and investment, China and other authoritarian governments have sunk vast sums into the developing world, enabling recipient governments to sidestep the standards of transparency and accountability required by the established international financial institutions.

Finally, illiberal regimes are scaling up their traditional- and new-media capabilities and broadcasting content to global audiences. On the surface, these enterprises seem like soft-power instruments. But China's CCTV and Russia's RT are not the BBC or Deutsche Welle, which operate according to a fundamentally different value system. Because editorial accountability for authoritarian media outlets ultimately rests with the political leadership, the content that they produce is compromised, through either editorial omission or commission. Thus if CCTV reports at all about controversial topics such as the Tiananmen Square Massacre, Tibet, or Taiwan, it is not in a dispassionate or critical way. RT, meanwhile, unfailingly follows the

Kremlin line, rationalizing the status quo that the regime seeks to maintain by cynically portraying all systems, whether authoritarian or democratic, as corrupt.

Similarly, the deepening commercial integration of the last two decades has enabled the Chinese and Russian governments to influence political affairs in both young and established democracies. These regimes have identified ways to compromise the values of transparency and accountability and to export corruption to the democracies. For example, under Vladimir Putin, a centerpiece of Russia's engagement with the West has been the corrupt and exploitative export of hydrocarbons, which has had an impact on Western financial, legal, and political institutions.[2] In short, the authoritarian toolkit enables illiberal regimes to project their influence into the democratic space in a variety of ways.

At the same time, authoritarian regimes have become adept at muffling voices from the democracies. Over time, Western universities, think tanks, and media and technology companies operating in China, Russia, Saudi Arabia, and other Gulf States have become more integrated commercially with these authoritarian systems. This has sometimes enabled these regimes to coopt their Western partners and induce self-censorship, thereby resetting norms of free expression through what is essentially economic coercion.

In addition, the authoritarians are trying to unmoor the institutions that have served as the glue of the post–Cold War order. Illiberal regimes work together within the regional and international rules-based organizations that have been crucial to the global political framework—the UN, the Organization of American States, the Council of Europe, and the Organization for Security and Co-operation in Europe (OSCE)—in order to neuter their human-rights and democracy components. Meanwhile, authoritarian governments are establishing their own organizations, including the Shanghai Cooperation Organization and the Eurasian Economic Union, which are promoting alternative, authoritarian-friendly norms.

In a relatively short period, the leading repressive regimes have forged a formidable infrastructure for challenging the democracies and their values, and a real competition over norms has emerged as the West's normative power has begun to unravel. As Alexander Cooley observes, leading authoritarian regimes are challenging the notion of universal human rights and propagating instead norms based on "state sovereignty" and security, "civilizational diversity," and the defense of "traditional values" against liberal democracy.

These all enjoy significant backing today. The effects are most visible in the narrowing of the political space for civil society, the shifting missions that regional organizations are embracing, and the growing clout of non-Western powers as international patrons.[3]

The Worst Get Worse

In the face of this authoritarian mobilization, the democracies have been caught flat-footed. Due in part to complacency but also to the "crisis of confidence" that set in after the 2008–2009 global economic crisis (and has been exacerbated by the European migrant crisis that began in 2015), the established democracies so far have had no coherent answer to the authoritarian surge. More troublingly, the West seems to have fallen into a political torpor that contributes to a larger "failure of imagination" in responding to the serious challenges that have emerged in the new, contested environment.[4] In order to understand the growing challenges to democracy posed by the authoritarian surge, we must examine the evolution of the authoritarian toolkit since the "backlash" against democracy began in the mid-2000s.

At first, the backlash was apparent only in a limited number of countries and was confined largely to the domestic level. In this early phase, authoritarian regimes used legal, regulatory, and informal measures, often restricting freedom of expression and association, to obstruct the emergence of democratic pluralism. Repression in authoritarian settings tends to exhibit an ebb and flow in which the government's grip is tightened and then, at some point, relaxed. The authoritarian backlash never eased, however. Instead, it has gained momentum and deepened in intensity over the past decade.

Freedom House's *Freedom in the World* report bears this out: In each of the past nine years, declines in political rights and civil liberties have outstripped improvements. Notably, a large share of those declines have occurred in countries already deemed Not Free by Freedom House. In other words, countries in the worst category have become even more repressive, sinking further *within* that category. This deepening authoritarianism in already repressive environments has been a crucial driver of the decline in Freedom House ratings often cited as evidence of a "democratic recession."

A big part of this story is found in the two regions that represent centers of authoritarianism: the former Soviet Union (FSU) and the Middle East and North Africa (MENA). In the FSU, rights and freedoms markedly declined in countries such as Azerbaijan, Kazakhstan, and Tajikistan between 2006 and 2015. Moreover, in Russia, whose intensifying authoritarianism has implications not just for its neighborhood but for the wider world, political rights and civil liberties worsened significantly during these years.

In the MENA region, fifteen of eighteen countries have become less free over the past ten years, and in many cases considerably so. (Tunisia, which has established a nascent democracy, is of course an exception.) Countries such as Bahrain, Iran, Jordan, and Saudi Arabia, which were already highly autocratic, have become even more so, especially since the Arab uprisings. Egypt under President Abdel Fattah al-Sisi is by most accounts even more repressive than it was during the Hosni Mubarak era.

China, with the world's largest population and second largest economy, ranks among the world's most politically repressive states. On Freedom House's combined 100-point scale[5] for political rights and civil liberties, China scores a paltry 17, the same as in 2006. Out of 40 possible points for political rights, China scores just 2, an astonishingly low number that reflects the systematic repression and denial of political rights in that country. As in Russia, deepening authoritarianism in an increasingly internationalist China reverberates beyond its borders.

Above all, authoritarian rulers are preoccupied with regime survival, and they study and learn from other authoritarian regimes, both past and present, in order to maintain power. The Chinese Communist Party (CCP) has scrutinized the collapse of the Soviet system in order to avoid the same fate,[6] while Vladimir Putin's Kremlin has carefully studied the durability of the Chinese system in the post-Tiananmen period. In the first case, the CCP seeks to draw lessons from Soviet failure; in the second, the post-Soviet Kremlin, like any number of other contemporary authoritarian governments, attempts to glean what it can from China's seeming success at repressing political opposition while growing its economy.

One sign of the priority given to regime security by authoritarian governments is their massive investment in internal security, which, tellingly, can outstrip even military and external-defense budgets. The Chinese and Iranian governments, for example, use public funds to build vast security apparatuses that are devoted to suppressing internal dissent.[7] Following the

Arab uprisings in 2011, Saudi Arabia increased the staff of its already amply manned interior ministry by sixty thousand.[8] These regimes have made the prevention of domestic dissent a cornerstone of their national (read "regime") security strategy.

Thwarting "Color Revolutions"

In countries where basic democratic rights are routinely denied, the menace of a "color revolution" has become the central organizing concept around which authoritarian regimes formulate their security and propaganda strategies. For example, the May 2014 Moscow Conference on International Security, sponsored by Russia's defense ministry, focused on the impact of popular protest—specifically color revolutions—on international security. Speakers included Russian defense minister Sergei Shoigu and foreign minister Sergei Lavrov. Senior officials from nondemocracies such as China, Egypt, Iran, Syria, and the United Arab Emirates attended the conference, along with officials from Burma, a country in the midst of a troubled transition. The Russian speakers warned attendees that "color revolutions are a new form of warfare invented by Western governments seeking to remove independently-minded national governments in favor of ones controlled by the West."[9]

In September 2015, Russia, Belarus, and EU-aspirant Serbia took part in a military-training exercise dubbed Slavic Brotherhood 2015, held in Novorossiysk, Russia. Army-General Valeriy Gerasimov, head of Russia's General Staff, explained that such exercises were needed because "'so-called color revolutions'" are "a form of armed struggle that must be met by military force." According to Gerasimov, interpreting color revolutions as a type of warfare allows for military-training adjustments and calls for the armed forces to devise ways to thwart such popular movements.[10] Through training exercises such as Slavic Brotherhood 2015, Russia and other authoritarian states are developing the hard-power capacity to contain democratic development and any form of organized dissent.

China has likewise devoted considerable attention to the concept of color revolutions. On 13 June 2015, for example, the *People's Daily*, a CCP mouthpiece, published five scholarly articles exploring the roots of color revolutions and what China might learn from the experience of the affected nations.

The CCP regime believes that the United States had a hand in these protest movements and that NGOs helped to foment them. China's official military strategy now states that "anti-China forces have never given up their attempt to instigate a 'color revolution' in this country."[11] By assigning responsibility for domestic dissent to external forces, these governments create a rationale for internationalizing their strategy of "democracy containment."

These kinds of cross-national military and security exercises show the extraordinary lengths to which these regimes and others are going to stifle political pluralism. This is part of a larger effort at authoritarian learning that has also helped authoritarians to craft more sophisticated methods for controlling civil society, the business community, and political opposition.

Authoritarian learning also has played a visible role in shaping how repressive regimes manage and censor the Internet, which they see as a growing threat. China is a leader in this regard, demonstrating that it is possible to expand Internet access—some 640 million people are now online in China—while maintaining effective control over political content. The authorities in Beijing, like illiberal governments in many other capitals, exploit the globalization of commerce to use the most modern technology available on the world market, often provided by Western firms, to censor the Internet. Facing this degree of online use and the challenge that it poses to the regime's ability to dominate key political narratives, the CCP has undertaken a vast, multilayered set of measures to maintain control.[12]

The CCP's censorship measures have also had a demonstration effect abroad. Other countries—both authoritarian and semi-authoritarian—see the "success" of Beijing's approach to controlling the Internet and other information and communications technologies and realize that systematic online censorship can be achieved. Over time, other countries have learned by observation or direct assistance from China, and have adapted methods of Internet repression to their own contexts.

In September 2013, Chinese authorities, citing the need to crack down on what they termed "online rumors," issued new guidelines for social media, which serve as vital popular forums for discussing politics. Under the new rules, Internet users who post defamatory comments that are seen by 5,000 users or reposted more than 500 times could face up to three years in jail. Since its adoption, this measure has effectively suppressed the most-followed civic voices in China on social media. The Kremlin clearly took notice, because less than a year later, in August 2014, it put into effect a new set of regulations similar to the Chinese guidelines. Russia's "blogger law" requires any person whose online presence draws more than 3,000 daily readers to register, disclose personal information, and submit to the same regulations as mass media.

Authoritarian regimes also are learning from each other how to choke off independent civil society. In recent years, trendsetting authoritarian regimes have adopted a cascade of laws restricting the civil society sector, and other countries, including some democracies, have followed suit.[13] Troublingly, the intensive learning that has taken place at the domestic level also has been crucial to the development of the authoritarians' methods for obstructing democracy beyond their borders. In other words, the most influential authoritarian regimes, Russia and China foremost among them, have served as incubators for the innovation of antidemocratic techniques that are now applied internationally. By and large, observers in the democracies have failed to appreciate this.

The Challenge from "Zombie" Democracy

Through experimentation and learning, authoritarian regimes have refined their techniques of manipulation at the domestic level. By constructing fake political parties, phony social movements, and state-controlled media enterprises that appear in many ways to be like those of their democratic counterparts, autocrats simulate democratic institutions as a way of preventing authentic democracy from taking root.

Authoritarian regimes have coupled their harsh crackdown on independent NGOs, for example, with a scaling up of government-backed GONGOs, entities that Moisés Naím describes as employing the "practices of democracy to subtly undermine democracy."[14] Beijing has moved aggressively to fill the public space with GONGOs and, as part of its larger ambitions, seeks to develop an array of state-backed think tanks. On 27 October 2014, at the sixth meeting of the Leading Group for Overall Reform, Chinese president Xi Jinping, who heads the group, called for the creation of a new set of CCP-directed think tanks: "Building a new type of think tank with Chinese characteristics is an important and pressing mission. It should be targeted [at] promoting scientific and democratic decision making, promoting modernization of the country's governing system and ability, as well as strengthening China's soft power."[15] The CCP already has taken the GON-GO concept one step further, requiring all domestic cultural, economic, and social organizations to establish Party-organized groups (sometimes called "PONGOs"), which will allow the authorities to assert even greater control in this sphere.[16]

As authoritarian "zombie democracy" has migrated from the domestic to the international level, China's state-backed GONGOs increasingly insinuate themselves into regional and supranational rules-based organizations. At sessions of the Universal Periodic Review (UPR), a component of the Geneva-based UN Human Rights Council (UNHRC) that reviews human rights in all UN member states, Beijing-aligned "nongovernmental" organizations take part in UN meetings in order to push the line of Chinese authorities and harass human-rights activists who criticize the Chinese government in this forum.

In October 2013, several Chinese GONGOs descended on Geneva as China's rights record was under review by the UNHRC. At such UPR sessions, representatives of GONGOs, sometimes in coordination with Chinese diplomats, use a variety of tactics to intimidate activists, taking unauthorized photos of them and filling up meeting halls with regime representatives to drown out accusations of rights abuses. According to a 2015 Reuters investigation, 47 NGOs from Mainland China, Hong Kong, and Macau are authorized to participate in UNHRC meetings. Of these, at least 34 are GONGOs, either under the authority of Chinese government ministries or CCP bodies, or headed by a current or retired government or Party official.[17]

In what has become an annual ritual at the OSCE's Human Dimension Implementation Meetings (HDIMs) in Warsaw, Poland, GONGOs from countries such as Azerbaijan, Belarus, Kazakhstan, and Russia take part in proceedings that were intended to allow authentic civil society groups to voice their views about human rights and democracy in their countries.[18] In 2014, Kremlin-backed GONGOs stayed true to form and sought to confuse the discussion about Russia's invasion of Ukraine. In September 2015, Azerbaijani GONGOs actively confronted independent Azerbaijani civil society participants and tried to muddy the waters regarding the country's rights record.

Similarly, the Cuban and Venezuelan governments brought GONGOs to the April 2015 Summit of the Americas in Panama, with the aim of presenting regime-backed groups as authentic civil society members. Many of these groups claim to be autonomous, yet they dutifully advocated the positions of their countries' governments.

Meanwhile, apart from influencing the proceedings of regional organizations, Russia sinks extensive resources into GONGOs in countries on its periphery and beyond. Through organizations such as Russky Mir and the Foundation for Defense of Rights of Compatriots Abroad, the Kremlin funds many initiatives of this kind. The Baltic states endure an especially heavy dose of Russian "soft power," as Kremlin-supported GONGOs try to influence the public debate and shape the views of these societies, which are home to large ethnic-Russian communities.

According to a 2015 report, the investigative-journalism initiative Re:Baltica found in 2013 that Russky Mir was making grants to support the promotion of "Russian language and culture" in the Baltic states, while the smaller Foundation for Defense of Rights of Compatriots Abroad funded "filmmakers that support and promote" the Russian version of twentieth-century history; "researchers who accuse the Baltic states and Ukraine of human rights violations"; ethnic Russians "who were tried [for] participating in the 2007 riots in Tallinn," Estonia's capital; and "active participants of the deportation of Lithuanians to Siberia" during and after World War II.[19] While the Kremlin ruthlessly represses the activities of independent NGOs in Russia, beyond its borders Russian authorities eagerly exploit the open space of the democracies, providing financial and political support to Kremlin-friendly GONGOs that operate unhindered in these democratic settings.

Authoritarian regimes also have begun using methods of election manipulation at the international level, supporting faux monitoring groups that endorse fraudulent elections with the aim of clouding the assessments made by established monitoring organizations. These "zombie" monitors have proliferated widely. Two authoritarian-led initiatives, the Commonwealth of Independent States Election Monitoring Organization and the Shanghai Cooperation Organization, have sent purported monitors to recent polls across Eurasia. In October 2013, Azerbaijan's government brought in zombie monitors from abroad to sanctify its patently manipulated presidential election. A host of ersatz monitoring organizations, with names such as the Observer Mission of the Standing Conference of Political Parties of Latin America and the Caribbean and the Observer Mission of the NGO Forum of the Organization of Black Sea Economic Cooperation, along with a motley group of fringe politicians from Europe, praised this Alice in Wonderland–like pseudo-election event.

A similar spectacle occurred in Crimea during a "referendum" held in March 2014 after Russia's "little green men" (as some Crimean locals called the Russian troops whose presence the Kremlin denied) had invaded the peninsula. During this pseudo-referendum, a mix of radical political figures who were brought to Crimea despite lacking credentials for authentic election monitoring appeared in Russian-government media outlets to present findings that went in lock step with those of the Kremlin. Even China, a country that itself does not hold real elections, has sent observers to recent elections in Burma and Zimbabwe.

The Battle over Information

The ideas and messages of zombie NGOs and election monitors are disseminated through state-backed media, which serve as instruments for manipulating audiences and suppressing democratic content. At home, the authoritarians can deploy a potent combination of censorship and propaganda, allowing them to dominate the media space and create an unchallenged alternate reality for their audiences. Beijing, Moscow, and Riyadh spare little expense to keep alternative ideas and information from entering mainstream political discussion. In a perfect example of the studious authoritarian avoidance of sensitive domestic issues, China's state-run media did not report at all on the country's massive stock-market collapse in August 2015.[20]

Abroad, however, Beijing and Moscow cannot impose censorship in the same way they do at home; instead, they use other techniques adapted from domestic experience and apply them to the international arena. In the online realm, for example, these regimes rely on trolls, cyberattacks, and disinformation to achieve their objectives. While these illiberal governments are committed to preventing the competition of ideas within their borders, they have taken big steps to make certain that their own point of view is heard abroad. The best-resourced among them have built formidable media outlets that enable them to project their messages into the global marketplace of ideas.

At home, these regimes repress domestic media and increasingly obstruct the work of Western news organizations, thereby cutting off one of the few remaining arteries for transmitting information on these politically closed countries. By manipulating the granting of visas and harassing and even jailing journalists (as in the case of *Washington Post* reporter Jason

Rezaian), these regimes set the terms of engagement. At the same time, authoritarian media outlets have exploited the openness of democracies by increasing their presence and activities in a number of democratic countries. Telesur, supported by Venezuela and several other countries, operates in Spanish-speaking Latin America. China's CCTV and Russia's RT have a large and growing presence in the United States; both have open access to dozens of cable and satellite systems in the United States and around the world for broadcasting their state-backed content.

CCTV offers programs in Arabic, French, Russian, and Spanish, while China's state news agency, Xinhua, is expanding worldwide. CCTV America's Washington headquarters employs about thirty journalists producing Mandarin-language content and more than a hundred producing English-language content. CCTV also has broadcasting facilities in New York and Los Angeles. China's media presence in the developing world is growing: It has twelve bureaus in Latin America and has built an enormous media foothold in sub-Saharan Africa. In November 2015, it came to light that China Radio International (CRI), Beijing's state-run radio network, is operating as a hidden hand behind a global web of stations on which the Chinese government controls much of the content. According to a Reuters investigation, 33 stations in 14 countries "primarily broadcast content created or supplied by CRI in the United States, Australia, and Europe." As part of this elaborate Chinese government effort to exploit the open media space, more than a dozen stations across the United States operate as part of the CCP's "borrowed boat" approach, in which existing media outlets in foreign countries are used to project China's messages.[21]

Beijing devotes elaborate efforts to limiting foreign reporting that it deems unfavorable. Over the past two decades, the Chinese government has developed tools to extend information controls to media outlets based outside of China. In many cases, Chinese officials directly impede independent reporting by media based abroad. More prevalent, however, and often more effective are methods of control that subtly induce self-censorship or inspire media owners, advertisers, and other international actors to take action on the CCP's behalf.[22]

Like CCTV, Russia's RT has a Washington, D.C., headquarters and broadcast facilities in New York, Miami, and Los Angeles. State or state-friendly media in Russia—Life News, NTV, Channel One Russia, and Russia 24—

disseminate not just the Kremlin's narratives but also outright fakery to domestic audiences and those in the Russian-speaking space. These outlets spread the same stories via social media as well. RT, meanwhile, pushes this manipulated content out to international audiences.

In addition to its English-language broadcasts, Russia's state media devote substantial attention to reaching the Balkans, Latin America, and the Middle East. Russia, like China and Iran, sees an opportunity to exploit the information space in the Balkans, where the democracies' already limited media presence is shrinking. A large part of Russia's editorial efforts, along with those of other authoritarian regimes, are aimed at assailing the West, distorting perceptions of democracy, and tarnishing the image of the United States and the EU. To the extent that these regimes have agreed on any ideology, it is anti-Americanism. This focus is best understood as a reflection of the absence of a positive ideology or vision of their own.

For a long time, the West did not worry about authoritarian international media enterprises. Over time, however, it has become clear that outlets such as CCTV and RT are able to exert real influence. Although it may be comforting to think that people in the democracies have a natural resistance to foreign propaganda, this is not always the case. One need only look at how warped and false arguments about Russia's invasion of Ukraine snaked their way into the debate in the United States and Europe.[23]

Authoritarian-backed media have become intertwined with the world of normal news, especially online. Western news outlets today are picking up key narratives pushed by Russian state media. Slick websites with phony news and Kremlin spins appear in the new democracies of Central Europe. In today's helter-skelter, fragmented media world, it is much easier for authoritarian governments to manipulate the global understanding of important issues, making it harder to distinguish between authentic and phony information.

Responding to Authoritarian Internationalism

A renewed struggle between democracy and authoritarianism has emerged. The decade-long democratic decline reported by Freedom House has been most dramatic within the ranks of already authoritarian regimes, which have become even more repressive. At the same time, the most influential among them—China, Russia, and Iran—have become more internationalist. In doing so, they have found ways to exploit integration and to broaden their influence in the democratic world. Through the development of the antidemocratic toolkit of simulated NGOs, think tanks, election monitors, and news media, the autocrats are actively seeking to undermine democracy from within.

Increasingly, these regimes show solidarity and coordination with one another, at least when it comes to contesting and containing democracy and the ideas central to it. Through this more internationalist approach and authoritarian learning, China, Russia, Iran, and other illiberal regimes have developed instruments to counter the democratic West's soft power. But the power that the authoritarians are exerting is not soft power as customarily understood. Indeed, the application of the term *soft power*—a benign concept generally applied to efforts made to bolster a country's image, contribute to open debate, and win friends and allies—to the ideas-related efforts of the authoritarians is problematic. What the authoritarian regimes are practicing is instead a more malign mirror image of soft power.

This misunderstanding has led observers in the West to assume that the authoritarians have established their international media outlets (CCTV, RT, and Iran's PressTV, for example) in order to build prestige and gain respect from the outside world—that is, to win hearts and minds. But this is a fundamental misapprehension. As China, Russia, and Iran have spent vast and increasing sums on media and other tools to exert international influence, the image of all three countries has remained very low in the West, and in some cases is sinking even lower.[24] Their principal aim is not to promote authoritarianism, but rather to contain the spread of democracy and reshape the norms of the international order. It will be increasingly important for observers in the West to understand the alternative (and more malevolent) explanation for these massive influence initiatives, because as Peter Pomerantsev observes, "illiberal regimes across the world are adopting similar strategies and uniting to create global networks of pseudorealities."[25]

Yet so far the democracies, whether out of complacency or willful ignorance, have not taken seriously the prospect that these emboldened illiberal powers could reshape the undefended post–Cold War liberal order. The challenge is particularly vexing because the authoritarians have turned integration, jiu jitsu–like, against the democracies. This unexpected twist requires some fresh and serious thinking about how the democratic world should respond to the growing authoritarian challenge.

Any such renewed thinking will first require dispensing with the false framing of this issue as a choice between shunning or engaging authoritarian regimes. Most of them are already thoroughly integrated into the international system, making some kind of engagement unavoidable. It is the nature of the democracies' engagement that must be rethought. The established democracies must pursue a more nimble and principled approach that takes into account the new environment in which authoritarian regimes are seeking to undermine democratic institutions and values.

The democracies need to renew and refresh their commitment to democratic institutions, and to take steps to stop the authoritarians from hollowing out the most important regional and global rules-based organizations. As China, Russia, and Iran scale up their media presence in places such as the Balkans, Central Europe, Latin America, and sub-Saharan Africa, so too should the United States and European democracies instead of scaling back as they have been doing. Moreover, the democratic states need to upgrade and modernize their international media capacity so that they can compete and flourish in this new and contested environment.

The democracies must pursue democratic learning—innovation by civil society but also renewal of commitment from democratic governments—with the same vigor that the authoritarians devote to their pursuit of authoritarian learning. If the democracies instead opt to pursue a reactive, status-quo policy that allows the authoritarians to keep the initiative, we can expect the grim prospect of an even greater erosion of democratic space in the years to come.

Notes

1. Joseph S. Nye Jr., "The Decline of America's Soft Power: Why Washington Should Worry," *Foreign Affairs* 83 (May–June 2004): 16–20.

2. Peter Pomerantsev and Michael Weiss, "The Menace of Unreality: How the Kremlin Weaponizes Information, Culture and Money," special report presented by *The Interpreter* (a project of the Institute of Modern Russia, New York), 2014.

3. Alexander Cooley, "Authoritarianism Goes Global: Countering Democratic Norms," in Larry Diamond, Marc F. Plattner, and Christopher Walker, eds., *Authoritarianism Goes Global: The Challenge to Democracy* (Baltimore: Johns Hopkins University Press, 2016), ch. 7.

4. Christopher Walker, "The West's Failure of Imagination," *Wall Street Journal*, 3 August 2015.

5. Freedom House rates countries as Free (1–2.5), Partly Free (3–5), or Not Free (5.5–7) based on their averaged combined scores for political rights and civil liberties, which in turn are based on a 40-point scale and a 60-point scale, respectively, that combine to make a 100-point scale. The declines of the past nine years are based on these more granular subdata rather than the overarching categories of Free, Partly Free, and Not Free, whose composition has not changed substantially. See *Freedom in the World* reports beginning in 2008 and "Freedom in the World: Aggregate and Subcategory Scores," *https://freedomhouse.org/report/freedom-world-aggregate-and-subcategory-scores*.

6. William Wan, "In China, Soviet Union's Failure Drives Decisions on Reform," *Washington Post*, 23 March 2013.

7. See Frederic Wehrey et al., "The Rise of Pasdaran: Assessing the Domestic Roles of Iran's Islamic Revolutionary Guards Corps," RAND Corporation, 2009; Saeid Golkar, *Captive Society: The Basij Militia and Social Control in Iran* (New York: Columbia University Press, 2015); Edward Wong, "Beijing Goes Quiet on Rise of Local Security Budgets," Sinosphere blog, *New York Times*, 6 March 2014, *http://sinosphere.blogs.nytimes.com/2014/03/06/beijing-goes-quiet-on-rise-of-local-security-budgets/?_r=0*.

8. Simeon Kerr, "Saudi Arabia Sets Lavish Spending Figure," *Financial Times*, 27 December 2011.

9. Dmitry Gorenburg, "Countering Color Revolutions: Russia's New Security Strategy and Its Implications for U.S. Policy," PONARS Eurasia Policy Memo No. 342, September 2014, *www.ponarseurasia.org/sites/default/files/policy-memos-pdf/Pepm342_Gorenburg_Sept2014.pdf*.

10. Roger McDermott, "Slavic Brotherhood 2015 Rehearses Anti–Color Revolution Operations," *Eurasia Daily Monitor* 12, no. 160, 8 September 2015, *www.jamestown.org/single/?tx_ttnews%5Btt_news%5D=44344&tx_ttnews%5BbackPid%5D=7&cHash=503b639c37a53036d98448683c3aac17#.VhBIEmflvIU*.

11. On the five articles, see Mimi Lau, "People's Daily Warns Against Colour Revolutions, Blames 'Spread of Western Ideology,'" *South China Morning Post*, 14 June 2015, *www.scmp.com/news/china/policies-politics/article/1822063/communist-party-paper-sees-red-over-colour-revolutions?page=all*; on CCP's belief in U.S. complicity, see David Shambaugh, *China's Communist Party: Atrophy and Adaptation* (Berkeley: University of California Press, 2009); for quote, see State Council Information Office of the People's Republic of China, "China's Military Strategy," May 2015, *http://eng.mod.gov.cn/Press/2015-05/26/content_4586805.htm*.

12. See, for example, Ronald Deibert, "Authoritarianism Goes Global: Cyberspace Under Siege," in Diamond, Plattner, and Walker, *Authoritarianism Goes Global*, ch. 13.

13. Douglas Rutzen, "Authoritarianism Goes Global (II): Civil Society Under Assault," in Diamond, Plattner, and Walker, *Authoritarianism Goes Global*, ch. 10.

14. Moisés Naím, "Democracy's Dangerous Impostors," *Washington Post*, 21 April 2007.

15. "Xi Calls for New Type of Think Tanks," Xinhua, 27 October 2014, *http://news.xinhuanet.com/english/china/2014-10/27/c_133746282.htm*.

16. Stanley Lubman, "China Asserts More Control Over Foreign and Domestic NGOs," China Real Time blog, *Wall Street Journal*, 16 June 2015, *http://blogs.wsj.com/chinarealtime/2015/06/16/china-asserts-more-control-over-foreign-and-domestic-ngos*.

17. Sui-Lee Wee and Stephanie Nebehay, "At UN, China Uses Intimidation Tactics to Silence Its Critics," *Reuters*, 6 October 2015.

18. The U.S. ambassador to the OSCE said that at the 2013 HDIM he overheard a putative representative of a registered NGO say, "We are happy to review your complaints about the new law we have drafted," momentarily forgetting that he was supposed to be acting like an NGO staff member rather than a government representative. See "Response to the Report by ODIHR on This Year's Human Dimension Implementation Meeting," delivered by Ambassador Daniel B. Baer to the Permanent Council, Vienna, 7 November 2013, *http://osce.usmission.gov/nov_7_13_hdim.html*.

19. Re:Baltica, "Money from Russia: Kremlin's Millions," 27 August 2015, *www.rebaltica.lv/en/investigations/money_from_russia/a/1257/kremlins_millions.html*.

20. Chris Buckley, "China's Party-Run Media Is Silent on Market Mayhem," *New York Times*, 25 August 2015, *www.nytimes.com/2015/08/26/world/asia/chinese-news-media-largely-silent-amid-stock-market-turmoil.html*.

21. Koh Gui Qing and John Shiffman, "Beijing's Covert Radio Network Airs China-Friendly News Across Washington, and the World," Reuters, 2 November 2015.

22. Sarah Cook, "The Long Shadow of Chinese Censorship: How the Communist Party's Media Restrictions Affect News Outlets Around the World," Center for International Media Assistance report, 22 October 2013.

23. Timothy Snyder, "Ukraine: The Haze of Propaganda," *New York Review of Books*, 1 March 2014.

24. Bruce Drake, "Even Before Ukraine Crisis, Views of Putin Had Grown More Negative in U.S., Europe," Pew Research Center, 20 March 2014, *www.pewresearch.org/fact-tank/2014/03/20/even-before-ukraine-crisis-views-of-putin-had-grown-more-negative-in-u-s-europe*; David Shambaugh, "China's Soft-Power Push: The Search for Respect," *Foreign Affairs* 94 (July–August 2015): 99–107.

25. Peter Pomerantsev, "Authoritarianism Goes Global: The Kremlin's Information War," in Diamond, Plattner, and Walker, *Authoritarianism Goes Global*, ch. 11.

ANNE APPLEBAUM, a columnist for the *Washington Post* and *Slate,* directs the Transitions Forum at the Legatum Institute in London. Her most recent book is *Iron Curtain: The Crushing of Eastern Europe, 1944–1956* (2012). "The Leninist Roots of Civil Society Repression" originally appeared in the October 2015 issue of the *Journal of Democracy.*

ANNE-MARIE BRADY, professor of political science at the University of Canterbury in New Zealand, is currently a Global Fellow at the Woodrow Wilson Center in Washington, D.C., Senior Fellow at the China Policy Institute, University of Nottingham, in the United Kingdom, and Editor-in-Chief of *The Polar Journal.* Her many books include *Marketing Dictatorship: Propaganda and Thought Work in Contemporary China* (2009) and *China's Thought Management* (2012). "China's Foreign Propaganda Machine" originally appeared in the October 2015 issue of the *Journal of Democracy.*

ALEXANDER COOLEY is director of the Harriman Institute at Columbia University and a professor of political science at Barnard College. His books include *Great Games, Local Rules: The New Great Power Contest in Central Asia* (2012) and *Ranking the World: Grading States as a Tool of Global Governance* (2015, coedited with Jack Snyder). "Countering Democratic Norms" originally appeared in the July 2015 issue of the *Journal of Democracy.*

JAVIER CORRALES is Dwight W. Morrow 1895 Professor of Political Science at Amherst College. He is the coauthor (with Michael Penfold) of *Dragon in the Tropics: The Legacy of Hugo Chávez,* now in its second edition (Brookings Institution Press, 2015). Portions of "Autocratic Legalism in Venezuela," which originally appeared in the April 2015 issue of the *Journal of Democracy,* draw from this book.

RON DEIBERT is director of the Citizen Lab at the Munk School of Global Affairs, University of Toronto. He is the author of *Black Code: Surveillance, Privacy, and the Dark Side of the Internet* (2013). He was a co-founder and principal investigator of the OpenNet Initiative (2003–14). "Cyberspace Under Siege" originally appeared in the July 2015 issue of the *Journal of Democracy*.

LARRY DIAMOND is founding coeditor of the *Journal of Democracy* and a senior fellow at the Hoover Institution and the Freeman Spogli Institute for International Studies at Stanford University.

PATRICK MERLOE is senior associate and director of electoral programs at the National Democratic Institute (NDI), where he has engaged in electoral-integrity activities in more than sixty countries. He publishes widely on elections, human rights, and international law. "Election Monitoring vs. Disinformation" originally appeared in the July 2015 issue of the *Journal of Democracy*.

ABBAS MILANI is the Hamid and Christina Moghadam Director of Iranian Studies at Stanford University and codirector of the Hoover Institution's Iran Democracy Project. He is the editor, with Larry Diamond, of *Politics and Culture in Contemporary Iran: Challenging the Status Quo* (2015). "Iran's Paradoxical Regime" originally appeared in the April 2015 issue of the *Journal of Democracy*.

ANDREW J. NATHAN is Class of 1919 Professor of Political Science at Columbia University and a member of the Editorial Board of the *Journal of Democracy*. His many books include *China's Search for Security* (coauthored with Andrew Scobell, 2012). "China's Challenge" originally appeared in the January 2015 issue of the *Journal of Democracy*.

MARC F. PLATTNER is founding coeditor of the *Journal of Democracy,* vice-president for research and studies at the National Endowment for Democracy (NED), and co-chair of the Research Council of NED's International Forum for Democratic Studies.

PETER POMERANTSEV, senior fellow at the Legatum Institute Transitions Forum, writes extensively on twenty-first-century propaganda. He is the author of *Nothing Is True and Everything Is Possible: The Surreal Heart of the New Russia* (2014). "The Kremlin's Information War" originally appeared in the October 2015 issue of the *Journal of Democracy*.

DOUGLAS RUTZEN Douglas Rutzen is president and CEO of the International Center for Not-for-Profit Law (ICNL, *www.icnl.org*). He is an adjunct professor of law at Georgetown University. "Civil Society Under Assault" originally appeared in the October 2015 issue of the *Journal of Democracy.*

LILIA SHEVTSOVA is a nonresident senior fellow in the Foreign Policy Program at the Brookings Institution. From 1995 to 2014, she was a senior associate at the Carnegie Moscow Center. Her books include *Putin's Russia* (2005) and *Lonely Power: Why Russia Has Failed to Become the West and the West Is Weary of Russia* (2010). "Forward to the Past in Russia" originally appeared in the April 2015 issue of the *Journal of Democracy.*

ALEX VATANKA, senior fellow at the Middle East Institute and Jamestown Foundation in Washington, D.C., specializes in Middle Eastern affairs, focusing particularly on Iran. A former editor of Jane's *Islamic Affairs Analyst,* his book *Iran and Pakistan: Security, Diplomacy and American Influence* was published in 2015. "Iran Abroad" originally appeared in the April 2015 issue of the *Journal of Democracy.*

CHRISTOPHER WALKER is executive director of the International Forum for Democratic Studies at the National Endowment for Democracy (NED). "Dealing with the Authoritarian Resurgence" appears in the January 2016 issue of the *Journal of Democracy.*

FREDERIC WEHREY is senior associate in the Middle East Program at the Carnegie Endowment for International Peace. He is the author of *Sectarian Politics in the Gulf: From the Iraq War to the Arab Uprisings* (2013). "Saudi Arabia's Anxious Autocrats" is a slightly updated version of an essay that originally appeared in the April 2015 issue of the *Journal of Democracy.*